RAMBLES AND RECOLLECTIONS
OF AN
INDIAN OFFICIAL

1809-1850

RAMBLES AND RECOLLECTIONS
OF AN
INDIAN OFFICIAL

1809-1850

WILLIAM H. SLEEMAN

A NEW EDITION
EDITED BY
VINCENT A. SMITH

IN TWO VOLUMES
VOLUME TWO

Published by

Gyan Publishing House
5, Ansari Road
Daryaganj, New Delhi-110002
Phone: 011-47034999, 9811692060
E-mail: books@gyanbooks.com

Distribution Network
gyanbooks.com
India, USA, Canada, UK, Australia, France

© **Publisher**

ISBN : 978-81-212-3935-6 (Set)
ISBN : 978-81-212-4750-4 (PB)
First Published, Westminister, 1893

2nd Impression 2020

Printed at: Gyan Press, Delhi.

Rambles and Recollections of An Indian Official Vol. II
Author: William H. Sleeman

RAMBLES

AND

RECOLLECTIONS

OF AN

INDIAN OFFICIAL

BY

MAJOR-GENERAL SIR W·H SLEEMAN K·C·B

IN TWO VOLUMES

VOL · II

A NEW EDITION

EDITED BY

VINCENT ARTHUR SMITH I·C·S

Westminster

ARCHIBALD CONSTABLE AND COMPANY

14 PARLIAMENT STREET S·W

MDCCCXCIII

CONTENTS OF VOLUME II

CONTENTS

CONTENTS

RAMBLES AND RECOLLECTIONS

CHAPTER I[1]

Govardhan, the Scene of Krishna's Dalliance with the Milk-maids.

On the 10th[2] we came on ten miles over a plain to
Govardhan, a place celebrated in ancient history as the
birthplace of Krishna, the seventh incarnation of the
Hindoo god of preservation, Vishnu, and the scene of his
dalliance with the milk-maids (gōpīs); and, in modern
days, as the burial or burning place of the Jāt chiefs of
Bharatpur and Dīg, by whose tombs, with their endowments, this once favourite abode of the god is prevented
from being entirely deserted.[3] The town stands upon a
narrow ridge of sandstone hills, about ten miles long, rising
suddenly out of an alluvial plain, and running north-east
and south-west. The population is now very small, and
composed chiefly of Brahmans, who are supported by the
endowments of these tombs, and the contributions of a few
pilgrims. All our Hindoo followers were much gratified
as we happened to arrive on a day of peculiar sanctity;
and they were enabled to bathe and perform their devotions to the different shrines with the prospect of great
advantage. This range of hills is believed by Hindoos to
be part of a fragment of the Himālaya mountains which

[1] Chapter VIII of Vol. II of original edition.
[2] January, 1836.
[3] See note on Govardhan, *ante*, Vol. I, p. 407.

Hanumān, the monkey general of Rāma, the sixth incarnation of Vishnu, was taking down to aid his master in the formation of his bridge from the continent to the island of Ceylon, when engaged in the war with the demon king of that island for the recovery of his wife Sītā. He made a false step by some accident in passing Govardhan, and this *small bit* of his load fell off. The rocks begged either to be taken on to the god Rāma, or back to their old place ; but Hanumān was hard pressed for time, and told them not to be uneasy, as they would have a comfortable resting-place, and be worshipped by millions in future ages—thus, according to popular belief, foretelling that it would become the residence of a future incarnation, and the scene of Krishna's miracles. The range was then about twenty miles long, ten having since disappeared under the ground. It was of full length during Krishna's days ; and, on one occasion, he took up the whole upon his little finger to defend his favourite town and its milk-maids from the wrath of Indra, who got angry with the people, and poured down upon them a shower of burning ashes.

As I rode along this range, which rises gently from the plains at both ends and abruptly from the sides, with my groom by my side, I asked him what made Hanumān drop all his burthen here.

" *All* his burthen ! " exclaimed he with a smile ; " had it been *all*, would it not have been an immense mountain, with all its towns and villages ? while this is but an insignificant belt of rock. A mountain upon the back of men of former days, sir, was no more than a bundle of grass upon the back of one of your grass-cutters in the present day."

Nathū, whose mind had been full of the wonders of this place from his infancy, happened to be with us, and he now chimed in.

" It was night when Hanumān passed this place, and the lamps were seen burning in a hundred towns upon the mountain he had upon his back—the people were all at their usual occupations, quite undisturbed ; this is a mere fragment of his great burthen."

"And how was it that the men of those towns should have been so much smaller than the men who carried them ? "

"God only knew; but the fact of the men of the plains having been so large was undisputed—their beards were as many miles long as those of the present, day are inches. . Did not Bhīm throw the forty-cubit stone pillar, that now stands at Eran,[1] a distance of thirty miles, after the man who was running away with his cattle ? "

I thought of poor Father Gregory at Agra, and the heavy sigh he gave when asked by Godby what progress he was making among the people in the way of conversion.[2] The faith of these people is certainly larger than all the mustard-seeds in the world.

I told a very opulent and respectable Hindoo banker one day that it seemed to us very strange that Vishnu should come upon the earth merely to sport with milk-maids, and to hold up an umbrella, however large, to defend them from a shower. "The earth, sir," said he, "was at that time infested with innumerable demons and giants, who swallowed up men and women as bears swallow white ants; and his highness, Krishna, came down to destroy them. His own mother's brother, Kans, who then reigned at Mathurā over Govardhan, was one of these horrible demons. Hearing that his sister would give birth to a son that was to destroy him, he put to death several of her progeny as soon as they were born.[3] When Krishna was

[1] *Ante*, Vol. I, p. 68, *note*.
[2] *Ante*, Vol. I, p. 407.
[3] This Hindoo version of the Massacre of the Innocents necessarily recalls to mind the story in St. Matthew's Gospel. Numerous incidents of the Gospel narrative, including the birth among the cattle, the stable, the manger, and the imperial census, are repeated in the Indian legends of Krishna. The exact channel of communication is not known, but the intercourse between Alexandria and India is, in

seven days old, he sent a nurse, with poison on her nipple,
to destroy him likewise; but his highness gave such a pull
at it, that the nurse dropped down dead. In falling, she
resumed her real shape of a she-demon, and her body
covered no less than six square miles, and it took several
thousand men to cut her up and burn her, to prevent the
pestilence that must have followed. His uncle then sent a
crane, which caught up his highness, who always looked very
small for his age, and swallowed him as he would swallow a
frog. But his highness kicked up such a rumpus in the bird's
stomach that he was immediately thrown up again. When
he was seven years old his uncle invited him to a feast, and
got the largest and most ferocious elephant in India to
tread him to death as he alighted at the door. His highness, though then not higher than my waist, took the
enormous beast by one tusk, and, after whirling him round
in the air with one hand half a dozen times, he dashed
him on the ground and killed him.[1] Unable any longer to
stand the wickedness of his uncle, he seized him by the
beard, dragged him from his throne, and dashed him to the
ground in the same manner."

I thought of poor old Father Gregory and the mustard-
seeds again, and told my rich old friend that it all appeared
to us indeed passing strange.

The orthodox belief among the Muhammadans is that
Moses was sixty yards high; that he carried a mace sixty
yards long; and that he sprang sixty yards from the
ground when he aimed the fatal blow at the giant Üj, the
son of Anak, who came from the land of Canaan, with a
mountain on his back, to crush the army of Israelites.
Still, the head of his mace could reach only to the ankle-bone
of the giant. This was broken with the blow. The giant
fell, and was crushed under the weight of his own mountain. Now a person whose ankle-bone was one hundred

general terms, the explanation of the coincidences. (Weber, *Die
Griechen in Indien*, 1890, and *Abh. über Krishna's Geburtfest*, 1868.)
[1] This story may be an adaptation of the similar Buddhist tale.

and eighty yards high must have been almost as prodigious as he who carried the fragment of the Himālaya upon his back ; and he who believes in the one cannot fairly find fault with his neighbour for believing in the other.[1]

I was one day talking with a very sensible and respectable Hindoo gentleman of Bundēlkhand about the accident which made Hanumān drop this fragment of his load at Govardhan. "All doubts upon that point," said the old gentleman, "have been put at rest by holy writ. It is related in our scriptures.

"Bharat, the brother of Rāma, was left regent of the kingdom of Ajodhya,[2] during his absence at the conquest of Ceylon. He happened at night to see Hanumān passing with the mountain upon his back, and thinking he might be one of the king of Ceylon's demons about mischief, he let fly one of his blunt arrows at him. It hit him on the leg, and he fell, mountain and all, to the ground. As he fell, he called out in his agony, 'Rām, Rām,' from which Bharat discovered his mistake. He went up, raised him in his arms, and with his kind attentions restored him to his senses. Learning from him the object of his journey, and fearing that his wounded brother Lachchhman would die before he could get to Ceylon with the requisite remedy, he offered to send Hanumān on upon the barb of one of his arrows, mountain and all. To try him Hanumān took up his mountain and seated himself with it upon the barb of the arrow as desired. Bharat placed the arrow to the string of his bow, and drawing it till the barb touched the bow, asked Hanumān whether he was ready. 'Quite ready,' said Hanumān, 'but I am now satisfied that you

---

[1] Uj is the Og, King of Bashan, of the Hebrew version of the legend. The extravagant stories quoted in the text are not in the Korān, but are the inventions of the commentators. Sale gives references in his notes to Chap. V of the Korān.

[2] The kingdom included the modern Oudh (Awadh). The capital was the ancient city, also named Ajodhya, adjoining Fyzabad, which is still a very sacred place of pilgrimage.

really are the brother of our prince, and regent of his
kingdom, which was all I desired. Pray let me descend ;
and be sure that I shall be at Ceylon in time to save your
wounded brother.' He got off, knelt down, placed his
forehead on Bharat's feet in submission, resumed his load,
and was at Ceylon by the time the day broke next morning,
leaving behind him the small and insignificant fragment,
on which the town and temples of Govardhan now stand.

"While little Krishna was frisking about among the
milk-maids of Govardhan," continued my old friend,
"stealing their milk, cream, and butter, Brahmā, the
creator of the universe, who had heard of his being an
incarnation of Vishnu, the great preserver of the universe,
visited the place, and had some misgivings, from his size
and employment, as to his real character. To try him, he
took off through the sky a herd of cattle, on which some of
his favourite playmates were attending, old and young,
boys and all. Krishna, knowing how much the parents of
the boys and owners of the cattle would be distressed,
created, in a moment, another herd and other attendants
so exactly like those that Brahmā had taken, that the
owners of the one, and the parents of the other, remained
ignorant of the change. Even the new creations themselves
remained equally ignorant; and the cattle walked into their
stalls, and the boys into their houses, where they recognized
and were recognized by their parents, as if nothing had
happened.

"Brahmā was now satisfied that Krishna was a true
incarnation of Vishnu, and restored to him the real herd
and attendants. The others were removed out of the way
by Krishna, as soon as he saw the real ones coming back."

"But," said I to the good old man, who told me this
with a grave face, "must they not have suffered in passing
from the life given to death ; and why create them merely
to destroy them again?"

"Was he not God the Creator himself?" said the old
man; "does he not send one generation into the world

after another to fulfil their destiny, and then to return to the earth from which they came, just as he spreads over the land the grass and corn? All is gathered in its season, or withers as that passes away and dies."

The old gentleman might have quoted Wordsworth :—

> We die, my friend,
> Nor we alone, but that which each man loved
> And prized in his peculiar nook of earth
> Dies with him, or is changed ; and very soon,
> Even of the good is no memorial left.[1]

I was one day out shooting with my friend, the Rājā of Maihar,[2] under the Vindhya range, which rises five or six hundred feet, almost perpendicularly. He was an excellent shot with an English double-barrel, and had with him six men just as good. I asked him whether we were likely to fall in with any hares, using the term "khargosh," or "ass-eared."

"Certainly not," said the Rājā, "if you begin by abusing them with such a name ; call them 'lambkanās,' sir, 'long-eared,' and we shall get plenty."

He shot one, and attributed my bad luck to the opprobrious name I had used. While he was reloading, I took

---

[1] It is, I think, absolutely impossible for the most sympathetic European to understand, or enter into, the mental position of the learned and devout Hindoo who implicitly believes the wild myth related in the text, and sees no incongruity in the congeries of inconsistent ideas which are involved in the story. We may dimly apprehend that Brahmā is conceived as a δημιουργός, or Architect of the Universe, working in subordination to an impersonal higher power, and not as the infinite, omniscient, omnipotent Creator whom the Hebrews reverenced, but we shall still be a long way from attaining the Hindoo point of view. The relations of Krishna, Vishnu, Brahmā, Rāma, Siva, and all the other deities, with one another and with mankind, seem to be conceived by the Hindoo in a manner so confused and contradictory that every attempt at elucidation or explanation must necessarily fail. A Hindoo is born, not made, and the "inwardness" of Hinduism is not to be penetrated, even by the most learned of "barbarian" pundits.

[2] *Ante,* Vol. I, p. 155, *note.*

occasion to ask him how this range of hills had grown up where it was?

"No one can say," replied the Rājā, "but we believe that when Rāma went to recover his wife Sītā from the demon king of Ceylon, Rāvan, he wanted to throw a bridge across from the continent to the island, and sent some of his followers up to the Himālaya mountains for stones. He had completed his bridge before they all returned, and a messenger was sent to tell those who had not yet come to throw down their burdens, and rejoin him in all haste. Two long lines of these people had got thus far on their return when the messenger met them. They threw down their loads here, and here they have remained ever since, one forming the Vindhya range to the north of this valley, and the other the Kaimūr range to the south."

The Vindhya range extends from Mirzapore, on the Ganges, nearly to the Gulf of Cambay, some six or seven hundred miles, so that my sporting friend's faith was as capacious as any priest could well wish it; and those who have it are likely never to die, or suffer much, from an overstretch of the reasoning faculties in a hot climate.

The town stands upon the belt of rocks, about two miles from its north-eastern extremity; and in the midst is the handsome tomb of Ranjīt Singh, who defended Bharatpur so bravely against Lord Lake's army. The tomb has on one side a tank filled with water, and, on the other, another much deeper than the first, but without any water at all. We were surprised at this, and asked what the cause could be. The people told us, with the air of men who had never known what it was to feel the uneasy sensation of doubt, that "Krishna, one hot day, after skying with the milk-maids, had drunk it all dry; and that no water would ever stay in it, lest it might be quaffed by less noble lips." No orthodox Hindoo would ever for a moment doubt that this was the real cause of the phenomenon. Happy people! How much do they escape of that pain which in hot climates wears us all down in our efforts to trace moral and physical phenomena to their real causes and sources! Mind! mind! mind! without any of it, those Europeans who eat and drink moderately might get on very well in this climate. Much of it weighs them down.

> "Oh, sir, the good die first, and those whose hearts (*brains*)
> Are dry as summer dust burn to the socket."[1]

One is apt sometimes to think that Muhammad, Manu, and Confucius would have been great benefactors in saving so many millions of their species from the pain of thinking too much in hot climates, if they had only written their books in languages less difficult of acquirement. Their works are at once "the bane and antidote" of despotism—the source whence it comes, and the shield which defends the people from its consuming fire.

The tomb of Sūraj Mal, the great founder of the Jāt power at Bharatpur, stands on the north-east extremity of this belt of rocks, about two miles from the town, and is an extremely handsome building, conceived in the very best taste, and executed in the very best style.[2] With its appendages of temples and smaller tombs, it occupies the whole of one side of a magnificent tank full of clear water; and on the other side it looks into a large and beautiful garden. All the buildings and pavements are formed of the fine white sandstone of Rūpbās, scarcely inferior either in quality or appearance to white marble. The stone is carved in relief with flowers in good taste. In the centre of the tomb is the small marble slab covering the grave, with the two feet of Krishna carved in the centre, and around them the emblems of the god, the discus, the skull, the sword, the rosary. These emblems of the god are put on that people may have something godly to fix their thoughts upon. It is by degrees, and with fear and trem-

---

[1] Wordsworth, *Excursion*, Book I.

[2] The original edition gives a coloured plate of this tomb, which is not noticed by Fergusson. That author's remarks on the palace at Dig would apply to this tomb also; the style is very good, but not quite the best.

bling, that the Hindoos imitate the Muhammadans in the magnificence of their tombs. The object is ostensibly to keep the ground on which the bodies have been burned from being defiled; and generally Hindoos have been content to raise small open terraces of brick and stucco work over the spot, with some image or emblem of the god upon it. The Jāts here, like the princes and Gosāins in Bundēlkhand, have gone a stage beyond this, and raised tombs equal in costliness and beauty to those over Muhammadans of the highest rank; still they do not venture to leave it without a divine image or emblem, lest the gods might become jealous, and revenge themselves upon the souls of the deceased and the bodies of the living. On one side of Sūraj Mal's tomb is that of his wife, or some other female member of his family; and upon the slab over her grave, that is, over the precise spot where she was burned, are the same emblems, except the sword, for which a necklace is substituted. At each end of this range of tombs stands a temple dedicated to Baldēo, the brother of Krishna; and in one of them I found his image, with large eyes, a jet black complexion, and an *African countenance.* Why is this that Baldēo should be always represented of this countenance and colour, and his brother Krishna, either white, or of an azure colour, and the *Caucasian countenance?* [1]

The inside of the tomb is covered with beautiful snow-white stucco work that resembles the finest marble; but this is disfigured by wretched paintings, representing, on one side of the dome, Sūraj Mal in "darbār," smoking his hookah, and giving orders to his ministers; in another, he is at his devotions; on the third, at his sports, shooting hogs and deer; and on the fourth, at war, with some French officers of distinction figuring before him. He is distinguished by his portly person in all, and by his favourite

---

[1] Baldēo, or in Sanskrit Bāladeva, Bālabhadra, or Bālarāma, was the elder brother of Krishna. His myth in some respects resembles that of Herakles, as that of Krishna is related to the myths of Apollo.

light-brown dress in three places. At his devotions he is
standing all in white before the tutelary god of his house,
Hardĕo.[1] In various parts, Krishna is represented at his
sports with the milk-maids. The colours are gaudy, and
apparently as fresh as when first put on eighty years ago ;
but the paintings are all in the worst possible taste and style.[2]
Inside the dome of Ranjit Singh's tomb the siege of
Bharatpur is represented in the same rude taste and style.
Lord Lake is dismounted, and standing before his white
horse giving orders to his soldiers. On the opposite side
of the dome, Ranjit Singh, in a plain white dress, is standing erect before his idol at his devotions, with his ministers
behind him. On the other two sides he is at his favourite
field sports. What strikes one most in all this is the entire
absence of priestcraft. He wanted all his revenue for his
soldiers ; and his tutelary god seems, in consequence, to
have been well pleased to dispense with the mediatory
services of priests.[3] There are few temples anywhere to be
seen in the territories of these Jāt chiefs ; and, as few of
their subjects have yet ventured to follow them in this
innovation upon the old Hindoo usages of building tombs,[4]
the countries under their dominion are less richly ornamented than those of their neighbours. Those who build
tombs or temples generally surround them with groves of
mango and other fine fruit-trees, with good wells to
supply water for them, and, if they have the means,
they add tanks, so that every religious edifice, or work

---

[1] *I.e.*, Hari deva, a form of Vishnu. The temple of Hari deva at
Govardhan was built about A.D. 1560. (*N. W. P. Gazetteer*, Vol.
VIII, p. 94.)

[2] All Hindoo paintings, excepting the ancient frescoes at Ajanta and
Bāgh, and the modern miniatures and a few portraits executed by the
Delhi craftsmen, are below criticism.

[3] The Jāts detest Brahmans. The members of a Jāt deputation
complained one day to the editor when in the Muzaffarnagar district
that they suffered many evils by reason of the Brahmans.

[4] The author's meaning is that building tombs is not an old Hindoo
usage.

of ornament, leads to one or more of utility. So it was in Europe; often the Northern hordes swept away all that had grown up under the institution of the Romans and the Saracens; for almost all the great works of ornament and utility, by which these countries became first adorned and enriched, had their origin in church establishments. That portion of India, where the greater part of the revenue goes to the priesthood will generally be much more studded with works of ornament and utility than that in which the greater part goes to the soldiery. I once asked a Hindoo gentleman, who had travelled all over India, what part of it he thought most happy and beautiful. He mentioned some part of Southern India, about Tanjore, I think, where you could hardly go a mile without meeting some happy procession, or coming to a temple full of priests, or find an acre of land uncultivated.

The countries under the Marāthā government improved much in appearance, and in happiness, I believe, after the mayors of the palace, who were Brahmans, assumed the government, and put aside the Satārā Rājās, the descendants of the great Sivajī.[1] Wherever they could, they conferred the government of their distant territories upon Brahmans, who filled all the high offices under them with men of the same caste, who spent the greater part of their incomes in tombs, temples, groves, and tanks, that

---

[1] Sivajī, the indomitable opponent of Aurangzēb in the Deccan, belonged to the agricultural Kunbī caste. He was born in May A.D. 1627, and died in April 1680. The Brahman ministers of the Rājās of Satārā were known by the title of Peshwā. Bājī Rāo I, who died in 1740, the second Peshwā, was the first who superseded in actual power his nominal master. The last of the Peshwās was Bājī Rāo II, who abdicated in 1818, after the termination of the great Marāthā war, and retired to Bithūr near Cawnpore. His adopted son was the notorious Nānā Sāhib. The Marquis of Hastings, in 1818, drew the Rājā of Satāra from captivity, and re-established his dignity and power. In 1839 the Rājā's treachery compelled the Government of India to depose him. His territory is now a district of the Bombay Presidency.

embellished and enriched the face of the country, and thereby diffused a taste for such works generally among the people they governed. The appearance of those parts of the Marāthā dominion so governed is infinitely superior to that of the countries governed by the leaders of the military class, such as Sindhia, Holkār, and the Bhonslā, whose capitals are still mere standing camps—a collection of hovels, and whose countries are almost entirely devoid of all those works of ornament and utility that enrich and adorn those of their neighbours.[1] They destroyed all they found in those countries when they conquered them; and they have had neither the wisdom nor the taste to raise others to supply their places. The Sikh government is of exactly the same character; and the countries they governed have, I believe, the same wretched appearance— they are swarms of human locusts, who prey upon all that is calculated to enrich and embellish the face of the land they infest, and all that can tend to improve men in their social relations, and to link their affection to their soil and their government.[2] A Hindoo prince is always running to the extreme; he can never take and keep a middle course. He is either ambitious, and therefore appropriates all his revenues to the maintenance of soldiers, to pour out in inroads upon his neighbours; or he is superstitious, and devotes all his revenue to his priesthood, who embellish his country at the same time that they weaken it, and invite

---

[1] The Rājā of Berār, also known as the Rājā of Nāgpur, was called the Bhonslā. The misrule of Gwālior has been described *ante*, in Chapters XXXVI and XLIX of Volume I.

[2] Since the annexation of the Panjāb in 1849, the Sikhs have justly earned so much praise as loyal and gallant soldiers, the flower of the Indian army, that their earlier less honourable reputation has been effaced. Captain Francklin, writing in 1803, and apparently express- ing the opinion of George Thomas, declares that "the Seiks are false, sanguinary, and faithless; they are addicted to plunder and the acquirement of wealth by any means, however nefarious." (*Military Memoirs of Mr. George Thomas, London reprint*, p. 112.) The Sikh states of the Panjāb are now sufficiently well governed.

invasion, as their prince becomes less and less able to repel it.

The more popular belief regarding this range of sand-stone hills at Govardhan is that Lachchhman, the brother of Rāma, having been wounded by Rāvan, the demon king of Ceylon, his surgeon declared that his wound could be cured only by a decoction of the leaves of a certain tree, to be found in a certain hill in the Himālaya mountains. Hanumān volunteered to go for it, but on reaching the place he found that he had entirely forgotten the description of the tree required ; and, to prevent mis-take, he took up the whole mountain upon his back, and walked off with it to the plains. As he passed Govardhan, where Bharat and Charat, the third and fourth brothers of Rāma, then reigned, he was seen by them.[1] It was night ; and, thinking him a strange sort of fish, Bharat let fly one of his arrows at him. It hit him in the leg, and the sudden jerk caused this small fragment of his huge burden to fall off. He called out in his agony, "Rām, Rām," from which they learned that he belonged to the army of their brother, and let him pass on ; but he remained lame for life from the wound. This accounts very satisfactorily, according to popular belief, for the halting gait of all the monkeys of that species ;[2] those who are descended lineally from the general inherit it, of course ; and those who are not, adopt it out of respect for his memory, as all the soldiers of Alexander contrived to make one shoulder higher than the other, because one of his happened to be so. When he passed, thousands and tens of thousands of lamps were burning upon his mountain, as the people remained entirely unconscious of the change, and at their

---

[1] I know of no authority for the name Charat (Churut). The sons of Dasaratha were Rāma, by the chief queen ; Bharat, by a second ; and Lachchhman (Lakshmaṇa), and Satrughna by a third consort.

[2] The species referred to is the long-tailed monkey called "Hanumān," and "langūr" in Hindī, the *Presbytis entellus* of Jerdon (=*P. anchises*, Elliot ;= *Semnopithecus*, Cuvier).

usual occupations. Hanumān reached Ceylon with his mountain, the tree ˉwas found upon it, and Lachchhman's wound cured.[1]

Govardhan is now within the boundary of our territory, and a native collector resides here from Agra.[2]

---

[1] The author seems to have forgotten that he has already told this story, *ante*, p. 5.

[2] It is now in the Mathurā district.

CHAPTER II [1]

Veracity.

THE people of Britain are described by Diodorus Siculus (Book V, chap. II) as in a very simple and rude state, subsisting almost entirely on the produce of the land, but as being "a people of much integrity and sincerity, far from the craft and knavery of men among us, contented with plain and homely fare, and strangers to the luxury and excesses of the rich." In India we find strict veracity most prevalent among the wildest and half-savage tribes of the hills and jungles in Central India, or the chain of the Himālaya mountains; and among those where we find it prevail most, we find cattle-stealing most common; the men of one tribe not deeming it to be any disgrace to *lift*, or steal, the cattle of another. I have known the man among the Gonds of the woods of Central India, whom nothing could induce to tell a lie, join a party of robbers to lift a herd of cattle from the neighbouring plains for nothing more than as much spirits as he could enjoy at one bout. I asked a native gentleman of the plains, in the valley of the Nerbudda, one day, what made the people of the woods to the north and south more disposed to speak the truth than those more civilized of the valley itself. "They have not yet learned the value of a lie," said he, with the greatest simplicity and sincerity, for he was a very honest and plain-spoken man.

Veracity is found to prevail most where there is least to tempt to falsehood, and most to be feared from it. In a

[1] Chapter IX of Vol. II of original edition.

very rude state of society, like that of which I have been speaking, the only shape in which property is accumulated is in cattle ; things are bartered for each other without the use of a circulating medium, and one member of a community has no means of concealing from the other the articles of property he has. If they were to steal from each other, they would not be able to conceal what they stole—to steal, therefore, would be no advantage. In such societies every little community is left to govern itself ; to secure the rights, and enforce the duties, of all its several members in their relations with each other ; they are too poor to pay taxes to keep up expensive establishments, and their governments seldom maintain among them any for the administration of justice, or the protection of life, property, or character. All the members of all such little communities will often unite in robbing the members of another community of their flocks and herds, the only kind of property they have, or in applauding those who most distinguish themselves in such enterprises ; but the well-being of the community demands that each member should respect the property of the others, and be punished by the odium of all if he does not.[1]

It is equally necessary to the well-being of the community that every member should be able to rely upon the veracity of the other upon the very few points where their rights, duties, and interests clash. In the very rudest state of society, among the woods and hills of India, the people

---

[1] Johnson says :—" Mountaineers are thievish because they are poor ; and, having neither manufactures nor commerce, can grow rich only by robbery. They regularly plunder their neighbours, for their neighbours are commonly their enemies ; and, having lost that reverence for property by which the order of civil life is preserved, soon consider all as enemies whom they do not reckon as friends, and think themselves licensed to invade whatever they are not obliged to protect." [W. H. S.] The quotation is from *A Journey to the Western Islands of Scotland.*

The observations in the text apply largely to the settled Hindoo villages, as well as to the forest tribes.

have some deity whose power they dread, and whose name they invoke, when much is supposed to depend upon the truth of what one man is about to declare. The "pīpal" tree (*Ficus religiosa*) is everywhere sacred to the gods, who are supposed to sit among its leaves, and listen to the music of their rustling. The deponent takes one of these leaves in his hand, and invokes the god who sits above him to crush him, or those dear to him, as he crushes the leaf in his hand, if he speaks anything but the truth ; he then plucks and crushes the leaf, and states what he has to say.[1]

The large cotton-tree is, among the wild tribes of India, the favourite seat of gods still more terrible,[2] because their superintendence is confined exclusively to the neighbourhood ; and having their attention less occupied, they can venture to make a more minute scrutiny into the conduct of the people immediately around them. The "pīpal" is occupied by one or other of the Hindoo triad, the god of creation, preservation, or destruction, who have the affairs of the universe to look after ;[3] but the cotton and other trees are occupied by some minor deities, who are vested with a

[1] *Ficus religiosa* is the Linnæan name for the "pīpal." Other botanists call it *Urostigma religiosum*. In the original edition the botanical name is erroneously given as *Ficus Indicus*. The *Ficus Indica* (*F. Bengalensis*, or *Urostigma B.*) is the banyan. A story is current that the traders of a certain town begged the magistrate to remove a pīpal-tree which he had planted in the market-place, because, so long as it remained, business could not be conducted. They knew "the value of a lie."

[2] The red cotton, or silk-cotton, tree, when in spring covered with its huge magnolia-shaped scarlet blossoms, is one of the most magnificent objects in nature. Its botanical name is *Salmalia Malabarica* (*Bombax Malabaricum ; B. heptaphyllum*). This is the tree referred to in the text. The white silk-cotton tree (*Eriodendron anfractuosum ; Bombax pentandrum* ; *Ceiba pentandra ; Gossampinus Rumphii*) has a more southern habitat. (Balfour's *Cyclopædia, s.v.* "Salmalia" and "Eriodendron.")

[3] The pīpal is usually regarded as sacred only to Vishnu, the Preserver. The *Ficus Indica*, or banyan, is sacred to Siva, the Destroyer, and the *Butea frondosa* (Hind. "dhāk," "palās," or "chhyūl") to Brahmā, the Creator, or δημιουργός.

local superintendence over the affairs of a district, or perhaps, of a single village.[1] These are always in the view of the people, and every man knows that he is every moment liable to be taken to their court, and to be made to invoke their vengeance upon himself, or those dear to him, if he has told a falsehood in what he has stated, or tells one in what he is about to state. Men so situated

---

[1] The sacred trees and plants of India are very numerous. Balfour (*Cyclop. s.v.* " Sacred ") enumerates eighty, and the list is by no means complete. The same author's article, " Tree," may also be consulted. The " minor deities " alluded to by the author are the real gods of popular rural Hinduism. The observations of Mr. William Crooke, probably the best authority on the subject of Indian popular religion, though made with reference to a particular locality, are generally applicable. " Hinduism certainly shows no signs of weakness, and is practically untouched by Christian and Muhammadan proselytism. The gods of the Vedas are as dead as Jupiter, and the Krishna worship only succeeds from its marvellous adaptability to the sensuous and romantic side of the native mind. But it would be too much to say that the creed exercises any real effect on life or morals. With the majority of its devotees it is probably more sympathetic than practical, and ranks with the periodical ablutions in the Ganges and Jumna, and the traditional worship of the local gods and ghosts, which really impress the rustic. He is enclosed on all sides by a ring of precepts, which attribute luck or ill-luck to certain things or actions. These and the bonds of caste, with its obligations for the performance of marriage, death, and other ceremonies, make up the religious life of the peasant. Nearly every village and hamlet has its local ghost, usually the shrine of a childless man, or one whose funeral rites remained for some reason unperformed. In the expressive popular phrase, he is " deprived of water " (*aud*). The pious make oblations to his cenotaph twice a year, and propitiate his ghost with offerings of water to allay his thirst in the lower world. The primeval serpent-worship is perpetuated in the reverence paid to traditional village-snakes. Of the local ghosts some are beneficent. Sometimes they are only mischievous, like Robin Goodfellow, and will milk the cows, and sour the milk, or pull your hair, if you wander about at night in certain well-known uncanny places. A more dangerous demon is heard in the crackling of the dry leaves of the date-tree in the night wind ; and some trees are haunted by a vampire, who will drag you up and devour you, if you venture near them in the darkness." (*N. W. P. Gazetteer*, Vol. VII, *Supplement*, p. 4.)

adhere habitually, and I may say religiously, to the truth ; and I have had before me hundreds of cases in which a man's property, liberty, or life has depended upon his telling a lie, and he has refused to tell it to save either ; as my friend told me, "they had not learned the value of a lie," or rather, they had not learned with how much impunity a lie could be told in the tribunals of civilized society. In their own tribunals, under the pīpal-tree or cotton-tree, imagination commonly did what the deities, who were supposed to preside, had the credit of doing ; if the deponent told a lie, he believed that the deity who sat on the sylvan throne above him, and searched the heart of man, must know it ; and from that moment he knew no rest—he was always in dread of his vengeance ; if any accident happened to him, or to those dear to him, it was attributed to this offended deity ; and if no accident happened, some evil was brought about by his own disordered imagination.[1]

In the tribunals we introduce among them, such people soon find that the judges who preside can seldom search deeply into the hearts of men, or clearly distinguish truth from falsehood in the declarations of deponents ; and when they can distinguish it, it is seldom that they can secure their conviction for perjury. They generally learn very soon that these judges, instead of being, like the judges of their own woods and wilds, the only beings who can search the hearts of men, and punish them for falsehood, are frequently the persons, of all others, most blind to the real state of the deponent's mind, and the degree of truth and falsehood in his narrative ; that, however well-intentioned, they are often labouring in the "darkness visible" created by the native officers around them. They not only learn this, but they learn what is still worse, that they may tell what lies they please in these tribunals ; and that not one

---

[1] Compare the story of Rāmkishan in Chap. XXV of Vol. I. Books on anthropology cite many instances of deaths caused by superstitious fears.

of them shall become known to the circle in which they move, and whose good opinion they value. If, by his lies told in such tribunals, a man has robbed another, or caused him to be robbed, of his property, his character, his liberty, or his life, he can easily persuade the circle in which he resides that it has arisen, not from any false statements of his, but from the blindness of the judge, or the wickedness of the native officers of his court, because all circles consider the blindness of the one, and the wickedness of the other, to be everywhere very great.

Arrian, in speaking of the class of supervisors in India, says :—"They may not be guilty of falsehood; and indeed none of the Indians were ever accused of that crime."[1] I believe that as little falsehood is spoken by the people of India, in their village communities, as in any part of the world with an equal area and population. It is in our courts of justice where falsehoods prevail most, and the longer they have been anywhere established, the greater the degree of falsehood that prevails in them. Those entrusted with the administration of a newly-acquired territory are surprised to find the disposition among both principals and witnesses in cases to tell the plain and simple truth. As magistrates, they find it very often difficult to make thieves

---

[1] Arrian, *Indica*, Ch. XII : " The sixth class consists of those called ' superintendents.' They spy out what goes on in country and town, and report everything to the king where the people have a king, and to the magistrates where the people are self-governed, and it is against use and wont for them to give a false report ;—but indeed no Indian is accused of lying." (McCrindle, *Ancient India*, p. 211.) Arrian uses the word ἐπίσκοποι ; in the Fragments of Megasthenes quoted by Diodorus and Strabo, the word is ἔφοροι. The people referred to seem to be the well-known " news-writers " employed by Oriental sovereigns (*ante*, Vol. I, p. 301) ; a simple explanation missed by McCrindle (*op. cit.* p. 43, *note*). The remark about the truthfulness of the Indians appears to be Arrian's addition. It is not in the Fragment of Megasthenes from which Arrian copies. But in Fragment XXVII (*op. cit.* p. 69) Megasthenes says, " Truth and virtue they hold alike in esteem"; and in Fragment XXXVI he asserts that " the ablest and most trustworthy men " are appointed ἔφοροι (p. 85).

and robbers tell lies, according to the English fashion, to avoid running a risk of criminating themselves. In England, this habit of making criminals tell lies arose from the severity of the penal code, which made the punishment so monstrously disproportionate to the crime, that the accused, however clear and notorious his crimes, became an object of general sympathy.[1] In India, punishments have nowhere been, under our rule, disproportionate to the crimes; on the contrary, they have generally been more mild than the people would wish them to be, or think they ought to be, in order to deter from similar crimes; and, in newly-acquired territories, they have generally been more mild than in our old possessions. The accused are, therefore, nowhere considered as objects of public sympathy; and in newly-acquired territories they are willing to tell the truth, and are allowed to do so, in order to save the people whom they have injured, and their neighbours generally, the great loss and annoyance unavoidably attending upon a summons to our courts. In the native courts, to which ours succeed, the truth was seen through immediately, the judges who presided could commonly distinguish truth from falsehood in the evidence before them, almost as well as the sylvan gods who sat in the pipal or cotton-trees; though they were seldom supposed by the people to be quite so just in their decisions. When we take possession of such countries, they, for a time at least, give us credit for the same sagacity, with a little more integrity. The prisoner knows that his neighbours expect him to tell the truth to save them trouble, and will detest him if he does not; he supposes that we shall have the sense to find out the truth whether he tells it or not, and then humanity to

---

[1] Up to the year 1827 " grand larceny," that is to say, stealing to a value exceeding twelve pence, was punishable with death. The Act 7 George IV, cap. 28, abolished the distinction of grand and petty larceny. In 1837, the first year of her present Majesty's reign, the punishment of death was abolished in the case of between thirty and forty offences. Other statutes have further mitigated the ferocity of the old law.

visit his crime with the punishment it merits, and no more.

The magistrate asks the prisoner what made him steal; and the prisoner enters at once into an explanation of the circumstances which reduced him to the necessity of doing so, and offers to bring witnesses to prove them; but never dreams of offering to bring witnesses to prove that he did not steal, if he really had done so; because the general feeling would be in favour of his doing the one, and against his doing the other. Tavernier gives an amusing sketch of Amīr Jumla presiding in a court of justice, during a visit he paid him in the kingdom of Golconda, in the year 1648. (*See* Book I, Part II, Chapter XI.)[1]

---

[1] The year was 1652, not 1648 (*Ball's Tavernier*, Vol. I, p. 260, *note*). The passages describing the criminal procedure of Amīr Jumla are not very long, and deserve quotation, as giving an accurate account of the administration of penal justice by an able native ruler. "On the 14th [September] we went to the tent of the Nawāb to take leave of him, and to hear what he had to say regarding the goods which we had shown him. But we were told that he was engaged examining a number of criminals, who had been brought to him for immediate punishment. It is the custom in this country not to keep a man in prison; but immediately the accused is taken he is examined and sentence is pronounced on him, which is then executed without any delay. If the person whom they have seized is found innocent, he is released at once; and whatever the nature of the case may be, it is promptly concluded. . . . On the 15th, at seven o'clock in the morning, we went to the Nawāb, and immediately we were announced he asked us to enter his tent, where he was seated with two of his secretaries by him. . . . The Nawāb had the intervals between his toes full of letters, and he also had many between the fingers of his left hand. He drew them sometimes from his feet, sometimes from his hand, and sent his replies through his two secretaries, writing some also himself. . . . While we were with the Nawāb he was informed that four prisoners, who were then at the door of the tent, had arrived. He remained more than half an hour without replying, writing continually and making his secretaries write, but at length he suddenly ordered the criminals to be brought in; and after having questioned them, and made them confess with their own mouths the crime of which they were accused, he remained nearly an hour without saying anything, continuing to write and to make his secretaries write.

I asked a native law officer, who called on me one day, what he thought would be the effect of an Act to dispense with oaths on the Korān and Ganges water, and substitute a solemn declaration made in the name of God, and under the same penal liabilities, as if the Korān or Ganges water had been in the deponent's hand. "I have practised in the courts thirty years, sir," said he, "and during that time I have found only three kinds of witnesses—two of whom would, by such an act, be left precisely where they were, while the third would be released by it from a very salutary check."

"And, pray, what are the three classes into which you divide the witnesses in our courts?"

"First, sir, are those who will always tell the truth, whether they are required to state what they know in the form of an oath or not."

"Do you think this a large class?"

"Yes, I think it is; and I have found among them many whom nothing on earth could make to swerve from the truth; do what you please, you could never frighten or bribe them into a deliberate falsehood. The second are those who will not hesitate to tell a lie when they have a motive for it, and are not restrained by an oath. In taking an oath they are afraid of two things, the anger of God and the odium of men. Only three days ago," continued my friend, "I required a power of attorney from a lady of

. . . Among these four prisoners who were brought into his presence there was one who had entered a house and slain a mother and her three infants. He was condemned forthwith to have his feet and hands cut off, and to be thrown into a field near the high road to end his days. Another had stolen on the high road, and the Nawāb ordered him to have his stomach slit open and to be flung in a drain. I could not ascertain what the others had done, but both their heads were cut off. While all this passed the dinner was served, for the Nawāb generally eats at ten o'clock, and he made us dine with him." (*Ibid.* p.p. 290-293.)

Such swift procedure and sharp punishments would still be highly approved of by the great mass of native opinion.

rank, to enable me to act for her in a case pending before the court in this town. It was given to me by her brother, and two witnesses came to declare that she had given it. 'Now,' said I, 'this lady is known to live under the curtain ; and you will be asked by the judge whether you saw her give this paper ; what will you say?' They both replied : —'If the judge asks us the question without an oath, we will say yes—it will save much trouble, and we know that she did give this paper, though we did not really see her give it ; but if he puts the Korān into our hands we must say no, for we should otherwise be pointed at by all the town as perjured wretches—our enemies would soon tell everybody that we had taken a false oath.' Now," my friend went on, "the form of an oath is a great check upon this sort of persons. The third class consists of men who will tell lies whenever they have sufficient motive, whether they have the Korān or Ganges water in their hands or not. Nothing will ever prevent their doing so ; and the declaration which you propose would be just as well as any other for them."

" Which class do you consider the most numerous of the three ? "

" I consider the second the most numerous,.and wish the oath to be retained for them."

" That is of all the men you see examined in our courts, you think the most come under the class of those who will, under the influence of strong motives, tell lies if they have not the Korān or Ganges water in their hands ? "

" Yes."

" But do not a great many of those, whom you consider to be included among the second class, come from the village communities—the peasantry of the country ? "

" Yes."

" And do you not think that the greatest part of those men who tell lies in the court, under the influence of strong motives, unless they bear the Korān or Ganges water in their hands, would refuse to tell lies, if questioned before the people of their villages among the circle in which they live?"

"Of course I do; three-fourths of those who do not scruple to lie in our courts, would be ashamed to lie before their neighbours, or the elders of their village."

"You think that the people of the village communities are more ashamed to tell lies before their neighbours than the people of towns?"

"Much more[1]—there is no comparison."

"And the people of towns and cities bear in India but a small proportion to the people of the village communities?"

"I should think a very small proportion indeed."

"Then you think that in the mass of the population of India *out of our courts*, and in their own circles, the first class, or those who speak truth, whether they have the Korān or Ganges water in their hands or not, would be found more numerous than the other two?"

"Certainly I do; if they were always to be questioned before their neighbours or elders, or so that they could feel that their neighbours and elders would know what they say."

This man is a very worthy and learned Muhammadan, who has read all the works on medicine to be found in Persian and Arabic; gives up his time from sunrise in the morning till nine, to the indigent sick of the town, whom he supplies gratuitously with his advice and medicines, that cost him thirty rupees a month, out of about one hundred and twenty that he can make by his labours all the rest of the day.

There can be no doubt that, even in England, the fear of the odium of society, which is sure to follow the man who has perjured himself, acts more powerfully in making men tell the truth, when they have the Bible in their hands before a competent and public tribunal, and with a strong

---

[1] Misprinted " much less " in original edition.

worldly motive to tell a lie, than the fear of punishment
by the Deity in the next world for having "taken his name
in vain" in this. Christians, as well as other people, are
too apt to think that there is yet abundance of time to
appease the Deity by repentance and reformation; but
they know that they cannot escape the odium of society,
with a free press and high tone of moral and religious feeling, like those of England, if they deliberately perjure
themselves in open court, whose proceedings are watched
with so much jealousy. They learn to dread the name of
"perjured villain" or "perjured wretch," which would
embitter the rest of their lives, and perhaps the lives of
their children.[1]

In a society much advanced in arts and the refinements
of life, temptations to falsehood become very great, and
require strong checks from law, religion or moral feeling.
Religion is seldom of itself found sufficient; for, though
men cannot hope to conceal their transgressions from the
Deity, they can, as I have stated, always hope in time to
appease him. Penal laws are not alone sufficient, for men
can always hope to conceal their trespasses from those who
are appointed to administer them, or at least to prevent
their getting that measure of judicial proof required for
their conviction; the dread of the indignation of their
circle of society is everywhere the more efficient of the
three checks; and this check will generally be found most
to prevail where the community is left most to self-government—hence the proverb, "There is honour among
thieves." A gang of robbers, who are outlaws, are, of

---

[1] The new Act, V of 1840, prescribes the following declaration :—
"I solemnly affirm, in the presence of Almighty God, that what I
shall state shall be the truth, the whole truth, and nothing but the
truth,"—and declares that a false statement made on this shall be
punished as perjury. [W. H. S.] The law now in force is to the
same effect. This form of declaration is absolutely worthless as a
check on perjury, and never hinders any witness from lying to his
heart's content. The use of the Koran and Ganges water in the
courts has been given up.

course, left to govern themselves; and, unless they could
rely on each other's veracity and honour in their relations
with each other, they could do nothing. If governments
were to leave no degree of self-government to the communities of which the society is composed, this moral check
would really cease—the law would undertake to secure
every right, and enforce every duty; and men would cease
to depend upon each other's good opinion and good
feelings.[1]

There is perhaps no part of the world where the communities of which the society is composed have been left
so much to self-government as in India. There has seldom
been any idea of a reciprocity of duties and rights between
the governing and the governed; the sovereign who has
possession feels that he has a right to levy certain taxes
from the land for the maintenance of the public establishments, which he requires to keep down rebellion against
his rule, and to defend his dominions against all who may
wish to intrude and seize upon them; and to assist him in
acquiring the dominions of other princes when favourable
opportunities offer; but he has no idea of a reciprocal duty
towards those from whom he draws his revenues. The
peasantry from whom the prince draws his revenues feel
that they are bound to pay that revenue; that, if they do
not pay it, he will, with his strong arm, turn them out and
give to others their possessions—but they have no idea of
any right on their part to any return from him. The
village communities were everywhere left almost entirely to

---

[1] The tendency of modern India is to rely too much on formal law
and the exercise of the powers of the central government. The con-
templation of the vast administrative machinery working with its
irresistible force and unfailing regularity in obedience to the will of
rulers, whose motives are not understood, undoubtedly has a paralyz-
ing influence on the life of the nations of India, which, if not
counteracted, would work deep mischief. Something in the way of
counteraction has been done, though not always with knowledge.
The difficulties inherent in the problem of reconciling foreign rule with
self-government in an Asiatic country are enormous.

self-government; and the virtues of truth and honesty, in all their relations with each other, were indispensably necessary to enable them to govern themselves.[1] A common interest often united a good many village communities in a bond of union, and established a kind of brotherhood over extensive tracts of richly cultivated land. Self-interest required that they should unite to defend themselves against attacks with which they were threatened at every returning harvest in a country where every prince was a robber upon a scale more or less large according to his means, and took the field to rob while the lands were covered with the ripe crops upon which his troops might subsist; and where every man who practised robbery with open violence followed what he called an "*imperial* trade" (pādshāhī kām)—the only trade worthy the character of a gentleman. The same interest required that they should unite in deceiving their own prince, and all his officers, great and small, as to the real resources of their estates; because they all knew that the prince would admit of no other limits to his exactions than their abilities to pay at the harvest. Though, in their relations with each other, all these village communities spoke as much truth as those of any other communities in the world; still, in their relation with the government, they told as many lies;—for falsehood, in the one set of relations, would have incurred the odium of the whole of their circles of society—truth, in in the other, would often have involved the same penalty. If a man had told a lie to *cheat* his neighbour, he would have become an object of hatred and contempt—if he told a lie to *save* his neighbour's fields from an increase of rent

[1] But panegyrics on the self-government of Indian villages must always be read with the qualification that the standard of such government was very low, and that hundreds of acts and omissions were tolerated which are intolerable to a modern European government. Hence comes the difficulty of enforcing numerous reforms loudly called for by European opinion. The vast native population hates reform and innovation for many reasons, and, above all, because they involve expense, which to the native mind appears wholly unwarrantable.

or tax, he would have become an object of esteem and respect.[1]   If the government officers were asked whether there was any truth to be found among such communities, they would say, *No, that the truth was not in them ;* because they would not cut each other's throats by telling them the real value of each other's fields.

If the peasantry were asked, they would say there was plenty of truth to be found everywhere except among a few scoundrels, who, to curry favour with the government officers, betrayed their trust, and told the value of their neighbours' fields.   In their ideas, he might as well have gone off, and brought down the common enemy upon them in the shape of some princely robber of the neighbourhood.

Locke says : "Outlaws themselves keep faith and rules of justice one with another—they practise them as rules of convenience within their own communities ; but it is impossible to conceive that they embrace justice as a practical principle who act fairly with their fellow highwaymen, and at the same time plunder or kill the next honest man they meet." (Vol. I, p. 37.)   In India, the difference between the army of a prince and the gang of a robber was, in the general estimation of the people, only in *degree* —they were both driving an *imperial trade*, a "padshāhī kām."   Both took the auspices, and set out on their expedition after the Dasahrā, when the autumn crops were ripening ; and both thought the Deity propitiated as soon as they found the omens favourable ;[2] one attacked palaces and capitals, the other villages and merchants' store-rooms. The members of the army of the prince thought as little of

---

[1] The same phenomenon is observable in rural Ireland, where, as in India, an unhappy history has generated profound distrust and dislike of official authority.   The Irish peasant has always been ready to give his neighbour "the loan of an oath," and a refusal to give it would be thought unneighbourly.   An Irish Land Commission and an Indian Settlement Officer must alike expect to receive startling information about the value of land.

[2] *Ante,* Vol. I, p. 359.

the justice or injustice of his cause as those of the gang of the robber ; the people of his capital hailed the return of the victorious prince who had contributed so much to their wealth, to his booty, and to their self-love by his victory. The village community received back the robber and his gang with the same feelings : by their skill and daring they had come back loaded with wealth, which they were always disposed to spend liberally with their neighbours. There was no more of truth in the prince and his army in their relations with the princes and people of neighbouring principalities, than in the robber and his gang in their relations with the people robbed. The prince flatters the self-love of his army and his people ; the robber flatters that of his gang and his village—the question is only in degree ; the persons whose self-love is flattered are blind to the injustice and cruelty of the attack—the prince is the idol of a people, the robber the idol of a gang. Was ever robber more atrocious in his attacks upon a merchant or a village than Louis XIV. of France in his attacks upon the Palatine and Palatinate of the Rhine? How many thousand similar instances might be quoted of princes idolized by their people for deeds equally atrocious in their relations with other people? What nation or sovereign ever found fault with their ambassadors for telling lies to the kings, courts, and people of other countries ?[1]

Rome, during the whole period of her history, was a mere den of execrable thieves, whose feelings were systematically

---

[1] Hume, in speaking of Scotland in the fifteenth century, says, "Arms more than laws prevailed ; and courage, preferably to equity and justice, was the virtue most valued and respected. The nobility, in whom the whole power resided, were so connected by hereditary alliances, or so divided by inveterate enmities, that it was impossible, without employing an armed force, either to punish the most flagrant guilt, or to give security to the most entire innocence. Rapine and violence, when employed against a hostile tribe, instead of making a person odious among his own clan, rather recommended him to their esteem and approbation ; and, by rendering him useful to the chieftain, entitled him to the preference above his fellows."

brutalized by the most revolting spectacles, that they
might have none of those sympathies with suffering
humanity, none of those " compunctious visitings of conscience," which might be found prejudicial to the interests
of the gang, and beneficial to the rest of mankind. Take,
for example, the conduct of this atrocious gang under
Æmilius Paulus, against Epirus and Greece generally after
the defeat of Perseus, all under the deliberate decrees of
the senate : take that of this gang under his son Scipio the
younger, against Carthage and Numantia ; under Cato, at
Cyprus—all in the same manner under the *deliberate decrees
of the senate.* Take indeed the whole of her history as a re-
public, and we find it that of the most atrocious band of robbers that was ever associated against the rest of their species.
In her relations with the rest of mankind Rome was collectively devoid of truth ; and her citizens, who were sent to
govern conquered countries, were no less devoid of truth individually—they cared nothing whatever for the feelings or
the opinions of the people governed ; in their dealings with
them, truth and honour were entirely disregarded. The
only people whose favourable opinion they had any desire
to cultivate were the members of the great gang ; and the
most effectual mode of conciliating them was to plunder the
people of conquered countries, and distribute the fruits
among them in presents of one kind or another. Can any
man read without shuddering that it was the practice
among this atrocious gang to have all the multitude of unhappy prisoners of both sexes, and of all ranks and ages, who
annually graced the triumphs of their generals, taken off
and murdered just at the moment when these generals
reached the Capitol, amid the shouts of the multitude, that
their joys might be augmented by the sight or conscious-
ness of the sufferings of others ? (See Hooke's Roman
History, Vol. III, p. 488 ; Vol. IV, p. 541.) " It was the
custom that, when the triumphant conqueror turned his
chariot towards the Capitol, he commanded the captives to
be led to prison, and there put to death, that so the glory

of the victor and the miseries of the vanquished might be
in the same moment at the utmost." How many millions
of the most innocent and amiable of their species must have
been offered up as human sacrifices to the triumphs of the
leaders of this great gang! The women were almost as
brutalized as the men ; lovers met to talk " soft nonsense,"
at exhibitions of gladiators. Valeria, the daughter and
sister of two of the first men in Rome, was beautiful, gay,
and lively, and of unblemished reputation. Having been
divorced from her husband, she and the monster Sylla
made love to each other at one of these exhibitions of
gladiators, and were soon after married. Gibbon, in
speaking of the lies which Severus told his two competitors
in the contest for empire, says, " Falsehood and insincerity, unsuitable as they seem to the dignity of public
transactions, offend us with a less degrading idea of mean-
ness than when they are found in the intercourse of private
life. In the latter, they discover a want of courage ; in
the other, only a defect of power ; and, as it is impossible for the most able statesmen to subdue millions of
followers and enemies by their own personal strength,
the world, under the name of *policy*, seems to have.
granted them a very liberal indulgence of craft and dissimulation." [1]

But the weak in society are often obliged to defend
themselves against the strong by the same weapons ; and
the world grants them the same liberal indulgence. Men
advocate the use of the ballot in elections that the weak
may defend themselves and the free institutions of the
country, by dissimulation, against the strong who would
oppress them. [2] The circumstances under which falsehood
and insincerity are tolerated by the community in the best
societies of modern days are very numerous ; and the worst
society of modern days in the civilized world, when slavery
does not prevail, is immeasurably superior to the best in

---

[1] Gibbon, Chapter V. The remark refers to Septimius Severus.
[2] The Ballot Act became law in 1872.

ancient days, or in the middle ages. Do we not every day hear men and women, in what are called the best societies, declaring to one individual or one set of acquaintances that the pity, the sympathy, the love, or the admiration they have been expressing for others is, in reality, all feigned to soothe or please? As long as the motive is not base, men do not spurn the falsehood as such. How much of untruth is tolerated in the best circles of the most civilized nations, in the relations between electors to corporate and legislative bodies, and the candidates for election? between nominators to offices under government and the candidates for nomination? between lawyers and clients, vendors and purchasers? (particularly of horses,)—between the recruiting sergeant and the young recruit, whom he has found a little angry with his widowed mother, whom he makes him kill by false pictures of what a soldier may hope for in the "bellaque matribus detestata" to which he invites him.[1]

There is, I believe, no class of men in India from whom it is more difficult to get the true statement of a case pending before a court than the Sepoys of our native regiments; and yet there are, I believe, no people in the world from whom it is more easy to get it in their own village communities, where they state it before their relations, elders, and neighbours, whose esteem is necessary to their happiness, and can be obtained only by an adherence to truth. Every case that comes before a regimental court involves, or is supposed to involve, the interest or feelings of some one or other of their companions; and the question which the deponent asks himself is—not what religion, public justice, the interests of

---

[1] All that the author says is true, and yet it does not alter the fact that Indian society is permeated and paralyzed by almost universal distrust. Such universal distrust does not prevail in England. This difference between the two societies is fundamental, and its reality is fully recognized by natives of India.

discipline and order, or the wishes of his officers require,
or what would appear manly and honourable before the
elders of his own little village, but what will secure
the esteem, and what will excite the hatred, of his comrades. This will often be downright, deliberate falsehood,
sworn upon the Korān or the Ganges water before his
officers.

Many a brave sepoy have I seen faint away from the
agitated state of his feelings, under the dread of the Deity
if he told lies with the Ganges water in his hands, and of
his companions if he told the truth, and caused them to
be punished. Every question becomes a party question,
and the "point of honour" requires that every witness
shall tell as many lies about it as possible.[1] When I go
into a village, and talk with the people in any part of India,
I know that I shall get the truth out of them on all subjects as long as I can satisfy them that I am not come on
the part of the government to inquire into the value of
their fields with a view to new impositions, and this I can
always do; but, when I go among the sepoys to ask about
anything, I feel pretty sure that I have little chance of
getting at the truth; they will take the alarm and try to
deceive me, lest what I learn should be brought up at some
future day against them or their comrades. The Duke of
Wellington says, speaking of the English soldiers:—"It is
most difficult to convict a prisoner before a regimental
court-martial; for, I am sorry to say, that soldiers have
little regard to the oath administered to them; and the
officers who are sworn well and truly to try and determine
according to the evidence, the matter before them, have too
much regard to the strict *letter* of that administered to
them." Again :—"The witnesses being in almost every
instance common soldiers, whose conduct this tribunal was
instituted to control, the consequence is that perjury is

[1] Compare the author's account of the fraudulent practices of the
Company's sepoys when on leave in Oudh. (*Journey through the
Kingdom of Oude,* Vol. I, p.p. 286-304.)

almost as common an offence as drunkenness and plunder, &c."[1]

In the ordinary civil tribunals of Europe and America a man commonly feels that, though he is removed far from the immediate presence of those whose esteem is necessary for him, their eyes are still upon him, because the statements he may give will find their way to them through the medium of the press. This he does not feel in the civil courts of India, nor in the military courts of Europe, or of any other part of the world, and the man who judges of the veracity of a whole people from the specimens he may witness in such courts, cannot judge soundly.

Shaikh Sādī, in his "Gulistān," has the following tale :—
" I have heard that a prince commanded the execution of a captive who was brought before him ; when the captive, having no hope of life, told the prince that he disgraced his throne. The prince, not understanding him, turned to one of his ministers and asked him what he had said. ' He says,' replied the minister, quoting a passage from the Korān, ' God loves those who subdue their passions, forgive injuries, and do good to his creatures.' The prince pitied the poor captive, and countermanded the orders for the execution. Another minister, who owed a spite to the one who first spoke, said, ' Nothing but truth should be spoken by such persons as we in the presence of the prince ; the captive spoke abusively and insolently, and you have not interpreted his words truly.' The prince frowned and said, ' His false interpretation pleases me more than thy true one, because his was given for a good, and thine for a malignant, purpose ; and wise men have said that "a peace-making lie is better than a factious or anger-exciting truth." ' "[2]

---

[1] The editor has failed to find these quotations in the Wellington Despatches.

[2] This is the first story in the first chapter of the "Gulistān." The Mishkāt-ul-Masābih (*Matthews*, Vol. II, p. 427) teaches the same doctrine as Sādī :—" That person is not a liar who makes peace between two people, and speaks good words to do away their quarrel although

He who would too fastidiously condemn this doctrine should think of the massacre of Thessalonica, and how much better it would have been for the great Theodosius to have had by his side the peace-making Ambrose, Archbishop of Milan, than the anger-exciting Rufinus, when he heard of the offence which that city had committed.[1]

In despotic governments, where lives, characters, and liberties are every moment at the mercy, not only of the prince, but of all his public officers from the highest to the lowest, the occasions in which men feel authorized and actually called upon by the common feelings of humanity to tell "peace-making lies" occur every day—nay, every hour, every petty officer of government, "armed with his little brief authority," is a little tyrant surrounded by men whose all depends upon his will, and who dare not tell him the truth—-the "point of honour" in this little circle demands that every one should be prepared to tell him "peace-making lies"; and the man who does not do so when the occasion seems to call for it, incurs the odium of the whole circle, as one maliciously disposed to speak "anger-exciting or factious truths." Poor Cromwell and Anne Boleyn were obliged to talk of *love* and *duty* towards their brutal murderer, Henry VIII., and tell "peace-making lies" on the scaffold to save their poor children from his resentment. European gentlemen in India often, by their violence, surround themselves with circles of the same kind, in which the "point of honour" demands that every member shall be prepared to tell "peace-making lies," to save the others from the effects of their master's ungovern-

they should be lies ; and that person who carries good words from one to another is not a tale-bearer."

[1] Gibbon, Chapter XXVII. In the year A.D. 390 Botheric, the general of Theodosius, was murdered by a mob at Thessalonica. Acting on the advice of Rufinus, the emperor avenged his officer's death by an indiscriminate massacre of the inhabitants, in which numbers variously estimated at from 7,000 to 15,000 perished. The emperor quickly felt remorse for the atrocity of which he had been guilty, and submitted to do public penance under the direction of Ambrose.

able passions—falsehood is their only safeguard ; and, consequently, falsehood ceases to be odious. Countenanced in the circles of the violent, falsehood soon becomes countenanced in those of the mild and forbearing ; their domestics pretend a dread of their anger which they really do not feel ; and they gain credit for having the same good excuse among those who have no opportunity of becoming acquainted with the real character of the gentlemen in their domestic relations — all are thought to be more or less *tigerish* in these relations, particularly *before breakfast*, because some are *known* to be so.[1]

I have known the native officers of a judge who was really a very mild and worthy man, but who lived a very secluded life, plead as their excuse for all manner of bribery and corruption, that their persons and character were never safe from his violence ; and urge that men whose tenure of office was very insecure, and who were every hour in the day exposed to so much indignity, could not possibly be blamed for making the most of their position. The society around believed all this, and blamed, not the native officers, but the judge, or the government, who placed them in such a situation. Other judges and magistrates have been known to do what this person was merely reported to do, otherwise society would neither have given credit to his officers, nor have held them excused for their malpractices.[2] Those European gentlemen who allow their passions to get the better of their reason among their domestics do much to lower the character of their countrymen in the estimation of the people ; but the high officials who forget what they owe to themselves and the native officers of their courts, when presiding on the bench of justice, do ten thousand times more ; and I grieve to say that I have known a few officials of this class.

[1] The sum total of truth in India would not, I fear, be appreciably increased if every European had the temper of an angel.

[2] The editor has never known a reputation for corruption in any way lower the social position of a native official.

We have in England known many occasions, particularly in the cases of prosecutions by the officers of government for offences against the state, where little circles of society have made it a "point of honour" for some individuals to speak untruths, and for others to give verdicts against their consciences; some occasions indeed where those who ventured to speak the truth, or give a verdict according to their conscience, were in danger from the violence of popular resentment. Have we not, unhappily, in England and among our countrymen in all parts of the world, experience of a wide difference between what is exacted from members of particular circles of society by the "point of honour," and what is held to be strict religious truth by the rest of society? Do we not see gentlemen cheating their tradesmen, while they dare not leave a gambling debt unpaid? The "point of honour" in the circle to which they belong demands that the one should be paid, because the non-payment would involve a breach of faith in their relations with each other, as in the case of the members of a gang of robbers; but the non-payment of a tradesman's bill involves only a breach of faith in a gentleman's relations with a lower-order. At least, some gentlemen do not feel any apprehension of incurring the odium of the circle in which they move by cheating of this kind. In the same manner the roué, or libertine of rank, may often be guilty of all manner of falsehoods and crimes to the females of the class below him, without any fear of incurring the odium of either males or females of his own circle; on the contrary, the more crimes he commits of this sort, the more sometimes he may expect to be caressed by males and females of his own order. The man who would not hesitate a moment to destroy the happiness of a family by the seduction of the wife or the daughter, would not dare to leave one shilling of a gambling debt unpaid—the one would bring down upon him the odium of his circle, but the other would not; and the odium of that circle is the only kind of odium he dreads. Appius Claudius apprehended no odium from his own order—the patrician—from the violation of the daughter of Virginius, of the plebeian order; nor did Sextus Tarquinius of the royal order, apprehend any from the violation of Lucretia, of the patrician order —neither would have been punished by their own order, but they were both punished by the injured orders below them.

Our own penal code punished with death the poor man who stole a little food to save his children from starvation, while it left to exult in the caresses of his own order, the wealthy libertine who robbed a father and mother of their only daughter, and consigned her to a life of infamy and misery. The poor victim of man's brutal passions and base falsehood suffered inevitable and exquisite punishment, while the laws and usages of society left the man himself untouched. He had nothing to apprehend if the father of his victim happened to be of the lower order, or a minister of the Church of Christ; because his own order would justify his refusing to meet the one in single combat, and the other dared not invite him to it, and the law left no remedy.[1]

Take the two parties in England into which society is politically divided. There is hardly any species of falsehood uttered by the members of the party out of power against the members of the party in power that is not tolerated and even applauded by one party; men state deliberately what they know to be utterly devoid of truth regarding the conduct of their opponents; they basely ascribe to them motives by which they know they were never actuated, merely to deceive the public, and to promote the interests of their party, without the slightest fear of incurring odium by so doing in the minds of any

---

[1] The argument in the author's mind seems to be that the unveracity practised and condoned by certain classes of the natives of India on certain occasions is, at least, not more reprehensible than the vices practised and condoned by certain classes of Europeans on certain occasions.

but their political opponents. If a foreigner were to judge of the people of England from the tone of their newspapers, he would say that there was assuredly neither honour, honesty, nor truth to be found among the classes which furnished the nation with its ministers and legislators ; for a set of miscreants more atrocious than the Whig and Tory ministers and legislators of England were represented to be in these papers never disgraced the society of any nation upon earth.

Happily, all foreigners who read these journals know that in what the members of one party say of those of the other, or are reported to say, there is often but little truth ; and that there is still less of truth in what the editors and correspondents of the ultra journals of one party write about the characters, conduct, and sentiments of the members of the other.

There is one species of untruth to which we English people are particularly prone in India, and, I am assured, everywhere else. It is this. Young "miss in her teens," as soon as she finds her female attendants in the wrong, no matter in what way, exclaims, "It is so like the natives ;" and the idea of the same error, vice, or crime, becomes so habitually associated in her mind with every native she afterwards sees, that she can no more separate them than she can the idea of ghosts and hobgoblins from darkness and solitude. The young cadet or civilian, as soon as he finds his valet, butler, or groom in the wrong, exclaims, "It is so like blacky—so like the niggers ; they are all alike, and what could you expect from him?" He has been constantly accustomed to the same vicious association of ideas in his native land—if he has been brought up in a family of Tories, he has constantly heard those he most reverenced exclaim, when they have found, or fancied they found, a Whig in the wrong, "It is so like the Whigs—they are all alike—there is no trusting any of them." If a Protestant, "It is so like the Catholics ; there is no trusting them in any condition of life." The members of Whig and

Catholic families may say the same, perhaps, of Tories and Protestants. An untravelled Englishman will sometimes say the same of a Frenchman; and the idea of everything that is bad in man will be associated in his mind with the image of a Frenchman. If he hears of an act of dishonour by a person of that nation, "It is so like a Frenchman—they are all alike; there is no honour in them." A Tory goes to America, predisposed to find in all who live under republican governments every species of vice and crime; and no sooner sees a man or woman misbehave, than he exclaims, "It is so like the Americans—they are all alike; but what could you expect from republicans?" At home, when he considers himself in relation to the members of the parties opposed to him in religion or politics, they are associated in his mind with everything that is vicious; abroad, when he considers the people of other countries in relation to his own, if they happen to be Christians, he will find them associated in his mind with everything that is good, or everything that is bad, in proportion as their institutions happen to conform to those which his party advocates. A Tory will abuse America and Americans, and praise the Austrians. A Whig will, *perhaps*, abuse the Austrians and others who live under paternal or despotic governments, and praise the Americans, who live under institutions still more free than his own.

This has properly been considered by Locke as a species of madness to which all mankind are more or less subject; and from which hardly any individual can entirely free himself. "There is," he says, "scarce a man so free from it, but that if he should always, on all occasions, argue or do as in some cases he constantly does, would not be thought fitter for Bedlam than civil conversation. I do not here mean when he is under the power of an unruly passion, but in the steady, calm course of his life. That which thus captivates their reason, and leads men of sincerity blindfold from common sense will, when examined, be found to be what we are speaking of. Some independent

ideas, of no alliance to one another, are, by education,
custom, and the constant din of their party, so coupled in
their minds, that they always appear there together, and
they can no more separate them in their thoughts than if
they were but one idea, and they operate as if they really
were so." (Book II, Chap. 33.)

Perjury had long since ceased to be considered disgraceful, or even discreditable, among the patrician order in
Rome before the soldiers ventured to break their oaths of
allegiance.   Military service had, from the ignorance and
selfishness of this order, been rendered extremely odious
to free-born Romans ; and they frequently mutinied and
murdered their generals, though they would not desert,
because they had sworn not to do so.   To break his oath
by deserting the standards of Rome was to incur the hatred
and contempt of the great mass of the people—the soldier
dared not hazard this.   But patricians of senatorial and
consular rank did not hesitate to violate their oaths whenever it promised any advantage to the patrician order
collectively or individually, because it excited neither contempt nor indignation in that order.   "They have been
false to their generals," said Fabius, " but they have never
deceived the gods.   I know they *can* conquer, and they
shall swear to do so."   They swore and conquered.

Instead of adopting measures to make the duties of a
soldier less odious, the patricians turned their hatred of
these duties to account, and at a high price sold an absolu-
tion from their oath.   While the members of the patrician
order bought and sold oaths among themselves merely to
deceive the lower orders, they were still respected among
the plebeians ; but when they began to sell dispensations
to the members of this lower order, the latter also, by
degrees, ceased to feel any veneration for the oath, and it
was no longer deemed disgraceful to desert duties which
the higher order made no effort to render less odious.

"That they who draw the breath of life in a court, and
pass all their days in an atmosphere of lies, should have

any very sacred regard for truth, is hardly to be expected.
They experience such falsehood in all who surround them,
that deception, at least suppression of the truth, almost
seems necessary for self-defence ; and, accordingly, if their
speech be not framed upon the theory of the French
cardinal, that language was given to man for the better
concealment of his thoughts, they at least seem to regard
in what they say, not its resemblance to the fact in question,
but rather its subserviency to the purpose in view."
(*Brougham's George IV.*) "Yet, let it never be forgotten,
that princes are nurtured in falsehood by the atmosphere
of lies which envelopes their palace ; steeled against natural
sympathies by the selfish natures of all that surround
them ; hardened in cruelty, partly indeed by the fears
incident to their position, but partly too by the unfeeling
creatures, the factions, the unnatural productions of a court
whom alone they deal with ; trained for tyrants by the
prostration which they find in all the minds which they
come in contact with ; encouraged to domineer by the
unresisting medium through which all their steps to power
and its abuse are made." (*Brougham's Carnot.*)

But Lord Brougham is too harsh. Johnson has observed
truly enough, "Honesty is not necessarily greater where
elegance is less ; " nor does a sense of supreme or despotic
power necessarily imply the exercise or abuse of it. Princes
have, happily, the same yearning as the peasant after the
respect and affection of the circle around them, and the
people under them ; and they must generally seek it by
the same means.

I have mentioned the village communities of India as
that class of the population among whom truth prevails
most ; but I believe there is no class of men in the world
more strictly honourable in their dealings than the mercantile classes of India. Under native governments a
merchant's books were appealed to as "holy writ," and the
confidence in them has certainly not diminished under our
rule. There have been instances of their being seized by

the magistrate, and subjected to the inspection of the officers of his court. No officer of a native government ventured to seize them; the merchant was required to produce them as proof of particular entries, and, while the officers of government did no more, there was no danger of false accounts.

An instance of deliberate fraud or falsehood among native merchants of respectable station in society is extremely rare. Among the many hundreds of bills I have had to take from them for private remittances, I have never had one dishonoured, or the payment upon one delayed beyond the day specified; nor do I recollect ever hearing of one who had. They are so careful not to speculate beyond their means, that an instance of failure is extremely rare among them. No one ever in India hears of families reduced to ruin or distress by the failure of merchants or bankers; though here, as in all other countries advanced in the arts, a vast number of families subsist upon the interest of money employed by them.[1]

There is no class of men more interested in the stability of our rule in India than this of the respectable merchants; nor is there any upon whom the welfare of our government and that of the people more depend. Frugal, first upon principle, that they may not in their expenditure encroach

[1] Since the author wrote the above remarks, the conditions of Indian trade have been revolutionized by the development of roads, railways, telegraphs, postal facilities, and exports. The Indian merchant has been drawn into the vortex of European and American commerce. He is, in consequence, not quite so cautious as he used to be, and is more liable to severe loss or failure, though he is still far more inclined to caution than are his Western rivals. The native banker is undoubtedly honest in ordinary banking transactions and anxious to maintain his commercial credit, but he will often stoop to the most discreditable devices in the purchase of a coveted estate, the foreclosure of a mortgage, and the like. His books, nowadays, are certainly not "appealed to as holy writ," and many merchants keep a duplicate set for income-tax purposes. The happy people of 1836 had never heard of income-tax. Private remittances are now seldom made through native bankers.

upon their capitals, they become so by habit; and when they advance in life they lay out their accumulated wealth in the formation of those works which shall secure for them, from generation to generation, the blessings of the people of the towns in which they have resided, and those of the country around. It would not be too much to say that one-half of the great works which embellish and enrich the face of India, in tanks, groves, wells, temples, &c., have been formed by this class of the people solely with the view of securing the blessings of mankind by contributing to their happiness in solid and permanent works.[1] "The man who has left behind him great works in temples, bridges, reservoirs, and caravanserais for the public good, does not die," says Shaikh Sādī,[2] the greatest of Eastern poets, whose works are more read and loved than those of any other uninspired man that has ever written, not excepting our own beloved Shakspeare.[3] He is as much loved and admired by Hindoos as by Muhammadans; and from boyhood to old age he continues the idol of the imaginations of both. The boy of ten, and the old man of seventy, alike delight to read and quote him for the music of his verses, and the beauty of his sentiments, precepts, and imagery.[4]

It was to the class last mentioned, whose incomes are derived from the profits of stock invested in manufactures and commerce, that Europe chiefly owed its rise and prog-

---

[1] These observations, which are perfectly true, form a corrective to the fashionable abuse of the Indian capitalist, whose virtues and merits are seldom noticed.

[2] The editor has not succeeded in tracing this quotation, but several passages to a similar effect occur in the Gulistān.

[3] I ought to except Confucius, the great Chinese moralist. [W. H. S.]

[4] For a brief notice of Sādī, see *ante,* Vol. I, p. 93, *note.* The Gulistān is everywhere used as a text-book in schools where Persian is taught. The author's extant correspondence shows that he was fascinated by the charms of Persian poetry, even during the first year of his residence in India.

ress after the downfall of the Roman empire, and the long night of darkness and desolation which followed it. It was through the means of mercantile industry, and the municipal institutions to which it gave rise, that the enlightened sovereigns of Europe were enabled to curb the licence of the feudal aristocracy, and to give to life, property, and character that security without which society could not possibly advance ; and it was through the same means that the people were afterwards enabled to put those limits to the authority of the sovereign, and to secure to themselves that share in the government without which society could not possibly be free or well constituted. Upon the same foundation may we hope to raise a superstructure of municipal corporations and institutions in India, such as will give security and dignity to the society ; and the sooner we begin upon the work the better.[1]

[1] The work was "begun upon" about thirty years ago, and "a superstructure of municipal corporations and institutions" now exists in every part of India. But "the same foundation" does not exist. The stout burghers of the mediæval English and German towns have no Indian equivalents. The superstructure of the municipal institutions is all that Acts of the legislature can make it ; the difficulty is to find or make a solid foundation. Still, it was right and necessary to establish municipal institutions in India, and, notwithstanding all weaknesses and defects, they are of considerable value, and are slowly developing.

CHAPTER III[1]

Declining Fertility of the Soil—Popular Notion of the Cause.

On the 13th[2] we came on ten miles to Sāhar, over a plain of poor soil, carelessly cultivated, and without either manure or irrigation. Major Godby left us at Govardhan to return to Agra. He would have gone on with us to Delhi; but having the command of his regiment, and being a zealous officer, he did not like to leave it so long during the exercising season. We felt much the loss of his society. He is a man of great observation and practical good sense; has an infinite fund of good humour, and a cheerfulness of temperament that never seems to flag—a more agreeable companion I have never met. The villages in these parts are literally crowded with peafowl. I counted no less than forty-six feeding close by among the houses of one hamlet on the road, all wild, or rather *unappropriated*, for they seemed on the best possible terms with the inhabitants. At Sāhar our water was drawn from wells eighty feet deep, and this is said to be the ordinary depth from which water is drawn; consequently irrigation is too expensive to be common. It is confined almost exclusively to small patches of garden cultivation in the vicinity of villages.

On the 14th we came on sixteen miles to Kosi, for the most part over a poor soil badly cultivated, and almost exclusively devoted to autumn crops, of which cotton is the principal. I lost the road in the morning before day-

[1] Chapter X of Vol. II of original edition.
[2] January, 1836.

light,[1] and the trooper, who usually rode with me, had not come up. I got an old landholder from one of the villages to walk on with me a mile, and put me in the right road. I asked him what had been the state of the country under the former government of the Jāts and Marāthās, and was told that the greater part was a wild jungle. " I remember," said the old man, " when you could not have got out of the road hereabouts without a good deal of risk. I could not have ventured a hundred yards from the village without the chance of having my clothes stripped off my back. Now the whole face of the country is under cultivation, and the roads are safe ; formerly the governments kept no faith with their landholders and cultivators, exacting ten rupees where they had bargained for five, whenever they found the crops good ; but, in spite of all this 'zulm'" (oppression), said the old man, "there was then more 'barkat' (blessings from above) than now. The lands yielded more returns to the cultivator, and he could maintain his little family better upon five acres than he can now upon ten."

"To what, my old friend, do you attribute this very unfavourable change in the productive powers of your soil ? "

"A man cannot, sir, venture to tell the truth at all times, and in all places," said he.

"You may tell it now with safety, my good old friend, I am a mere traveller ('musāfir') going to the hills in search of health, from the valley of the Nerbudda, where the people have been suffering much from blight, and are much perplexed in their endeavour to find a cause."

"Here, sir, we all attribute these evils to the dreadful system of *perjury*, which the practices of your judicial courts have brought among the people. You are perpetually putting the Ganges water into the hands of the Hindoos, and the Korān into those of Muhammadans ; and all kinds of lies are every day told upon them. God

---

[1] The old Anglo-Indian rose much earlier than his successor of the present day commonly does.

Almighty can stand this no longer; and the lands have
.ceased to be blessed with that fertility which they had before
this sad practice began.   This, sir, is almost the only fault
we have, any of us, to, find with your government; men,
by this system of perjury, are able to cheat each other out
of their rights, and bring down sterility upon the land, by
which the innocent are made to suffer for the guilty."

On reaching our tents, I asked a respectable farmer, who
came to pay his respects to the Commissioner of the division, Mr. Fraser, what he thought of the matter, telling him
what I had heard from my old friend on the road.   " The
diminished fertility is," said he, "owing no doubt to the
want of those salutary fallows which the fields got under
former governments, when invasions and civil wars were
things of common occurrence, and kept at least two-thirds
of the land waste; but there is, on the other hand, no
doubt that you have encouraged perjury a good deal in your
courts of justice; and this perjury must have some effect
in depriving the land of the blessing of God.[1]   Every
man now, who has a cause in your civil courts, seems to
think it necessary either to swear falsely himself, or to get
others to do it for him.   The European gentlemen, no
doubt, do all they can to secure every man his right, but,
surrounded as they are by perjured witnesses, and corrupt
native officers, they commonly labour in the dark."

Much of truth is to be found among the village communities of India, where they have been carefully maintained, if people will go among them to seek it.   Here, as
almost everywhere else, truth is the result of self-government, whether arising from choice, under municipal institutions, or necessity, under despotism and anarchy; self-
government produces self-esteem and pride of character.

Close to our tents we found the people at work, irrigat-

---

[1] For other native explanations of the alleged decrease in fertility of
the soil, *see ante*, Vol. I, Chap. XXVII, where three explanations are
offered, namely, the eating of beef, the prevalence of adultery, and the
impiety of surveys.

ing their fields from several wells, whose waters were all brackish. The crops watered from these wells were admirable—likely to yield at least fifteen returns of the seed. Wherever we go, we find the signs of a great government passed away—signs that must tend to keep alive the recollections, and exalt the ideas of it in the minds of the people. Beyond the boundary of our military and civil stations we find as yet few indications of our reign or character, to link us with the affections of the people. There is hardly anything to indicate our existence as a people or a government in this country; and it is melancholy to think that in the wide extent of country over which I have travelled there should be so few signs of that superiority in science and arts which we boast of, and really do possess, and ought to make conducive to the welfare and happiness of the people in every part of our dominions. The people and the face of the country are just what they might have been had they been governed by police officers and tax-gatherers from the Sandwich Islands, capable of securing life, property, and character, and levying honestly the means of maintaining the establishments requisite for the purpose.[1] Some time after the journey here described, in the early part of November, after a heavy fall of rain, I was driving alone in my buggy from Garhmuktesar on the Ganges to Meerut. The roads were very bad, the stage a double one, and my horse became tired, and unable to go on.[2] I got out at a small village to give him a little rest and food; and sat down, under the shade of one old tree, upon the trunk

[1] The inapplicability of these observations of the author to the present time is a good measure of the material progress of India during the last sixty years. The Ganges Canal, the bridges over the Indus, Ganges, and other great rivers, and numberless engineering works throughout the empire, are permanent witnesses to the scientific superiority of the ruling race. Buildings, which can claim any high degree of architectural excellence are, unfortunately, still rare, but the public edifices of Bombay will not suffer by comparison with those of most capital cities.

[2] The road is now an excellent one.

E 2

of another that the storm had blown down, while my
groom, the only servant I had with me, rubbed down and
baited my horse.. I called for some parched gram from the
same shop which supplied my horse, and got a draught of
good water, drawn from the well by an old woman in a
brass jug lent to me for the purpose by the shopkeeper.[1]

While I sat contentedly and happily stripping my parched
gram of its shell, and eating it grain by grain, the farmer,
or head landholder of the village, a sturdy old Rājpūt,
came up and sat himself, without any ceremony, down by
my side, to have a little conversation. To one of the
dignitaries of the land, in whose presence the aristocracy
are alone entitled to chairs, this easy familiarity on the
part of a poor farmer seems at first somewhat strange and
unaccountable ; he is afraid that the man intends to offer
him some indignity, or, what is still worse, mistakes him for
something less than the dignitary. The following dialogue
took place.

"You are a Rājpūt, and a 'zamīndār'?" (landholder.)

"Yes ; I am the head landholder of this village."

"Can you tell me how that village in the distance is
elevated above the ground ? Is it from the débris of old
villages, or from a rock underneath ? "

"It is from the débris of old villages. That is the
original seat of all the Rājpūts around ; we all trace our
descent from the founders of that village who built and
peopled it many centuries ago."

"And you have gone on subdividing your inheritances
here, as elsewhere, no doubt, till you have hardly any of you
anything to eat ? "

"True, we have hardly any of us enough to eat ; but
that is the fault of the government, that does not leave us

---

[1] Parched gram, or chick-pea, is commonly used by native travellers
as a convenient and readily portable form of food. The "brass
jug" lent to the author could be purified by fire after his use of it.

enough, that takes from us as much when the season is bad as when it is good."[1]

" But your assessment has not been increased, has it ? "

" No, we have concluded a settlement for twenty years upon the same footing as formerly."

" And if the sky were to shower down upon you pearls and diamonds, instead of water, the government would never demand more from you than the rate fixed upon ? "

" No."

" Then why should you expect remissions in the bad seasons ? "

" It cannot be disputed that the ' barkat' (blessing from above) is less under you than it used to be formerly, and that the lands yield less to our labour."

" True, my old friend, but do you know the reason why ? "

" No."

" Then I will tell you. Forty or fifty years ago, in what you call the times of the ' barkat ' (blessing from above), the cavalry of Sikh freebooters from the Panjāb used to sweep over this fine plain, in which stands the said village from which you are all descended ; and to massacre the whole population of some villages, and a certain portion of that of every other village ; and the lands of those killed used to lie waste for want of cultivators. Is not this all true ? "

" Yes, quite true."

" And the fine groves which had been planted over the plain by your ancestors, as they separated from the great parent stock, and formed independent villages and hamlets for themselves, were all swept away and destroyed by the same hordes of freebooters, from whom your poor imbecile emperors, cooped up in yonder large city of Delhi, were utterly unable to defend you ? "

[1] Growls of this kind must not be interpreted too literally. Any native village landholder, if encouraged, would grumble in the same strain.

—"Quite true," said the old man with a sigh. "I remember when all this fine plain was as thickly studded with fine groves of mango-trees as Rohilkhand, or any other part of India."

"You know that the land requires rest from labour, as well as men and bullocks, and that, if you go on sowing wheat and other exhausting crops, it will go on yielding less and less returns, and at last not be worth the tilling?"

"Quite well."

"Then why do you not give the land rest by leaving it longer fallow, or by a more frequent alternation of crops relieve it?"

"Because we have now increased so much that we should not get enough to eat were we to leave it to fallow; and unless we tilled it with exhausting crops we should not get the means of paying our rents to the government."

"The Sikh hordes in former days prevented this; they killed off a certain portion of your families, and gave the land the *rest* which you now refuse it. When you had exhausted one part, you found another recovered by a long fallow, so that you had better returns; but now that we neither kill you, nor suffer you to be killed by others, you have brought all the cultivable lands into tillage; and under the old system of cropping to exhaustion, it is not surprising that they yield you less returns."[1]

By this time we had a crowd of people seated around us upon the ground, as I went on munching my parched gram, and talking to the old patriarch.

They all laughed at the old man at the conclusion of my last speech, and he confessed I was right.

"This is all true, sir, but still your government is not considerate; it goes on taking kingdom after kingdom, and adding to its dominions without diminishing the burthen upon us, its old subjects. Here you have had armies away

[1] This is the permanent difficulty of Indian revenue administration, which no government measures can seriously diminish.

taking Afghānistān, but we shall not have one rupee the less to pay."[1]

" True, my friend, nor would you demand a rupee less from those honest cultivators around us, if we were to leave you all your lands untaxed. You complain of the government—they complain of you." (Here the circle around us laughed at the old man again.) " Nor would you subdivide the lands the less for having it rent-free ; on the contrary, it would be every generation subdivided the more, inas- much as there would be more of local ties, and a greater disinclination of families to separate and seek service abroad."

"True, sir, very true—that is, no doubt, a very great evil."

"And you know it is not an evil produced by us, but one arising out of your own laws of inheritance. You have heard, no doubt, that with us the eldest son gets the whole of the land, and the younger sons all go out in search of service, with such share as they can get of the other property of their father ? "

"Yes, sir ; but when shall we get service ?—you have none to give us. I would serve to-morrow if you would take me as a soldier," said he, stroking his white whiskers.

The crowd laughed heartily ; and some wag observed that I should perhaps think him too old.

· " Well," said the old man, smiling, " the gentleman him- self is not very young, and yet I dare say he is a good servant of his government."

This was paying me off for making the people laugh at his expense.

---

[1] The mission to Kābul, under Captain Alexander Burnes, was not despatched till September, 1837, and troops did not assemble before the conclusion of the treaty with the Sikhs in June 1838. The army crossed the Indus in January, 1839. The conversation in the text is stated to have taken place " some time after the journey herein described," and must, apparently, be dated in November, 1839. The author was in the North-Western Provinces in that year.

"True, my old friend," said I, "but I began to serve, when I was young, and have been long learning."

"Very well," said the old man, "but I should be glad to serve the rest of my life upon a less salary than you got when you began to learn."

"Well, my friend, you complain of our government; but you must acknowledge that we do all we can to protect you, though it is true that we are often acting in the dark."

"Often, sir? you are always acting in the dark; you, hardly any of you, know anything of what your revenue and police officers are doing: there is no justice or redress to be got without paying for it, and it is not often that those who pay can get it."

"True, my old friend, that is bad all over the world. You cannot presume to ask anything even from the Deity himself, without paying the priest who officiates in his temples; and if you should, you would none of you hope to get from your Deity what you asked for."

Here the crowd laughed again, and one of them said that "there was this certainly to be said for our government, that the European gentlemen themselves never took bribes, whatever those under them might do."

"You must not be too sure of that, neither. Did not the Lāl Bībī, the Red Lady, get a bribe for soliciting the judge, her husband, to let go Amīr Singh, who had been confined in jail?"

"How did this take place?"

"About three years ago Amīr Singh was sentenced to imprisonment, and his friends spent a great deal of money in bribes to the native officers of the court, but all in vain. At last they were recommended to give a handsome present to the Red Lady. They did so, and Amīr Singh was released."

"But did they give the present into the lady's own hand?"

"No, they gave it to one of her women."

"And how do you know that she ever gave it to her

mistress, or that her mistress ever heard of the transaction ? "

" She might certainly have been acting without her mistress' knowledge ; but the popular belief is that the Lāl Bībī got the present."

I then told the story of the affair at Jubbulpore, when Mrs. Smith's name had been used for a similar purpose, and the people around us were all highly amused ; and the old man's opinion of the transaction with the Red Lady evidently underwent a change.[1]

We became good friends, and the old man begged me to have my tents, which he supposed were coming up, pitched among them, that he might have an opportunity of showing that he was not a bad subject, though he grumbled against the government.

The next day at Meerut I got a visit from the chief native judge, whose son, a talented youth, is in my office. Among other things, I asked him whether it might not be possible to improve the character of the police by increasing the salaries of the officers, and mentioned my conversation with the landholder.

" Never, sir," said the old gentleman ; " the man that now gets twenty-five rupees a month is contented with making perhaps fifty or seventy-five more ; and the people subject to his authority pay him accordingly. Give him a

---

[1] Some of Mr. Smith's suitors entered into a combination to defraud a suitor in his court of a large sum of money, which he was to pay to Mrs. Smith as she walked in the garden. A dancing girl from the town of Jubbulpore was made to represent Mrs. Smith, and a suit of Mrs. Smith's clothes was borrowed for her from the washerman. The butler took the suitor to the garden, and introduced him to the supposed Mrs. Smith, who received him very graciously, and condescended to accept his offer of five thousand rupees in gold mohurs. The plot was afterwards discovered, and the old butler, washerman, and all, were sentenced to work in a rope on the roads. [W. H. S.]

Penal labour on the roads has long since been discontinued. Similar plots have probably often escaped detection. The whole conversation is a valuable illustration of native habits and modes of thought.

hundred, sir, and he will put a shawl over his shoulders, and the poor people will be obliged to pay him at a rate that will make up his income to four hundred. You will only alter his style of living, and make him a greater burthen to the people. He will always take as long as he thinks he can with impunity."

"But do you not think that when people see a man adequately paid by the government they will the more readily complain of any attempt at unauthorized exactions?"

"Not a bit, sir, as long as they see the same difficulties in the way of prosecuting him to conviction. In the administration of civil justice" (the old gentleman is a civil judge), "you may occasionally see your way, and understand what is doing; but in revenue and police you never have seen it in India, and never will, I think. The officers you employ will all add to their incomes by unauthorized means; and the lower these incomes, the less their pretensions, and the less the populace have to pay."[1]

[1] The subject of the police administration is more fully discussed *post*, in Chapter XIV.

CHAPTER IV[1]

Concentration of Capital and its Effects.

Kosi[2] stands on the borders of Firōzpur, the estate of the late Shams-ud-din, who was hanged at Delhi on the 3rd of October, 1835, for the murder of William Fraser, the representative of the Governor-General in the Delhi city and territories.[3] The Mewātis of Firōzpur are notorious thieves and robbers. During the Nawāb's time they dared not plunder within his territory, but had a free licence to plunder wherever they pleased beyond it.[4] They will now be able to plunder at home, since our tribunals have been introduced to worry prosecutors and their witnesses to death by the distance they have to go, and the tediousness of our process; and thereby to secure impunity to offenders, by making it the interest of those who have been robbed, not only to bear with the first loss without complaint, but largely to bribe police officers to conceal the crimes from

[1] Chapter XI of Vol. II of original edition.
[2] Kosī is twenty-nine miles north-west of Mathurā.
[3] The story of the murder of Mr. Fraser is fully detailed *post* in Chapter IX. After the execution of Shams-ud-din the estate of the criminal was taken possession of by Government, and the town of Firōzpur is now the headquarters of a sub-collectorship of the Gurgāon district in the Panjāb. The Delhi territories were placed under the government of the Lieutenant-Governor of the Panjāb in 1858.
[4] The Mewātī depredations had gone on for centuries. The Sultān Balban (Ghiās-ud-din, alias Ulūgh Khān), who reigned from A.D. 1265–1287, temporarily suppressed them by punishments of awful cruelty, flaying them alive, and so forth. They now supply men to a few robber gangs, but are incapable of mischief on a large scale.

their master, the magistrate, when they happen to come to their knowledge. Here it was that Jeswant Rāo Holkār gave a grand ball on the 14th of October, 1804, while he was with his cavalry covering the siege of Delhi by his regular brigade. In the midst of the festivity he had an European soldier of the King's 76th Regiment, who had been taken prisoner, strangled behind the curtain, and his head stuck upon a spear and placed in the midst of the assembly, where the "nāch" (nautch) girls were made to dance round it. Lord Lake reached the place the next morning in pursuit of this monster; and the gallant regiment, who here heard the story, had soon an opportunity of revenging the foul murder of their comrade in the battle of Dīg, one of the most gallant passages of arms we have ever had in India.[1]

Near Kosī there is a factory in ruins belonging to the late firm of Mercer and Company. Here the cotton of the district used to be collected and screwed under the superin-

---

[1] Delhi was most nobly defended against Holkār by a very small force under Lieutenant-Colonel Burn, who "repelled an assault, and defended a city ten miles in circumference, and which had ever before been given up at the first appearance of an enemy at its gates."

The battle of Dīg was fought on the 13th November, 1804, by the division under the command of General Fraser on the one side, and Holkār's infantry and artillery on the other. "The 76th led the way, with its wonted alacrity and determination," and forced its way into the village in advance of its supports. The fight resulted in the total defeat of the Marāthās, who lost nearly two thousand men, and eighty-seven pieces of cannon. The English loss also was heavy, amounting to upwards of six hundred and forty killed and wounded, including the brave commander, who was mortally wounded, and survived the victory only a few days.

On the night of the 17th November, General Lake in person routed Holkār and his cavalry, killing about three thousand men. The English loss on this occasion amounted to only two men killed, and about twenty wounded.

The fort of Dīg, with a hundred guns and a considerable quantity of ammunition and military stores, was captured on the 24th December of the same year. (Thornton, *History of British India*, p.p. 316–319, 2nd edn., 1859.)

tendence of European agents, preparatory to its embarkation for Calcutta on the river Jumna. On the failure of the firm, the establishment was broken up, and the work, which was then done by one great European merchant, is now done by a score or two of native merchants. There is, perhaps, nothing which India wants more than the concentration of capital; and the failure of all the great commercial houses in Calcutta, in the year 1833, was, unquestionably, a great calamity. They none of them brought a particle of capital into the country, nor does India want a particle from any country; but they *concentrated* it; and had they employed the whole, as they certainly did a good deal of it, in judiciously improving and extending the industry of the natives, they might have been the source of incalculable good to India, its people, and government.[1]

To this concentration of capital in great commercial and manufacturing establishments, which forms the grand characteristic of European in contradistinction to Asiatic societies in the present day, must we look for those changes which we consider desirable in the social and religious institutions of the people. Where land is liable to eternal subdivision by the law and the religion of both the Muhammadan and Hindoo population; where every great work that improves its productive powers, and facilitates the distribution of its produce among the people, in canals, roads, bridges, &c., is made by government; where capital is nowhere concentrated in great commercial or manufacturing establishments, there can be no upper classes in

---

[1] The author was grievously mistaken in supposing that India did not require "a particle" of foreign capital. The railways, and the great tea, coffee, indigo, and other industries, which have been built up and developed during the last fifty years, owe their existence to the hundreds of millions sterling of English capital poured into the country, and could not possibly have been financed from Indian resources. The author seems not to have expected the construction of railways in India, although when he wrote a beginning of the railway system in England had been made.

society but those of office ; and of all societies, perhaps that is the worst in which the higher classes are so exclusively composed. In India, public office has been, and must continue to be, the only road to distinction, until we have *a law of primogeniture*, and *a concentration of capital.* In India no man has ever thought himself respectable, or been thought so by others, unless he is armed with his little "hukūmat;" his "little brief authority" under government, that gives him the command of some public establishment paid out of the revenues of the state.[1] In Europe and America, where capital has been concentrated in great commercial and manufacturing establishments, and free institutions prevail almost as the natural consequence, *industry* is everything ; and those who direct and command it are, happily, looked up to as the source of the wealth, the strength, the virtue, and the happiness of the nation. The concentration of capital in such establishments may, indeed, be considered, not only as the natural consequence, but as the pervading cause of the free institutions by which the mass of the people in European countries are blessed.[2] The mass of the people were as much brutalized and oppressed by the landed aristocracy as they could have been by any official aristocracy before towns and higher classes were created by the concentration of capital.

The same observations are applicable to China. There the land all belongs to the sovereign, as in India ; and, as in India, it is liable to the same eternal subdivision among the sons of those who hold it under him. Capital is nowhere more concentrated in China than in India ; and all the great works that add to the fertility of the soil, and facilitate the distribution of the land labour of the country are formed by the sovereign out of the public revenue.

---

[1] This sentiment is still potent, and explains the eagerness often shown by wealthy landholders of high social rank to obtain official appointments, which to the European mind seem unworthy of their acceptance.

[2] Few readers are likely to accept this proposition.

The revenue is, in consequence, one of office ;[1] and no man considers himself respectable,[2] unless invested with some office under government, that is, under the Emperor. Subdivision of labour, concentration of capital, and machinery render an Englishman everywhere dependent upon the co-operation of multitudes ; while the Chinaman, who as yet knows little of either, is everywhere independent, and able to work his way among strangers. But this very dependence of the Englishman upon the concentration of capital is the greatest source of his strength and pledge of his security, since it supports those members of the higher orders who can best understand and assert the rights and interests of the whole.[3]

If we had any great establishment of this sort in which Christians could find employment and the means of religious and secular instruction, thousands of converts would soon flock to them ; and they would become vast sources of future improvement in industry, social comfort, municipal institutions, and religion. What chiefly prevents the spread of Christianity in India is the dread of exclusion from caste and all its privileges ; and the utter hopelessness of their ever finding any respectable circle of society of the adopted religion, which converts, or would-be converts, to Christianity now everywhere feel. Form such circles for them, make the members of these circles happy in the exertion of honest and independent industry, let those who rise to eminence in them feel that they are considered as respectable and as important in the social system as the servants of Government, and converts will flock around you from all parts, and from all classes of the Hindoo community. I have, since I have been in India,

---

[1] This clause is not intelligible to the editor. The word "revenue" is probably a misprint for "Society."

[2] The original edition prints, "No man considers himself less respectable," which is nonsense.

[3] This sentiment reads oddly in these days of social democracy and continual conflict between capital and labour.

had, I may say, at least a score of Hindoo grass-cutters turn Musalmāns, merely because the grooms and the other grass-cutters of my establishment happened to be of that religion, and they could neither eat, drink, nor smoke with them. Thousands of Hindoos all over India become every year Musalmāns from the same motive ;[1] and we do not get the same number of converts to Christianity, merely because we cannot offer them the same advantages. I am persuaded that a dozen such establishments as that of Mr. Thomas Ashton of Hyde, as described by a physician at Manchester, and noticed in Mr. Baines's admirable work on the *Cotton Manufactures of Great Britain* (page 447), would do more in the way of conversion among the people of India than has ever yet been done by all the religious establishments, or ever will be done by them, without such aid.[2]

I have said that the great commercial houses of Calcutta, which in their ruin involved that of so many useful establishments scattered over India, like that of Kosī, brought no capital into the country. They borrowed from one part of the civil and military servants of government at a high interest that portion of their salary which they saved ; and lent it at a higher interest to others of the same establishment, who for a time required or wished to spend more than they received ; or they employed it at a higher rate of profit for great commercial and manufacturing establishments scattered over India, or spread over the ocean. Their great error was in mistaking nominal for real profits. Calculating their dividend on the nominal profits, and never supposing that there could be any such things as

---

[1] This statement may be a slight exaggeration. Recent converts to Islām are said to be numerous in Eastern Bengal.

[2] The author's whimsical notion that a development of commercial and manufacturing organization in India would cause converts to flock from all parts, and from all classes of the Hindoo community, has not been verified by experience. Much capital is now concentrated in the great cities, and the number of cotton, jute, and other factories is considerable, but Christian converts are not among the goods produced.

losses in commercial speculation, or bad debts from misfortunes and bad faith, they squandered them in lavish
hospitality and ostentatious display, or allowed their
retiring members to take them to England and to every
other part of the world where their creditors might not find
them, till they discovered that all the real capital left at
their command was hardly sufficient to pay back with the
stipulated interest one-tenth of what they had borrowed.
The members of those houses who remained in India up to
the time of the general wreck were of course reduced to
ruin, and obliged to bear the burthen of the odium and
indignation which the ruin of so many thousands of
confiding constituents brought down upon them. Since
that time the savings of civil and military servants
have been invested either in government securities at
a small interest, or in banks, which make their profit
in the ordinary way, by discounting bills of exchange,
and circulating their own notes for the purpose, or
by lending out their money at a high interest of ten
or twelve per cent. to other members of the same
services.[1]

On the 16th of January we went on to Horal, ten miles
over a plain, with villages numerous and large, and in
every one some fine large building of olden times—sarāi,
palace, temple, or tomb, but all going to decay. The
population much more dense than in any of the native
states I have seen; villages larger and more numerous;
trade in the transit of cotton, salt, sugar, and grain, much

[1] The three Presidency Banks, the Bank of Bengal, the Bank of
Madras, and the Bank of Bombay, in which the Indian Government is
interested, are the leading Indian banks. The Bank of Bengal was
opened in 1806. No bank in India is allowed to issue notes. The
paper money in use is issued by the Paper Currency Department of the
Government of India, and the notes are known as "currency notes."
The issue of these notes began in 1862-63. (Balfour's *Cyclopædia*,
s.v. "Bank and Paper Currency.") Much Indian capital is now
invested in joint-stock companies of every kind.

brisker. A great number of hares were here brought to us for sale at threepence apiece, a rate at which they sell at this season in almost all parts of Upper India, where they are very numerous, and very easily caught in nets.

CHAPTER V[1]

Transit Duties in India—Mode of Collecting them.

AT Horal resides a Collector of Customs with two or three uncovenanted European assistants as patrol officers.[2] The rule now is to tax only the staple articles of produce from the west on their transit down into the valley of the Jumna and Ganges, and to have only one line on which these articles shall be liable to duties.[3] They are free to

[1] Chapter XII of Vol. II of original edition.

[2] The term "uncovenanted" may require explanation for readers not familiar with the details of Indian administration. The Indian Civil Service, which supplies most of the higher administrative and judicial officers, is known as the Covenanted service, because its members sign a covenant with the Secretary of State. All the other services, Public Works, Postal, and the rest, were, until recently, grouped together as uncovenanted. In accordance with the report of the Public Service Commission, the future distinction will be between the Imperial and the Provincial services.

[3] The text refers to what was known as the "customs hedge." Before the establishment of the British supremacy each of the innumerable native jurisdictions levied transit duties on many kinds of goods at each of its frontiers, to the infinite vexation of traders. These duties were gradually abolished in British territory, and few, if any, are now enforced by native states. Salt cannot be manufactured in British India without a licence, and the Salt (formerly called Inland Customs) Department is charged with the duty of preventing the manufacture or sale of illicit salt. In its later developments the Customs hedge was used for the collection of the salt duty only. Sir John Strachey took a leading part in its abolition. To secure the levy of the duty on salt, he writes, "there grew up gradually a monstrous system, to which it would be almost impossible to find a parallel in any tolerably civilized country. A Customs line was established which stretched across the whole of India, which in 1869

pass everywhere else without search or molestation. This has, no doubt, relieved the people of these provinces from an infinite deal of loss and annoyance inflicted upon them by the former system of levying the Customs duties, and that without much diminishing the net receipts of Government from this branch of its revenues. But the time may come when Government will be constrained to raise a greater proportion of its collective revenues than it has hitherto done from indirect taxation, and when this time comes, the rule which confines the impost to a single line must of course be abandoned.[1] Under the former system, one great man, with a very high salary, was put in to preside over a host of native agents with very small salaries, and without any responsible intermediate agent whatever to aid

extended from the Indus to the Mahānadī in Madras, a distance of 2,300 miles; and it was guarded by nearly 12,000 men and petty officers, at an annual cost of £162,000. It would have stretched from London to Constantinople. . . . It consisted principally of an immense impenetrable hedge of thorny trees and bushes . . . A similar line, 280 miles in length, was maintained in the north-eastern part of the Bombay Presidency from Dohud to the Runn of Cutch." In 1878 the salt duties were revised, and the necessary arrangements with the native states were made. With effect from the 1st April, 1879, the whole Customs line was abolished, with the exception of a small portion on the Indus. (Sir J. Strachey, *The Finances and Public Works of India*, 1869–1881, London, 1882, p.p. 219, 220, 225.) Great mines of rock salt are worked near the Indus.

[1] Most people who know India intimately are of opinion that indirect taxation is more suitable to the circumstances of the country than direct taxation. Unhappily, however, the opposite policy has prevailed, and the Indian Government has been compelled to surrender most of its sea Customs duties, and the excise duties on salt, opium, and liquor, are the objects of incessant attack. For municipal purposes, indirect taxation, under the name of octroi, is levied by most considerable towns, and attempts to obtain the necessary income by direct taxation are extremely unpopular and unsuccessful. Precautions are taken to prevent the octroi duties from hampering through trade. The above remarks on the suitability of indirect taxation for India are not intended as a defence of the barbarous device of the " Customs hedge," which was indefensible.

him, and to watch over them.[1]   The great man was selected
without any reference to his knowledge of, or fitness for,
the duties entrusted to him, merely because he happened
to be of a certain standing in a certain exclusive service,
which entitled him to a certain scale of salary, or because
he had been found unfit for judicial or other duties requiring more intellect and energy of character.   The consequence was that for every one rupee that went into the
public treasury, ten were taken by these harpies from the
merchants, or other people over whom they had, or could
pretend to have, a right of search.

Some irresponsible native officer who happened to have
the confidence of the great man (no matter in what capacity
he served him) sold for his own profit, and for that of those
whose good-will he might think it worth while to conciliate,
the offices of all the subordinate agents immediately
employed in the collection of the duties.   A man who was
to receive an avowed salary of seven rupees a month would
give him three or four thousand for his post, because it
would give him charge of a detached post, in which he
could soon repay himself with a handsome profit.   A poor
" peon," who was to serve under others, and could never
hope for an independent charge, would give five hundred
rupees for an office which yielded him avowedly only four
rupees a month.   All arrogated the right of search, and

1 This unsound system seems to have prevailed in all departments
during the early years of the present century. " In Bengal, the
monopoly of salt in one form or other dates at least from the establishment of the Board of Trade there in 1765. The strict monopoly of salt
commenced in 1780, under a system of agencies. The system
introduced in 1780 continued in force with occasional modifications
till 1862, when the several salt agencies were gradually abolished,
leaving the supply of salt, whether by importations or excise
manufacture, to private enterprise. Since then, for Bengal Proper, the
supply of the condiment has been obtained chiefly by importation, but
in part by private manufacture under a system of excise." (Balfour's
Cyclopædia, s.v. Salt.) At present the Salt Department is controlled
by a single Commissioner with the Government of India. The fee
payable for a license to manufacture salt is fifty rupees.

the state of Indian society and the climate were admirably suited to their purpose. A person of any respectability would feel himself dishonoured were the females of his family to be *seen*, much less *touched*, while passing along the road in their palanquin or covered carriage ; and to save himself from such dishonour he was everywhere obliged to pay these custom-house officers. Many articles that pass in transit through India would suffer much damage from being opened along the road at any season, and be liable to be spoiled altogether during that of the rains ; and these harpies could always make the merchants open them, unless they paid liberally for their forbearance. Articles were rated to the duty according to their value ; and articles of the same weight were often, of course, of very different values. These officers could always pretend that packages liable to injury from exposure contained within them, among the articles set forth in the invoice, others of greater value in proportion to their weight. Men who carried pearls, jewels, and other articles very valuable compared with their bulk, always depended for their security from robbers and thieves on their concealment ; and there was nothing which they dreaded so much as the insolence and rapacity of these custom-house officers, who made them pay large bribes, or exposed their goods. Gangs of thieves had members in disguise at such stations, who were soon able to discover through the insolence of the officers, and the fears and entreaties of the merchants, whether they had anything worth taking or not.

A party of thieves from Datiyā, in 1832, followed Lord William Bentinck's camp to the bank of the river Jumna near Mathurā, where they found a poor merchant humbly entreating an insolent custom-house officer not to insist upon his showing the contents of the little box he carried in his carriage, lest it might attract the attention of thieves, who were always to be found among the followers of such a camp, and offering to give him anything reasonable for his forbearance. Nothing he could be got to offer would satisfy the rapacity of the man ; the box was taken out and opened. It contained jewels which the poor man hoped to sell to advantage among the European ladies and gentlemen of the Governor-General's suite. He replaced his box in his carriage ; but in half an hour it was travelling post-haste to Datiyā, by relays of thieves who had been posted along the road for such occasions. They quarrelled about the division ; swords were drawn, and wounds inflicted. One of the gang ran off to the magistrate at Sāgar, with whom he had before been acquainted ;[1] and he sent him back with a small party, and a letter to the Datiyā Rājā requesting that he would get the box of jewels for the poor merchant. The party took the precaution of searching the house of the thieves before they delivered the letter to their friend the minister, and by this means recovered about half the jewels, which amounted in all to about seven thousand rupees. The merchant was agreeably surprised when he got back so much of his property through the magistrate of Mathurā, and confirmed the statement of the thief regarding the dispute with the custom-house officer which enabled them to discover the value of the box.

Should Government by-and-by extend the system that obtains in this single line to the Customs all over India they may greatly augment their revenue without any injury, and with but little necessary loss and inconvenience to merchants. The object of all just taxation is to make the subjects contribute to the public burthen in proportion to their means, and with as little loss and inconvenience to themselves as possible. The people who reside west of this line enjoy all their salt, cotton, and other articles which are taxed on crossing the line without the payment of any duties, while those to the east of it are obliged to pay. It is, therefore, not a just line. The advantages are, firstly, that it interposes a body of most efficient officers between

---

[1] The author.

the mass of harpies and the heads of the department, who now virtually superintend the whole system, whereas they used formerly to do so merely ostensibly. They are at once the *tapis* of Prince Husain and the telescope of Prince Ali; they enable the heads of departments to be everywhere and see everything, whereas before they were nowhere and saw nothing.[1]   Secondly, it makes the great staple articles of general consumption alone liable to the payment of duties, and thereby does away in a great measure with the odious right of search.

At Kosī our friend, Charles Fraser, left us to proceed through Mathurā to Agra.   He is a very worthy man and excellent public officer, one of those whom one always meets again with pleasure, and of whose society one never tires.   Mr. Wilmot, the Collector of Customs, and Mr. Wright, one of the patrol officers, came to dine with us. The wind blew so hard all day that the cook and khānsā-mān (butler) were long in despair of being able to give us any dinner at all.   At last we managed to get a tent, closed at every crevice to keep out the dust, for a cook-room; and they were thus able to preserve their master's credit, which no doubt, according to their notions, depended altogether on the quality of his dinner.

---

[1] The same observations, *mutatis mutandis*, are applicable to the magistracy of the country; and the remedy for all the great existing evils must be sought in the same means, the interposition of a body of efficient officers between the magistrate and the "thānadārs," or present head police officers of small divisions. [W. H. S.]   Much has been done to carry out this advice.   The "most efficient officers" of the Customs department alluded to in the text were the European or Eurasian uncovenanted Collectors of Customs and their assistants. The editor's inquiries have failed to trace the source of the author's repeated allusions to Prince Husain and Prince Ali.

CHAPTER VI[1]

Peasantry of India attached to no existing Government—Want of
Trees in Upper India[2]—Cause and Consequence—Wells and
Groves.

WHAT strikes one most after crossing the Chambal is,
I think, the improved size and bearing of the men ; they
are much stouter, and more bold and manly, without being
at all less respectful.   They are certainly a noble peasantry,
full of courage, spirit, and intelligence ; and heartily do I
wish that we could adopt any system that would give our
Government a deep root in their affections, or link their
interests inseparably with its prosperity ; for, with all its
defects, life, property, and character are certainly more
secure, and all their advantages more freely enjoyed under
our Government than under any other they have ever heard
of, or that exists at present in any other part of the country.
The eternal subdivivion of the landed property reduces
them too much to one common level, and prevents the
formation of that middle-class which is the basis of all
that is great and good in European societies—the great
vivifying spirit which animates all that is good above it in
the community.[3]   It is a singular fact that the peasantry,

---

[1] Chapter XIII of Vol. II of original edition.

[2] This phrase is misleading.   There is no want of trees in Upper
India generally ; only certain limited areas are ill-wooded.   Most of
the districts in the plains of the Ganges and Jumna are well
wooded.

[3] This is a favourite doctrine of the author, often reiterated.   The
absence of a powerful middle class is a characteristic, not of India
only, but of all Oriental despotisms, and the subdivision of landed
property is only one of the causes of the non-existence of such a
class.

and, I may say, the landed interest of the country generally, have never been the friends of any existing government, have never considered their interests and that of their government the same ; and, consequently, have never felt any desire for its success or its duration.[1]

The towns and villages all stand upon high mounds formed of the débris of former towns and villages, that have been accumulating, most of them for thousands of years. They are for the most part mere collections of wretched hovels built of frail materials, and destined only for a brief period.

> " Man wants but little here below,
> Nor wants that little long."[2]

And certainly there is no climate in the world where man wants less than in this of India generally, and Upper India particularly. The peasant lives in the open air ; and a house to him is merely a thing to eat and sleep in, and to give him shelter in the storm, which comes upon him but seldom, and never in a pitiless shape. The society of his friends he enjoys in the open air, and he never furnishes his house for their reception or for display. The peasantry of India, in consequence of living and talking so much in the open air, have all stentorian voices, which they find it exceedingly difficult to modulate to our taste when they come into our rooms.

Another thing in this part of India strikes a traveller from other parts—the want of groves of fruit-trees around the villages and along the roads. In every other part of India he can at every stage have his tents pitched in a grove of mango-trees, that defend his followers from the

[1] This is quite true. The rural population want two things, first a light assessment, secondly the minimum of official interference. They do not care a straw who the ruler is, and they like best that ruler, be his name or nationality what it may, who worries them least, and takes least money from them.

[2] Goldsmith, *The Hermit* (in Chap. VIII. of the *Vicar of Wakefield*.)

direct rays of the sun in the daytime, and from the cold
dews at night ; but in the district above Agra, he may go
for ten marches without getting the shelter of a grove in
one.[1]   The Sikhs, the Marāthās, the Jāts, and the Pathāns
destroyed them all during the disorders attending the
decline of the Muhammadan empire ; and they have never
been renewed, because no man could feel secure that they
would be suffered to stand ten years.   A Hindoo believes
that his soul in the next world is benefited by the blessings
and grateful feelings of those of his fellow-creatures who
unmolested eat the fruit and enjoy the shade of the trees
he has planted during his sojourn in this world ; and,
unless he can feel assured that the traveller and the public
in general will be permitted to do so, he can have no hope
of any permanent benefit from his good work.   It might
as well be cut down as pass into the hands of another
person who had no feeling of interest in the eternal repose
of the soul of the planter.   That person would himself
have no advantage in the next world from giving the fruit
and the shade of the trees to the public, since the prayers
of those who enjoyed them would be offered for the soul
of the planter, and not for his—he, therefore, takes all
their advantage to himself in this world, and the planter
and the public are defrauded.   Our Government thought
they had done enough to encourage the renewal of these
groves, when by a regulation they gave to the present
lessees of villages the privilege of planting them themselves, or permitting others to plant them ; but where they
held their leases for a term of only five years, of course
they would be unwilling to plant them.   They might lose
their lease when the term expired, or forfeit it before ; and
the successor would have the land on which the trees
stood, and would be able to exclude the public, if not the
proprietor, from the enjoyment of any of their advantages.
Our Government has, in effect, during the thirty-five years

[1] Groves are still scarce in the Agra country, but much planting has
been done on the roads.

that it has held the dominion of the North-Western Provinces,[1] prohibited the planting of mango groves, while the old ones are every year disappearing. On the resumption of rent-free lands, even the ground on which the finest of these groves stand has been recklessly resumed, and the proprietors told me that they may keep the trees they have, but cannot be allowed to 'renew them, as the lands are become the property of Government. The lands of groves that have been the pride of families for a century and a half have been thus resumed. Government is not aware of the irreparable mischief they do the country they govern by such measures.[2]

[1] Gorakhpur, Azamgarh, and some other districts, forming half of the old province of Oudh, were ceded by the ruler of Oudh in 1801, and were long known as the Ceded Provinces. The western districts of the North-Western Provinces, known as the Conquered Provinces, were taken from the Marāthās in 1803–1805. The Province of Benares became British territory in 1775. The hill districts of the Kumaun Division were annexed in 1816, at the close of the war with Nepāl.

[2] The author's remarks are not readily intelligible to readers unversed in the technicalities of Indian revenue administration. The author writes on the assumption that Government was the proprietor of the soil. While he was writing, the settlements under Regulation IX. of 1833 were in progress. These settlements, or revenue contracts, were ordinarily sanctioned for periods of thirty years, and the landholders, whom the author calls "lessees," have gradually changed into "proprietors," with full power over their land, subject only to the State lien for the land revenue, and to the laws of inheritance and succession. The "resumption of rent-free lands" simply means the subjection of those lands to the payment of land revenue. It is inaccurate to say that the lands are become "the property of Government" by reason of their being assessed. Even when land generally was regarded as the property of the State, and the landholders were considered to be only lessees, no objection would have been made to the planting of groves if payment of the land revenue had been continued for the planted area as for cultivated land. Since landholders have been recognized as proprietors, there is nothing to prevent them planting as much land as they like with trees, though the State has not always been willing to exempt the whole planted area from assessment. No one ever objected to the renewal of trees except on the ground that the area under trees might be excluded from assess-

On my way back from Meerut, after the conversation already related with the farmer of the small village (*ante*, p. 52), my tents were one day pitched, in the month of December, amidst some very fine garden cultivation in the district of Alīgarh;[1] and in the evening I walked out as usual to have some talk with the peasantry. I came to a neighbouring well at which four pair of bullocks were employed watering the surrounding fields of wheat for the market, and vegetables for the families of the cultivators. Four men were employed at the well, and two more in guiding the water into the little embanked squares into which they divide their fields.

I soon discovered that the most intelligent of the four was a Jāt; and I had a good deal of conversation with him as he stood landing the leather buckets, as the two pair of bullocks on his side of the well drew them to the top, a distance of forty cubits from the surface of the water beneath.

"Who built this well?" I began.

"It was built by one of my ancestors, six generations ago."

"How much longer will it last?"

"Ten generations more, I hope; for it is now just as good as when first made. It is of 'pakkā' bricks without mortar cement."[3]

ment. For many years past the Government of India has been most anxious to encourage tree-planting, and has sanctioned very liberal rules respecting the exemption of grove land from assessment to land revenue, or rent, as the author calls it. The Government of the North-Western Provinces and Oudh is certainly not now liable to reproach for indifference to the value of groves. Enormous progress in the planting of road avenues has also been made. The deficiency of trees in the country about Agra is partly due to nature. Much of the ground is cut up by ravines, and is unfavourable for planting.

[1] The Alīgarh district lies to the north and east of the Mathurā district. The fort of Alīgarh is fifty-five miles north of Agra, and eighty-four miles south-east of Delhi.

[3] "Pakkā" here means "burned in a kiln," as distinguished from "sun-dried."

"How many waterings do you give?"

"If there should be no rain, we shall require to give the land six waterings, as the water is sweet; had it been brackish four would do. Brackish water is better for wheat than sweet water; but it is not so good for vegetables or sugar-cane."

"How many 'bīghās' are watered from this well?"

"We water twenty 'bīghās,' or one hundred and five 'jarībs,' from this well."[1]

"And you pay the Government how much?"

"One hundred rupees, at the rate of five rupees the bīghā. But only the five immediately around the well are mine, the rest belong to others."

"But the well belongs to you; and I suppose you get from the proprietors of the other fifteen something for your water?"

"Nothing. There is more water for my five bīghās, and I give them what they require gratis; they acknowledge that it is a gift from me, and that is all I want."

"And what does the land beyond the range of your water of the same quality pay?"

"It pays at the rate of two rupees the bīghā, and it is with difficulty that they can be made to pay that. Water, sir, is a great thing, and with that and manure we get good crops from the land."[2]

"How many returns of the seed?"

"From these twenty bīghās with six waterings, and cross ploughing, and good manure, we contrive to get twenty returns; that is, if God is pleased with us and blesses our efforts."

---

[1] The "bīghā" is the unit of superficial land measure, varying, but often taken as five-eighths of an acre. The "jarīb" is a smaller measure.

[2] The rules now in force require assessing officers to make allowance for permanent improvements, such as the well described in the text, so as to give the fair benefit of the improvement to the maker. In the early settlements this important matter was commonly neglected.

" And you maintain your family comfortably out of the return from your five ? "

" If they were mine I could ; but we had two or three bad seasons seven years ago, and I was obliged to borrow eighty rupees from our banker at twenty-four per cent., for the subsistence of my family. I have hardly been able to pay him the interest with all I can earn by my labour, and I now serve him upon two rupees a month."

" But that is not enough to maintain you and your family ? "

" No ; but he only requires my services for half the day, and during the other half I work with others to get enough for them."

" And when do you expect to pay off your debt ? "

" God only knows ; if I exert myself, and keep a good ' niyat ' (pure mind or intentions), he will enable me or my children to do so some day or other. In the meantime he has my five bīghās of land in mortgage, and I serve him in the cultivation."

" But under those misfortunes, you could surely venture to demand something from the proprietors of the other fifteen bīghās for the water of your well ? "

" Never, sir ; it would be said all over the country that such an one sold God's water for his neighbours' fields, and I should be ashamed to show my face. Though poor, and obliged to work hard, and serve others, I have still too much pride for that."

" How many bullocks are required for the tillage of these twenty bīghās watered from your well ? "

" These eight bullocks do all the work ; they are dear now. This was purchased the other day on the death of the old one, for twenty-six rupees. They cost about fifty rupees a pair—the late famine has made them dear."[1]

" What did the well cost in making ? "

[1] Tolerable bullocks, fit for use at the well and in the plough, would now cost much more. This conversation appears to have taken place in the year 1839. The famine alluded to is that of 1837-8.

" I have heard that it cost about one hundred and twenty rupees ; it would cost about that sum to make one of this kind in the present day, not more."

" How long have the families of your caste been settled in these parts ? "

" About six or seven generations ; the country had before been occupied by a peasantry of the Kalār caste. Our ancestors came, built up mud fortifications, dug wells, and brought the country under cultivation ; it had been reduced to a waste ; for a long time we were obliged to follow the plough with our swords by our sides, and our friends around us with their matchlocks in their hand, and their matches lighted."

" Did the water in your well fail during the late seasons of drought ? "

" No, sir, the water of this well never fails."

" Then how did bad seasons affect you ? "

" My bullocks all died one after the other from want of fodder, and I had not the means to till my lands ; subsistence became dear, and to maintain my family, I was obliged to contract the debt for which my lands are now mortgaged.   I work hard to get them back, and, if I do not succeed, my children will, I hope, with the blessing of God.' [1]

The next morning I went on to Kākā, fifteen miles ; and finding tents, people, and cattle, without a tree to shelter them, I was much pleased to see in my neighbourhood a plantation of mango and other fruit-trees. It had, I was told, been planted only three years ago by Hirāman and Mōtīrām, and I sent for them, knowing that they would be pleased to have their good work noticed by any European gentleman.   The trees are now covered with cones of

---

[1] This conversation gives a very vivid and truthful picture of rural life in Northern India.   Most revenue officers have held similar conversations with rustics, but the author is almost the only writer on Indian affairs who has perceived that exact notes of casual chats in the fields would be found interesting and valuable.

thatch to shelter them from the frost. The merchants came, evidently much pleased, and I had a good deal of talk with them.

"Who planted this new grove?"

"We planted it three years ago."

"What did your well cost you, and how many trees have you?"

"We have about four hundred trees, and the well has cost us two hundred rupees, and will cost us two hundred more."

"How long will you require to water them?"

"We shall require to water the mango and other large trees ten or twelve years; but the orange, pomegranate, and other small trees will always require watering."

"What quantity of ground do the trees occupy?"

"They occupy twenty-two 'bighas' of one hundred and five 'jaribs.' We place them all twelve yards from each other, that is, the large trees; and the small ones we plant between them."

"How did you get the land?"

"We were many years trying in vain to get a grant from the government through the collector; at last we got him to certify on paper that, if the landholder would give us land to plant our grove upon, the government would have no objection. We induced the landholder, who is a constituent of ours, to grant us the land; and we made our well, and planted our trees."

"You have done a good thing; what reward do you expect?"

"We hope that those who enjoy the shade, the water, and the fruit, will think kindly of us when we are gone. The names of the great men who built the castles, palaces, and tombs at Delhi and Agra have been almost all forgotten, because no one enjoys any advantage from them; but the names of those who planted the few mango groves we see are still remembered and blessed by all who eat of their fruit, sit in their shade, and drink of their water, from whatever part of the world they come. Even the European gentlemen remember their names with kindness; indeed, it was at the suggestion of a European gentleman, who was passing this place many years ago, and talking with us as you are now, that we commenced this grove. 'Look over this plain,' said he; 'it has been all denuded of the fine groves with which it was, no doubt, once studded; though it is tolerably well cultivated, the traveller finds no shelter in it from the noonday sun—even the birds seem to have deserted you, because you refuse them the habitations they find in other parts of India.' We told him that we would have the grove planted, and we have done so; and we hope God will bless our undertaking."

"The difficulty of getting land is, I suppose, the reason why more groves are not planted, now that property is secure?"

"How could men plant without feeling secure of the land they planted upon, and when government would not guarantee it? The landholder could guarantee it only during the five years of lease;[1] and, if at the end of that time government should transfer the lease of the estate to another, the land of the grove would be transferred with it. We plant not for worldly or immediate profits, but for the benefit of our souls in the next world—for the prayers of those who may derive benefit from our works when we are gone. Our landholders are good men, and will never resume the lands they have given us; and if the lands be sold at auction by government, or transferred to others, we hope the certificate of the collector will protect us from his grasp."[2]

"You like your present government, do you not?"

"We like it much. There has never been a government that gave so much security to life and property; all we want is a little more of public service, and a little more of

---

[1] The early settlements were made for short terms.

[2] The certificate would not be of much avail in a civil court.

trade ; but we have no cause to complain ; it is our own fault if we are not happy."

" But I have been told that the people find the returns from the soil diminishing, and attribute it to the perjury that takes place in our courts occasionally."

" That, sir, is no doubt true ; there has been a manifest falling off in the returns ; and people everywhere think that you make too much use of the Korān and the Ganges water in your courts. God does not like to hear lies told upon one or other, and we are apt to think that we are all punished for the sins of those who tell them. May we ask, sir, what office you hold ? "

" It is my office to do the work which God assigns to me in this world."

" The work of God, sir, is the greatest of all works, and those are fortunate who are chosen to do it."

Their respect for me evidently increased when they took me for a clergyman. I was dressed in black.

" In the first place, it is my duty to tell you that God does not punish the innocent for the guilty, and that the perjury in courts has nothing to do with the diminution of returns from the soil. Where you apply water and manure, and alternate your crops, you always get good returns, do you not ? "

" Very good returns ;. but we have had several bad seasons that have carried away the greater part of our population ; but a small portion of our lands can be irrigated for want of wells, and we had no rain for two or three years, or hardly any in due season ; and it was this deficiency of rain which the people thought a chastisement from heaven."

" But the wells were not dried up, were they ? "

" No."

" And the people whose fields they watered had good returns, and high prices for produce ? "

" Yes, they had ; but their cattle died for want of food, for there was no grass anywhere to be found."

G 2

"Still they were better off than those who had no wells to draw water from for their fields; and the only way to provide against such evils in future is to have a well for every field. God has given you the fields, and he has given you the water; and when it does not come from the clouds, you must draw it from your wells."[1]

"True, sir, very true; but the people are very poor, and have not the means to form the wells they require."

"And if they borrow the money from you, you charge them with interest?"

"From one to two per cent. a month according to their character and circumstances; but interest is very often merely nominal, and we are in most cases glad to get back the principal alone."[2]

"And what security have you for the land of your grove in case the landholder should change his mind, or die and leave sons not so well disposed."

"In the first place, we hold his bonds for a debt of nine thousand rupees which he owes us, and which we have no hopes of his ever paying. In the next, we have on stamped paper his deed of *gift*, in which he declares that he has given us the land, and that he and his heirs for ever shall be bound to make good the rents, should government sell the estate for arrears of revenue. We wanted him to write this document in the regular form of a deed of sale; but he said that none of his ancestors had ever yet sold their lands, and that he would not be the first to disgrace his family, or record their disgrace on stamped paper—it should, he was resolved, be a deed of gift."

"But, of course, you prevailed upon him to take the price?"

"Yes, we prevailed upon him to take two hundred rupees for the land, and got his receipt for the same; indeed, it is so mentioned in the deed of gift; but still the

---

[1] The Aligarh district is now irrigated by canals.

[2] This is the lender's view of his business; the borrowers might have a different story.

landlord, who is a near relation of the late chief of Hatrās would persist in having the paper made out as a deed, not of sale, but of gift. God knows whether, after all, our grove will be secure—we must run the risk now we have begun upon it."

CHAPTER VII[1]

Public Spirit of the Hindoos—Tree Cultivation and Suggestions for
extending it.

I MAY here be permitted to introduce as something
germane to the matter of the foregoing chapter a recollection of Jubbulpore, although we are now far past that
locality.

My tents are pitched where they have often been before,
on the verge of a very large and beautiful tank in a fine
grove of mango-trees, and close to a handsome temple.
There are more handsome temples and buildings for
accommodation on the other side of the tank, but they are
gone sadly out of repair. The bank all round this noble
tank is beautifully ornamented by fine banyan and pipal
trees, between which and the water's edge intervene
numerous clusters of the graceful bamboo. These works
were formed about eighty years ago by a respectable agricultural capitalist who resided at this place, and died about
twenty years after they were completed. No relation of
his can now be found in the district, and not one in a
thousand of those who drink of the water or eat of the
fruit knows to whom he is indebted. There are round the
place some beautiful " bāolīs," or large wells with flights of
stone steps from the top to the water's edge, imbedded in
clusters of beautiful trees. They were formed about the
same time for the use of the public by men whose grandchildren have descended to the grade of cultivators of the
soil, or belted attendants upon the present native collectors,

[1] Chapter XIV of Vol. II of original edition.

without the means of repairing any of the injury which time is inflicting upon these magnificent works. Three or four young pipal-trees have begun to spread their delicate branches and pale green leaves rustling in the breeze from the dome of this fine temple; which these infant Herculeses hold in their deadly grasp and doom to inevitable destruction. Pigeons deposit the seeds of the pipal-tree, on which they chiefly feed, in the crevices of buildings.

No Hindoo dares, and no Christian or Muhammadan will condescend to lop off the heads of these young trees, and if they did, it would only put off the evil and inevitable day; for such are the vital powers of their roots, when they have once penetrated deeply into a building, that they will send out their branches again, cut them off as often as you may, and carry on their internal attack with undiminished vigour.

No wonder that superstition should have consecrated this tree, delicate and beautiful as it is, to the gods. The palace, the castle, the temple, and the tomb, all those works which man is most proud to raise to spread and to perpetuate his name, crumble to dust beneath her withering grasp. She rises triumphant over them all in her lofty beauty, bearing high in air amidst her light green foliage fragments of the wreck she has made, to show the nothingness of man's greatest efforts.

While sitting at my tent-door looking out upon this beautiful sheet of water, and upon all the noble works around me, I thought of the charge, so often made against the people of this fine land, of the total want of *public spirit* among them, by those who have spent their Indian days in the busy courts of law, and still more busy commercial establishments of our great metropolis.

If by the term public spirit be meant a disposition on the part of individuals to sacrifice their own enjoyments, or their own means of enjoyment for the common good, there is perhaps no people in the world among whom it abounds so much as among the people of India. To live in the grateful recollections of their countrymen for benefits conferred upon them in great works of ornament and utility is the study of every Hindoo of rank and property.[1] Such works tend, in his opinion, not only to spread and perpetuate his name in this world, but, through the good wishes and prayers of those who are benefited by them, to secure the favour of the Deity in the next.

According to their notions, every drop of rain-water or dew that falls to the ground from the green leaf of a fruit-tree, planted by them for the common good, proves a refreshing draught for their souls in the next [world]. When no descendant remains to pour the funeral libations in their name, the water from the trees they have planted for the public good is destined to supply its place. Everything judiciously laid out to promote the happiness of their fellow-creatures will in the next world be repaid to them tenfold by the Deity.

In marching over the country in the hot season, we every morning find our tents pitched on the green sward amid beautiful groves of fruit-trees, with wells of " pakkā " (brick or stone) masonry, built at great expense, and containing the most delicious water ; but how few of us ever dream of asking at whose cost the trees that afford us and our followers such agreeable shade were planted, or the wells that afford us such copious streams of fine water in the midst of dry, arid plains were formed—we go on enjoying all the advantages which arise from the *noble public spirit* that animates the people of India to benevolent exertions, without once calling in question the truth of the assertion of our metropolitan friends that " the people of India have no public spirit."

Mānmōr, a respectable merchant of Mirzapore, who traded chiefly in bringing cotton from the valley of the Nerbudda and Southern India through Jubbulpore to Mirzapore, and in carrying back sugar and spices in return, learning how much travellers on this great road suffered

[1] This proposition is too general.

from the want of water near the Hiliyā pass, under the Vindhya range of hills, commenced a work to remedy the evil in 1822. Not a drop of wholesome water was to be found within ten miles of the bottom of the pass, where the laden bullocks were obliged to rest during the hot months, when the greatest thoroughfare always took place. Mānmōr commenced a large tank and garden, and had laid out about twenty thousand rupees in the work, when he died. His son, Lalū Mānmōr, completed the work soon after His father's death, at a cost of eighty thousand rupees more, that travellers might enjoy all the advantages that his good old father had benevolently intended for them. The tank is very large, always full of fine water even in the driest part of the dry season, with flights of steps of cut freestone from the water's edge to the top all round. A fine garden and shrubbery, with temples and buildings for accommodations, are attached, with an estab· lishment of people to attend and keep them in order.[1]

All the country around this magnificent work was a dreary solitude—there was not a human habitation within many miles on any side. Tens of thousands who passed this road every year were blessing the name of the man who had created it where it was so much wanted, when the new road from the Nerbudda to Mirzapore was made by the British Government to descend some ten miles to the north

---

[1] The Hiliyā, or Haliyā, Pass is near the town of the same name in the Mirzāpur district, 31 miles south-west of Mirzāpur. A bilingual inscription, in English and Hindī, on a large slab on the bank of the river, records the capture of the fort of Bhūpārī in 1811 by the 21st Regiment Native Infantry. The tank described in the text is at Dibhōr, 12 miles south of Haliyā, and is 430 feet long by 352 broad. The full name of the builder is Srīmān Nāyak Mānmōr, who was the head of the Banjāra merchants of Mirzāpur. The inscription on his temple is dated 23 February, 1825, A.D. "I suppose," remarks Cunningham, "that the vagrant instinct of the old Banjāra preferred a jungle site. No doubt he got the ground cheap; and from this vantage point he was able to supply Mirzāpur with both wood and charcoal." (*Archæol. Survey Reports*, vol. xxi, p.p. 121-125.)

of it. As many miles were saved in the distance by the
new cut, and the passage down made comparatively easy at
great cost, travellers forsook the Hiliyā road, and poor
Mānmōr's work became comparatively useless. I brought
the work to the notice of Lord William Bentinck, who, in
passing Mirzapore some time after, sent for the son, and
conferred upon him a rich dress of honour, of which he has
ever since been extremely proud.[1]

Hundreds of works like this are undertaken every year
for the benefit of the public by benevolent and unosten-
tatious individuals, who look for their reward, not in the
applause of newspapers and public meetings, but in the
grateful prayers and good wishes of those who are benefited
by them ; and in the favour of the Deity in the next world,
for benefits conferred upon his creatures in this.[2]

What the people of India want is not public spirit, for
no men in the world have more of it than the Hindoos,
but a disposition on the part of private individuals to com-

---

[1] The new road passes through the Katrā Pass. The pass _viâ_
Dibhōr and Haliyā, which the author calls the Hiliyā Pass, is properly
called the Kerahi (Kerāi) Pass. Both old and new roads are now
little used. The construction of railways has altogether changed the
course of trade, and Cawnpore has risen on the ruins of Mirzāpur.
Lalū, Nāyak's "grandson, died in comparative obscurity some years
ago, and only a few female relatives remain to represent the family—a
striking example, if one were needed, of the instability of Oriental
fortunes." (_Archæol. Surv. Rep._, vol. xxi, p. 124, _quoting Gazetteer_.)

[2] Within a few miles of Gosalpur, at the village of Talwā, which
stands upon the old high road leading to Mirzapore, is a still more
magnificent tank with one of the most beautiful temples in India, all
executed two or three generations ago at the expense of two or three
lakhs of rupees for the benefit of the public, by a very worthy man,
who became rich in the service of the former government. His
descendants, all save one, now follow the plough ; and that one has a
small rent-free village held on condition of appropriating the rents to
the repair of the tank. [W. H. S.]

The name Talwā is only the rustic way of pronouncing "tāl,"
meaning the tank. Gosalpur is nineteen miles north-east of Jabalpur.
Two or three lakhs of rupees were then (in eighteenth century) worth
about £22,000 to £33,000 sterling.

bine their efforts and means in effecting great objects for the public good. With this disposition they will be, in time, inspired under our rule, when the enemies of all settled governments may permit us to divert a little of our intellect and our revenue from the duties of war to those of peace.[1]

In the year 1829, while I held the civil charge of the district of Jubbulpore, in this valley of the Nerbudda, I caused an estimate to be made of the public works of utility and ornament it contained. The population of the district at that time amounted to 500,000 souls, distributed among 4,053 occupied towns, villages and hamlets. There were 1,000 villages more which had formerly been occupied, but were then deserted. There were 2,288 tanks, 209 "bãolis," or large wells with flights of steps extending from the top down to the water when in its lowest stage ; 1,560 wells lined with brick and stone, cemented with lime, but without stairs ; 360 Hindoo temples, and 22 Muhammadan mosques. The estimated cost of these works in grain at the present price, had the labour been paid in kind at the ordinary rate was ₨86,66,043 (£866,604 sterling).[2]

[1] India, except on the frontiers, has been at peace since 1858, and much revenue has been spent on the duties of peace, but the power of combination for public objects has developed among the natives to a less degree than the author seems to have expected, though some development undoubtedly has taken place.

[2] In the original edition these statistics are given in words. Figures have been used in this edition as being more readily grasped. The *Gazetteer* (1870) gives the following figures :—Area of district, 4,261 square miles ; population, 620,201 ; villages, 2,707 ; wells in use, 5,515. The *Gazetteer* figures apparently include wells of all kinds, and do not reckon hamlets separately. Wells are, of course, an absolute necessity, and their construction could not be avoided in a country occupied by a fixed population. The number of temples and mosques was very small for so large a population. Many of the tanks, too, are indispensably necessary for watering the cattle employed in agriculture. The "bãolis" may fairly be reckoned as the fruit of the public spirit of individuals. This chapter is a reprint of a paper entitled "On the Public Spirit of the Hindoos." *See* Bibliography.

The labourer was estimated to be paid at the rate of about two-thirds the quantity of corn he would get in England if paid in kind, and corn sells here at about one-third the price it fetches in average seasons in England. In Europe, therefore, these works, supposing the labour equally efficient, would have cost at least four times the sum here estimated; and such works formed by private individuals for the public good, without any view whatever to return in profits, indicate a very high degree of *public spirit.*

The whole annual rent of the lands of this district amounts to R650,000 (£65,000 sterling), that is, 500,000 demandable by the government, and 150,000 by those who hold the lands at lease immediately under government, over and above what may be considered as the profits of their stock as farmers. These works must, therefore, have cost about thirteen times the amount of the annual rent of the whole of the lands of the district, or the whole annual rent for above thirteen years.[1]

But I have not included the groves of mango and tamarind, and other fine trees with which the district abounds. Two-thirds of the towns and villages are imbedded in fine groves of these trees, mixed with the banyan (*Ficus Indica*) and the pīpal (*Ficus religiosa*). I am sorry they were not numbered; but I should estimate them at three thousand, and the outlay upon a mango grove is, on an average, about four hundred rupees.

The groves of fruit-trees planted by individuals for the

---

[1] The *Gazetteer* states that in 1868-69 the land-revenue was R5,70,434, as compared with R500,000 in the author's time. It has since been largely enhanced. The lessees (zamīndārs) have now become proprietors, and the land-revenue, according to the rule in force for many years past, should not exceed half the estimated profit rental. The early settlements were made in accordance with the theory of native governments that the land is the property of the State, and that the lessees are entitled only to subsistence, and a small percentage sa payment for the trouble of collection from the actual cultivators. The author's estimate gives the zamīndārs only 15/16ths, or 1/16ths of the profit rental.

use of the public, without any view to a return in profit, would in this district, according to this estimate, have cost twelve lākhs [12,00,000] more, or about twice the amount of the annual rent of the whole of the lands. It should be remarked that the whole of these works had been formed under former governments. Ours was established in the year 1817.[1]

The Upper Doāb and the Delhi Territories were denuded of their trees in the wars that attended the decline and fall of the Muhammadan empire, and the rise and progress of the Sikhs, Jāts, and Marāthās in that quarter. These lawless freebooters soon swept all the groves from the face of every country they occupied with their troops, and they never attempted to renew them or encourage the renewal. We have not been much more sparing; and the finest groves of fruit-trees have everywhere been recklessly swept down by our barrack-masters to furnish fuel for their brick-kilns; and I am afraid little or no encouragement is given for planting others to supply their place in those parts of India where they are most wanted.

We have a regulation authorizing the lessee of a village to plant a grove in his grounds, but where the settlements of the land-revenue have been for short periods, as in all Upper and Central India, this authority is by no means sufficient to induce them to invest their property in such works. It gives no sufficient guarantee that the lessee for the next settlement shall respect a grant made by his pre-

---

[1] The people of the Jabalpur district must have been very different from those of the rest of India if they planted their groves solely for the public benefit. The editor has never known the fruit, not to mention the timber and firewood, of a grove to be available for the use of the general public. Universal custom allows all comers to use the shade of any established grove, but the fruit is always jealously guarded and gathered by the owners. Even one tree is often the property of many sharers, and disputes about the division of mangoes and other fruits are extremely frequent. The framing of a correct record of rights in trees is one of the most embarrassing tasks of a revenue officer.

decessors ; and every grove of mango-trees requires outlay and care for at least ten years. Though a man destines the fruit, the shade, and the water for the use of the public, he requires to feel that it will be held for the public in his name, and by his children and descendants, and never be exclusively appropriated by any man in power for his own use.

If the lands were still to belong to the lessee of the estate under government, and the trees only to the planter and his heirs, he to whom the land belonged might very soon render the property in the trees of no value to the planter or his heirs.[1]

If Government wishes the Upper Doāb, the Delhi, Mathurā, and Agra districts again enriched and embellished with mango groves, they will not delay to convey this feeling to the hundreds, nay, thousands, who would be willing to plant them upon a single guarantee that the lands upon which the trees stand shall be considered to belong to them and their heirs as long as these trees stand upon them.[2] That the land, the shade, the fruit, and the water will be left to the free enjoyment of the public we may take for granted, since the good which the planter's soul is to derive from such a work in the next world must depend upon their being so ; and all that is required to be stipulated in such grants is that mango, tamarind, pīpal, or "bar" (*i.e.* banyan) trees, at the rate of twenty-five the English acre, shall be planted and kept up in every piece of land granted for the purpose ; and that a well of "pakkā" masonry shall

[1] Under the modern system it very often happens that the land belongs to one party, and the trees to another. Disputes, of course, occur, but, as a rule, the rights of the owner of the trees are not interfered with by the owner of the land. In thousands of such cases both parties exercise their rights without friction.

[2] This sentence shows very clearly how remote from the author's mind was the idea of private property in land in India. Government has long since parted with the power of giving grants such as the author recommends. The Upper Doāb districts of Meerut, Muzaffarnagar, and Sahāranpur have now plenty of groves.

be made for the purpose of watering them, in the smallest, as well as in the largest, piece of ground granted, and kept always in repair.

If the grantee fulfil the conditions, he ought, in order to cover part of the expense, to be permitted to till the land under the trees till they grow to maturity and yield their fruit ; if he fails, the lands, having been declared liable to resumption, should be resumed. The person soliciting such grants should be required to certify in his application that he had already obtained the sanction of the present lessee of the village in which he wishes to have his grove, and for this sanction he would, of course, have to pay the full value of the land for the period of his lease. When his lease expires, the land in which the grove is planted would be excluded from the assessment ; and when it is considered that every good grove must cost the planter more than fifty times the annual rent of the land, government may be satisfied that they secure the advantage to their people at a very cheap rate.[1]

Over and above the advantage of fruit, water, and shade for the public, these groves tend much to secure the districts that are well studded with them from the dreadful calamities that in India always attend upon deficient falls of rain in due season. They attract the clouds, and make them deposit their stores in districts that would not otherwise be blessed with them ; and hot and dry countries denuded of their trees, and by that means deprived of a great portion of that moisture to which they had been accustomed, and which they require to support vegetation, soon become dreary and arid wastes. The lighter particles, which formed the richest portion of their soil, blow off, and

---

[1] The cost of establishing a grove varies much according to circumstances, of which the distance of water from the surface is the most important. Where water is distant, the cost of constructing and working a well is very high. Where water is near, these items of expense are small, and the roots of the trees soon reach a moist stratum, and can dispense with irrigation.

leave only the heavy arenaceous portion; and hence, perhaps, those sandy deserts in which are often to be found the signs of a population once very dense.

In the Mauritius, the rivers were found to be diminishing under the rapid disappearance of the woods in the interior, when government had recourse to the measure of preventing further depredations, and they soon recovered their size.

The clouds brought up from the southern ocean by the south-east trade wind are attracted, as they pass over the island, by the forests in the interior, and made to drop their stores in daily refreshing showers. In many other parts of the world governments have now become aware of this mysterious provision of nature; and have adopted measures to take advantage of it for the benefit of the people; and the dreadful sufferings to which the people of those of our districts, which have been the most denuded of their trees, have been of late years exposed from the want of rain in due season, may, perhaps, induce our Indian Government to turn its thoughts to the subject.[1]

[1] The author was, in his appreciation of the value of arboriculture and forest conservancy, far in advance of his Anglo-Indian contemporaries. A modern meteorologist might object to some of his phraseology, but the substance of his remarks is quite sound. His statement of the ways in which trees benefit climate is incomplete. One important function performed by the roots of trees is the raising of water from the depths below the surface, to be dispersed by the leaves in the form of vapour. Trees act beneficially in many other ways also, which it would be tedious to specify.

The Indian Government long remained blind to the importance of the duty of saving the country from denudation. The first forest conservancy establishments were organized in 1852 for Madras and Burma, and, by Act VII of 1865, the Forest Department was established on a legal basis. Its operations have since been largely extended, and trained foresters are now sent out each year to India. The Department at the present time controls many thousand square miles of forest. The reader may consult the article "Forests" in Balfour's *Cyclopædia*, and sundry official reports for further details.

A yearly grant for arboriculture is now made to every district. Thousands of miles of roads have been lined with trees, and multi-

The province of Mālwā, which is bordered by the Nerbudda on the south, Guzerāt on the west, Rājputāna on the north, and Allahabad on the east, is said never to have been visited by a famine ; and this exemption from so great a calamity must arise chiefly from its being so well studded with hills and groves. The natives have a couplet, which, like all good couplets on rural subjects, is attributed to Sahdĕo, one of the five demigod brothers of the Mahābhārata, to this effect—" If it does not thunder on such a night, you, father, must go to Mālwā, and I to Guzerāt," meaning, " the rains will fail us here, and we must go to those quarters where they never fail."

tudes of groves have been established both by Government and private individuals. The author was himself a great tree-planter. In a letter dated 15th December, 1844, he describes the avenue which he had planted along the road from Maihar to Jabalpur in 1829 and 1830, and another, 86 miles long, from Jhānsī Ghāt on the Nerbudda to Chāka. The trees planted were banyan, pīpal, mango, tamarind, and "jāman" (*Eugenia jambolana*). He remarks that these trees will last for centuries.

CHAPTER VIII[1]

Cities and Towns, formed by Public Establishments, disappear as
Sovereigns and Governors change their Abodes.

ON the 17th and 18th,[2] we went on twenty miles to
Palwal,[3] which stands upon an immense mound, in some
places a hundred feet high, formed entirely of the débris of
old buildings. There are an immense number of fine brick
buildings in ruins, but not one of brick or stone at present
inhabited. The place was once evidently under the former
government the seat of some great public establishments,
which, with their followers and dependents, constituted
almost the entire population. The occasion which keeps
such establishments at a place no sooner passes away than
the place is deserted and goes to ruin as a matter of
course. Such is the history of Nineveh, Babylon,[4] and
all cities which have owed their origin and support
entirely to the public establishments of the sovereign—
any revolution that changed the seat of government de-
populated a city.

[1] Chapter XV of Vol. II of original edition.
[2] January, 1836.
[3] A small town, forty-one miles south of Delhi, situated in the
Gurgāon district, which is now included in the Panjāb, but was, in the
author's time, attached to the North-Western Provinces. The town
is the chief place in the "pargana" of the same name.
[4] Nineveh is not a well-chosen example, inasmuch as its decay was
due to deliberate destruction, and not to mere desertion by a sovereign.
It was deliberately burned and ruined by Nabopolassar, viceroy of
Babylon, and his allies shortly after B.C. 625. The decay of Babylon
was gradual. See note post, p. 100.

Sir Thomas Roe, the ambassador of James the First of England to the court of Delhi during the reign of Jahāngīr, passing through some of the old capital cities of Southern India, then deserted and in ruins, writes to the Archbishop of Canterbury :—" I know not by what policy the Emperors seek the ruin of all the ancient cities which were nobly built, but now lie desolate and in rubbish. It must arise from a wish to destroy all the ancient cities in order that there might appear nothing great to have existed before their time."[1] But these cities, like all which are supported in the same manner, by the residence of a court and its establishments, become deserted as the seat of dominion is changed. Nineveh, built by Ninus out of the spoils he brought back from the wide range of his conquests, continued to be the residence of the court and the principal seat of its military establishments for thirteen centuries to the reign of Sardanapalus. During the whole of this time it was the practice of the sovereigns to collect from all the provinces of the empire their respective quotas of troops, and to canton them within the city for one year, at the expiration of which they were relieved by fresh troops. In the last years of Sardana-palus, four provinces of the empire, Media, Persia, Babylonia, and Arabia, are said to have furnished a quota of four hundred thousand ; and, in the rebellion which closed his reign, these troops were often beaten by those from the other provinces of the empire, which could not have been much less in number. The successful rebel, Arbaces, transferred the court and its appendages to its capital, and Nineveh became deserted,

[1] Extract from a letter to the Archbishop of Canterbury, dated from Ajmīr, 29th January, 1615. The words immediately following "rub-bish" are "His own [i.e. the King's] houses are of stone, hand-some and uniform. His great men build not, for want of inheritance ; but, as far as I have yet seen, live in tents, or in houses worse than our cottages. Yet, when the King likes, as at Agra, because it is a city erected by him, the buildings, as is reported, are fair and of carved stone." (Pinkerton's *Collection*, vol. viii, p. 45.)

and for more than eighteen centuries lost to the civilized world.[1]

Babylon in the same manner; and Susa, Ecbatana, Persepolis, and Seleucia, all, one after the other, became deserted as sovereigns changed their residence, and with it the seats of their public establishments, which alone supported them. Thus Thebes became deserted for Memphis, Memphis for Alexandria, and Alexandria for Cairo, as the sovereigns of Egypt changed theirs; and thus it has always been in India, where cities have been almost all founded on the same bases—the residence of princes, and their public establishments, civil, military, or ecclesiastical.

The city of Kanauj, on the Ganges, when conquered by

---

[1] The site of Nineveh was forgotten for even a longer period than that stated by the author. Mr. Claudius Rich, the Resident at Baghdad, was the first European to make a tentative identification of Nineveh with the mounds opposite Mosal, in 1818. Botta's excavations began in 1843, and Layard's in 1845, and real knowledge of the site and its history dates from those years. (Bonomi, *Nineveh and its Palaces*, 2nd ed. 1853.) The author's account of the fall of Nineveh is based on that of Diodorus Siculus, but is not in accordance with the conclusions of the best modern authorities. The destruction of the city in or about B.C. 606 was really effected some years after the death of Sardanapalus (Assur-banipal), in B.C. 625, by Nabopolassar (Nabupal-uzur), the rebel viceroy of Babylon, in alliance with Necho of Egypt, Cyaxares of Media, and the King of Armenia. The Assyrian monarch who perished in the assault was not Sardanapalus (Assurbanipal), but his son Assur-ebel-ili, or, according to Professor Sayce, a king called Saracus. After the destruction of Nineveh, Babylon became the capital of the Mesopotamian empire, and under Nebuchadnezzar, son of Nabopolassar, who came to the throne in 604 B.C., attained the height of glory and renown. It was occupied by Cyrus in B.C. 539, and gradually decayed, but was still a place of importance in the time of Alexander the Great. The eponymous hero, Ninus, is of course purely mythical. Professor Sayce's article "Babylonia" in the ninth edition of the *Encyclopædia Britannica*, and the articles "Babylonia," "Assyria," and "Nineveh," in Balfour's *Cyclopædia* give the results of modern research. The history of Cyrus, as given by the Greek and Hebrew writers, has been greatly modified by the discovery of an inscribed cylinder of his. (Laing, *Human Origins*, London, 1892, p. 73.)

Mahmūd of Ghaznih,[1] is stated by the historians of the conqueror to have contained a standing army of five hundred thousand infantry, with a due proportion of cavalry and elephants, thirty thousand shops for the sale of "pān" alone, and sixty thousand families of opera girls.[2] The "pān" dealers and opera girls were part and parcel of the court and its public establishments, and as much dependent on the residence of the sovereign as the civil, military, and ecclesiastical officers who ate their "pān," and enjoyed their dancing and music; and this great city no sooner ceased to be the residence of the sovereign, the great proprietor of all the lands in the country, than it became deserted.

After the establishment of the Muhammadan dominion in India almost all the Hindoo cities, within the wide range of their conquest, became deserted as the necessary consequence, as the military establishments were all destroyed or disbanded, and the religious establishments scattered, their lands confiscated, their idols broken, and their temples either reduced to ruins in the first ebulition of fanatical zeal, or left deserted and neglected to decay from want of those revenues by which alone they had been, or could be, supported.[3] The towns and cities of the Roman empire which owed their origin to the same cause, the residence of governors and their legions or other public establishments, resisted similar shocks with more endurance, because they

---

[1] Kanauj, now in the Farrukhābād district of the North-Western Provinces, was sacked by Mahmūd of Ghaznih in 1016 A.D. The name of Mahmūd's capital is correctly spelled Ghaznih, though the forms Ghazni and Ghaznīn are also in use. (Major Raverty, in *J. As. Soc., Bengal*, Part i, vol. lxi, p. 156, *note*.)

[2] "Pān," the well-known Indian condiment (*ante*, Vol. I, p. 263, *note*). "Opera girls" is a rather whimsical rendering of the more usual phrase "nāch (nautch) girls," or "dancing girls."

[3] This statement is much too general. Benares, Allahabad (Prayāg), and many other important Hindoo cities, were never deserted, and continued to be populous through all vicissitudes. It is true that in most places the principal temples were desecrated or destroyed, and were frequently converted into mosques.

had most of them ceased to depend upon the causes in which they originated, and began to rest upon other bases. When destroyed by wave after wave of barbarian conquest, they were restored for the most part by the residence of church dignitaries and their establishments; and the military establishments of the new order of things, instead of remaining as standing armies about the courts of princes, dispersed after every campaign like militia, to enjoy the fruits of the lands assigned for their maintenance, when alone they could be enjoyed in the rude state to which society had been reduced—upon the lands themselves.

For some time after the Muhammadan conquest of India, that part of it which was brought effectually under the new dominion can hardly be considered to have had more than one city with its dependent towns and villages; because the Emperor chose to concentrate the greater part of his military establishments around the seat of his residence, and this great city became deserted whenever he thought it necessary or convenient to change that seat.

But when the Emperor began to govern his distant provinces by viceroys, he was obliged to confide to them a share of his military establishments, the only public establishments which a conqueror thought it worth while to maintain; and while they moved about in their respective provinces, the imperial camp became fixed. The great officers of state, enriched by the plunder of conquered provinces, began to spend their wealth in the construction of magnificent works for private pleasure or public convenience. In time, the viceroys began to govern their provinces by means of deputies, who moved about their respective districts, and enabled their masters, the viceroys of provinces, to convert their camps into cities, which in magnificence often rivalled that of the Emperor their master. The deputies themselves in time found that they could govern their respective districts from a central point; and as their camps became fixed in the chosen spots, towns of considerable magnitude rose, and sometimes rivalled the capitals of the viceroys. The Muhammadans had always a greater taste for architectural magnificence, as well in their private as in their public edifices, than the Hindoos,[1] who sought the respect and good wishes of mankind through the medium of groves and reservoirs diffused over the country for their benefit. Whenever a Muhammadan camp was converted into a town or city almost all the means of individuals were spent in the gratification of this taste. Their wealth in money and movables would be, on their death, at the mercy of their prince—their offices would be conferred on strangers ; tombs and temples, canals, bridges, and caravanserais, gratuitously for the public good, would tend to propitiate the Deity, and conciliate the goodwill of mankind, and might also tend to the advancement of their children in the service of their sovereign. The towns and cities which rose upon the sites of the standing camps of the governors of provinces and districts in India were many of them as much adorned by private and public edifices as those which rose upon the standing camps of the Muhammadan conquerors of Spain.[2]

Standing camps converted into towns and cities, it became in time necessary to fortify with walls against any surprise under any sudden ebullition among the conquered people ; and fortifications and strong garrisons often sug-

[1] This proposition is not true of Southern India at all, and in Northern India applies only to secular buildings. The temples of Khajurāho, Mount Abū, and numberless other places, equal in magnificence the architecture of the Muhammadans, or, indeed, of any people in the world.

[2] The author's remarks seem to the editor likely to convey wrong notions. Very few of the capitals of the Muhammadan viceroys and governors were new foundations. Nearly all of them were ancient Hindoo towns adopted as convenient official residences, and enlarged and beautified by the new rulers, much of the old beauties being at the same time destroyed. Fyzabad certainly was a new foundation of the Nawāb Wazīrs of Oudh, but it lies so close to the extremely ancient city of Ajodhya that it should rather be regarded as a Muhammadan extension of that city. Lucknow occupies the site of a Hindoo city of great antiquity.

gested to the bold and ambitious governors of distant provinces attempts to shake off the imperial yoke.[1] That portion of the annual revenue, which had hitherto flowed in copious streams of tribute to the imperial capital, was now arrested, and made to augment the local establishments, adorn the cities, and enrich the towns of the viceroys, now became the sovereigns of independent kingdoms. The lieutenant-governors of these new sovereigns, possessed of fortified towns, in their turn often shook off the yoke of their masters in the same manner, and became in their turn the independent sovereigns of their respective districts. The whole resources of the countries subject to their rule being employed to strengthen and improve their condition, they soon became rich and powerful kingdoms, adorned with splendid cities and populous towns, since the public establishments of the sovereigns, among whom all the revenues were expended, spent all they received in the purchase of the produce of the land and labour of the surrounding country, which required no other market.

Thus the successful rebellion of one viceroy converted Southern India into an independent kingdom ; and the successful rebellion of his lieutenant-governors in time divided it into four independent kingdoms, each with a standing army of a hundred thousand men, and adorned with towns and cities of great strength and magnificence.[2]

---

[1] It would be difficult to point out an example of a *Muhammadan* standing camp which was first converted into an open, and then into a fortified town.

[2] This abstract of the history of the Deccan, or Southern India, is not quite accurate. The Emperor Muhammad Tughlak, in A.D. 1325, reduced the Deccan to a certain extent to submission, but the country revolted in A.D. 1347, when Hasan Gango founded the Bāhmani dynasty of Kulburga, afterwards known as that of Bīdar. At the end of the fifteenth, and the beginning of the sixteenth century, the kingdom so founded broke up into five, not four, separate states, namely, Bījāpur, Ahmadnagar, Golconda, Berār, and Bīdar. The Berār state had a separate existence for less than eighty years, and then became merged in the kingdom of Ahmadnagar.

But they continued to depend upon the causes in which they originated—the public establishments of the sovereign ; and when the Emperor Akbar and his successors, aided by their own [*sic*] intestine wars, had conquered these sovereigns, and again reduced their kingdoms to tributary provinces, almost all these cities and towns became de-populated as the necessary consequence. The public establishments were again moving about with the courts and camps of the Emperor and his viceroys ; and drawing in their train all those who found employment and subsist-ence in contributing to their efficiency and enjoyment. It was not, as our ambassador, in the simplicity of his heart supposed, the disinclination of the Emperors to see any other towns magnificent; save those in which they resided, which destroyed them, but their ambition to reduce all independent kingdoms to tributary provinces.

CHAPTER IX[1]

Murder of Mr. Fraser, and Execution of the Nawāb Shams-ud-dīn.

AT Palwal Mr. Wilmot and Mr. Wright, who had come on business, and Mr. Gubbins, breakfasted and dined with us. They complained sadly of the solitude to which they were condemned, but admitted that they should not be able to get through half so much business were they placed at a large station, and exposed to all the temptations and distractions of a gay and extensive circle, nor feel the same interest in their duties, or sympathy with the people, as they do when thrown among them in this manner. To give young men good feelings towards the natives, the only good way is to throw them among them at those out-stations in the early part of their career, when all their feelings are fresh about them. This holds good as well with the military as the civil officer, but more especially with the latter. A young officer at an outpost with his corps, or part of it, for the first season or two, commonly lays in a store of good feeling towards his men that lasts him for life ; and a young gentleman of the Civil Service lays in, in the same manner, a good store of sympathy and fellow-feeling with the natives in general.[2]

Mr. Gubbins is the Magistrate and Collector of one of

---

[1] Chapter XVI of Vol. II of original edition.

[2] The author's remarks concerning military officers refer to officers serving with native regiments. Before the institution of the reformed police in 1861 the native troops used to be much scattered in detachments, guarding treasuries, and performing other duties now entrusted to the police. Detachments are now rarely sent out, except on frontier service.

the three districts into which the Delhi territories are divided, and he has charge of Firōzpur, the resumed estate of the late Nawāb Shams-ud-dīn, which yields a net revenue of about two hundred thousand rupees a year.[1] I have already stated that this Nawāb took good care that his Mewātī plunderers should not rob within his own estate; but he not only gave them free permission to rob over the surrounding districts of our territory, but encouraged them to do so, that he might share in their booty.[2] He was a handsome young man, and an extremely agreeable companion ; but a most unprincipled and licentious character. No man who was reputed to have a handsome wife or daughter was for a moment safe within his territories.   The following account of Mr. William Fraser's assassination by this Nawāb may, I think, be relied upon.[3]

The Firōzpur Jāgīr was one of the principalities created under the principle of Lord Cornwallis's second administration, which was to make the security of the British dominions dependent upon the divisions among the independent native chiefs upon their frontiers.   The person receiving the grant or confirmation of such principality from the British government "pledged himself to relinquish all claims to aid, and to maintain the peace · in his own possessions."[4]   Firōzpur was conferred by Lord Lake, in 1805,

---

[1] Firōzpur is now the headquarters of a sub-collectorate in the Gurgāon district.   The rest of the Delhi Territories is chiefly comprised in the Delhi and Hissar districts.   All these districts have been since 1858 included in the Panjāb, where the district officer has the title of Deputy Commissioner, instead of that of Magistrate and Collector, which is used in the North-Western Provinces.

[2] *Ante*, Vol. I, p. 283.   Some great landholders of the present day pursue the same policy.

[3] Miniature medallion portraits of Nawāb Shams-ud-dīn and his servant Karīm Khān are given on the frontispiece of Volume II in the original edition.

[4] The inglorious second administration of Lord Cornwallis lasted only from 30th of July, 1805, the date on which he relieved the Marquis Wellesley, to the 5th of October of the same year, the date of his death at Ghāzīpur.   "The Marquis Cornwallis arrived in

upon Ahmad Baksh, for his diplomatic services, out of
the territories acquired by us west of the Jumna during the
Marāthā wars.   He had been the agent on the part of the
Hindoo chiefs of Alwar in attendance upon Lord Lake
during the whole of that war.   He was a great favourite,
and his lordship's personal regard for him was thought by
those chiefs to have been so favouràble to their cause that
they conferred upon him the "pargana" of Lohārū in
hereditary rent-free tenure.

In 1822, Ahmad Baksh declared Shams-ud-dīn, his eldest
son, his heir, with the sanction of the British government
and the Rājās of Alwar.   In February 1825, Shams-ud-dīn,
at the request of his father, by a formal deed assigned over
the pargana of Lohārū as a provision for his younger
brothers by another mother, Amīn-ud-dīn and Ziā-ud-dīn ;[1]
and in October 1826 he was finally invested by his father
with the management ; and the circumstance was notified
to the British government, through the Resident at Delhi,
Sir Charles Metcalfe.   Ahmad Baksh died in October 1827.
Disputes soon after arose between the brothers, and they
expressed a desire to submit their claims to the arbitration

India, prepared to abandon, as far as might be practicable, all the
advantages gained for the British government by the wisdom, energy,
and perseverance of his predecessor ; to relax the bands by which the
Marquis Wellesley had connected the greater portion of the states of
India with the British government ; and to reduce that government
from the position of arbiter of the destinies cf India, to the rank of
one among many equals."   His policy was zealously carried out by
Sir George Barlow, who succeeded him, and held office till July 1807.
This statesman was not ashamed to write that "the British possessions
in the Doāb will derive additional security from the contests of the
neighbouring states."   (Thornton, *The History of the British Empire
in India*, chapter xxi.)   This fatuous policy produced twelve years
of anarchy, which were terminated by the Marquis of Hastings' great
war with the Marāthās and Pindhārīs in 1817, so often referred to in
this book.   Lord Lake addressed the most earnest remonstrances to
Sir George Barlow without avail.
    [1] Amīn-ud-dīn and Ziā-ud-dīn's mother was the Bhāo Bēgam, or
wife ; Shams-ud-dīn's the Bhāo Khānum, or mistress. [W. H. S.]

of Sir Edward Colebrooke,[1] who had succeeded Sir Charles Metcalfe in the Residency of Delhi.[2] He referred the matter to the Supreme Government; and by their instructions, under date 11th of April, 1828, he was authorized to adjust the matter. He decided that Shams-ud-din should make a complete and unencumbered cession to his younger brothers of the pargana of Lohārū, without the reservation of any right of interference in the management, or of any condition of obedience to himself whatever; and that Amin-ud-din should, till his younger brother came of age, pay into the Delhi treasury for him the annual sum of five thousand two hundred and ten rupees, as his half share of the net proceeds, to be there held in deposit for him; and that the estate should, from the time he came of age, be divided between them in equal shares. This award was confirmed by government; but Sir Edward was recommended to alter it for an annual money payment to the two younger brothers, if he could do so with the consent of the parties.

The pargana was transferred, as the money payment could not be agreed upon; and in September Mr. Martin, who had succeeded Sir E. Colebrooke, proposed to government that the pargana of Lohārū should be restored to Shams-ud-din in lieu of a fixed sum of twenty-six thousand rupees a year to be paid by him annually to his two younger brothers. This proposal was made on the ground that Amin-ud-din could not collect the revenues from the refractory landholders (instigated, no doubt, by the emissaries of Shams-ud-din), and consequently could not pay his younger brother's revenue into the treasury. In calculating

[1] The son and biographer of Sir Henry Thomas Colebrooke, Baronet, the greatest of Anglo-Indian Sanskritists.

[2] Sir Charles Metcalfe was for a time Assistant Resident at Delhi, and was first appointed to the Residency at the extraordinarily early age of twenty-six. He was then transferred to other posts. In 1824 he returned to the Delhi Residency, superseding Sir David Ochterlony, whose measures had been disapproved by the Government of India.

the annual *net* revenue of 10,420 rupees, 15,000 of the *gross* revenue had been estimated as the annual expenses of the mutual [*sic*] establishments of the two brothers. To the arrangement proposed by Mr. Martin the younger brothers strongly objected ; and proposed in preference to make over the pargana to the British government, on condition of receiving the net revenue, whatever might be the amount. Mr. Martin was desired by the Governor-General to effect this arrangement, should Amin-ud-din appear still to wish it ; but he preferred retaining the management of it in his own hands, in the hope that circumstances would improve.

Shams-ud-din, however, pressed his claim to the restoration of the pargana so often that it was at last, in September, 1833, insisted upon by Government, on the ground that Amin-ud-din had failed to fulfil that article of the agreement which bound him to pay annually into the Delhi treasury 5,210 rupees for his younger brother, though that brother had never complained ; on the contrary, lived with him on the best possible terms, and was as averse as himself to the retransfer of the pargana, on condition that they gave up their claims to a large share of the movable property of their late father, which had been already decided in their favour in the court of first instance. Mr. W. Fraser, who had succeeded to the office of Governor-General's representative in the Delhi Territories, remonstrated strongly against this measure ; and wished to bring it again under the consideration of government, on the grounds that Zia-ud-din had never made any complaint against his brother Amin-ud-din for want of punctuality in the payment of his share of the net revenue after the payment of their mutual establishments ; that the two brothers would be deprived by this measure of an hereditary estate to the value of sixty thousand rupees a year in perpetuity, burthened with the condition that they relinquished a suit already gained in the court of first instance, and likely to be gained in appeal, involving a sum that would of itself yield them that annual sum at the moderate interest of 6 per cent. The grounds alleged by him were not considered valid, and the pargana was made over to Shams-ud-din. The pargana now yields 40,000 rupees a year, and under good management may yield 70,000.

At Mr. Fraser's recommendation, Amīn-ud-din went himself to Calcutta, and is said to have prevailed upon the government to take his case again into their consideration. Shams-ud-dīn had become a debauched and licentious character; and having criminal jurisdiction within his own estate, no one's wife or daughter was considered safe; for, when other means failed him, he did not scruple to employ assassins to effect his hated purposes, by removing the husband or father.[1] Mr. Fraser became so disgusted with his conduct that he would not admit him into his house when he came to Delhi, though he had, it may be said, brought him up as a child of his own; indeed he had been as fond of him as he could be of a child of his own; and the boy used to spend the greater part of his time with him. One day after Mr. Fraser had refused to admit the Nawāb to his house, Colonel Skinner,[2] having some apprehensions that by such slights he might be driven to seek revenge by assassination, is said to have remonstrated with Mr. Fraser as his oldest and most valued friend. Mr. Fraser told him that he considered the Nawāb to be still but a boy, and the only way to improve him was to treat him as such. It was, however, more by these slights than by any supposed injuries that Shams-ud-din was exasperated; and from that day he determined to have Mr. Fraser assassinated.

Having prevailed upon a man, Karīm Khān, who was

---

[1] The editor once had occasion to deal with a similar case, which resulted in the loss by the offending Rājā of his rank and title. The orders were passed by the Government of Lord Dufferin.

[2] Colonel Skinner, who raised the famous troops known as Skinner's Horse, died in 1841, and was buried in the church at Delhi which he had built. The church still exists.

at once his servant and boon companion, he sent him to
Delhi with one of his carriages, which he was to have sold
through Mr. McPherson, a European merchant of the
city.   He was ordered to stay there ostensibly for the
purpose of learning the process of extracting copper from
the fossil containing the ore, and purchasing dogs for the
Nawāb.   He was to watch his opportunity and shoot Mr.
Fraser whenever he might find him out at night, attended
by only one or two orderlies ; to be in no haste, but to
wait till he found a favourable opportunity, though it
should be for several months.   He had with him a groom
named Rūplā, and a Mewātī attendant named Aniā, and
they lodged in apartments of the Nawāb's at Daryāoganj.
He rode out morning and evening, attended by Aniā on
foot, for three months, during which he often met Mr.
Fraser, but never under circumstances favourable to his
purpose ; and at last, in despair, returned to Firōzpur.
Aniā had importuned him for leave to go home to see his
children, who had been ill, and Karīm Khān did not like
to remain without him.   The Nawāb was displeased with
him for returning without leave, and ordered him to return
to his post, and effect the object of his mission.   Aniā
declined to return, and the Nawāb recommended Karīm to
take somebody else, but he had, he said, explained all his
designs to this man, and it would be dangerous to entrust
the secret to another ; and he could, moreover, rely
entirely upon the courage of Aniā on any trying occasion.

Twenty rupees were due to the treasury by Aniā on
account of the rent of the little tenement he held under
the Nawāb ; and the treasurer consented, at the request of
Karim Khān, to receive this by small instalments, to be
deducted out of the monthly wages he was to receive from
him.   He was, moreover, assured that he should have
nothing to do but to cook and eat ; and should share
liberally with Karīm in the one hundred rupees he was
taking with him in money, and the letter of credit upon
the Nawāb's bankers at Delhi for one thousand rupees

more. The Nawāb himself came with them as far as the village of Nagīna, where he used to hunt; and there Karīm requested permission to change his groom, as he thought Rūplā too shrewd a man for such a purpose. He wanted, he said, a stupid, sleepy man, who would neither ask nor understand anything; but the Nawāb told him that Rūplā was an old and quiet servant, upon whose fidelity. he could entirely rely; and Karīm consented to take him. Aniā's little tenement, upon which his wife and children resided, was only two miles distant, and he went to give instructions about gathering in the harvest, and to take leave of them. He told his wife that he was going to the capital on a difficult and dangerous duty, but that his companion Karīm would do it all, no doubt. Aniā asked Karīm before they left Nagīna what was to be his reward; and he told him that the Nawāb had promised them five villages in rent-free tenure. Aniā wished to learn from the Nawāb himself what he might expect; and being taken to him by Karīm, was assured that he and his family should be provided for handsomely for the rest of their lives, if he did his duty well on this occasion.

On reaching Delhi they took up their quarters near Colonel Skinner's house, in the Bulvemar's Ward,[1] where they resided for two months. The Nawāb had told Karīm to get a gun made for his purpose at Delhi, or purchase one, stating that his guns had all been purchased through Colonel Skinner, and would lead to suspicion if seen in his possession. On reaching Delhi, Karīm purchased an old gun, and desired Aniā to go to a certain man in the Chāndnī Chauk, and get it made in the form of a short blunderbuss, with a peculiar stock, that would admit of its being concealed under a cloak; and to say that he was going to Gwālior to seek service, if any one questioned him. The barrel was cut, and the instrument made exactly as Karīm wished it to be by the man whom he

---

[1] I print this word "Bulvemar's" as it stands in the original edition, not knowing what it means.

pointed out. They met Mr. Fraser every day, but never at night; and Karīm expressed regret that the Nawāb should have so strictly enjoined him not to shoot him in the daytime, which he, thought he might do without much risk. Aniā got an attack of fever, and urged Karīm to give up the attempt and return home, or at least permit him to do so. Karīm himself became weary, and said he would do so very soon if he could not succeed; but that he should certainly shoot *some European gentleman* before he set out, and tell his master that he had taken him for Mr. Fraser—to save appearances. Aniā told him that this was a question between him and his master, and no concern of his.

At the expiration of two months, a peon came to learn what they were doing. Karīm wrote a letter by him to the Nawāb, saying that "*the dog* he wished was never to be seen without ten or twelve people about him; and that he saw no chance whatever of finding him, except in the midst of them; but that if he wished, he would purchase this *dog* in the midst of the crowd." The Nawāb wrote a reply, which was sent by a trooper, with orders that it should be opened in presence of no one but Aniā. The contents were:—"I command you not to purchase *the dog* in presence of many persons, as its *price* will be greatly raised. You may purchase him before one person, or even two, but not before more; I am in no hurry, the longer the time you take the better; but do not return without purchasing *the dog*."[1] That is, without killing Mr. Fraser.

They wait on every day to watch Mr. Fraser's movements. Leaving the horse with the groom, sometimes in one old ruin of the city, and sometimes in another, ready saddled for flight, with orders that he should not be exposed to the

---

[1] The habits of Europeans have now changed, and to most people escorts have become very distasteful. High officials now constantly go about unattended, and could be assassinated with little difficulty. Happily crimes of the kind are rare, except on the Afghān frontier, where special precautions are taken.

view of passers-by, Karīm and Aniā used to pace the streets, and on several occasions fell in with him, but always found him attended by too many. followers of one kind or another for their purpose. At last, on Sunday, the 13th of March, 1835, Karīm heard that Mr. Fraser was to attend a "nāch" (dance), given by Hindoo Rāo, the brother of the Baiza Bāi,[1] who then resided at Delhi; and determining to try whether he could not shoot him from horseback, he sent away his groom as soon as he had ascertained that Mr. Fraser was actually at the dance. Aniā went in and mixed among the assembly; and as soon as he saw Mr. Fraser rise to depart, he gave intimátion to Karim, who ordered him to keep behind, and make off as fast as he could, as soon as he should hear the report of his gun.

A little way from Hindoo Rao's house the road branches off; that to the left is straight, while that to the right is circuitous. Mr. Fraser was known always to take the straight road, and upon that Karim posted himself, as the road up to the place where it branched off was too public for his purpose. As it happened, Mr. Fraser, for the first time, took the circuitous road to the right, and reached his home without meeting Karīm. Aniā placed himself at the cross way, and waited there till Karim came up to him. On hearing that he had taken the right road, Karim said that "a man in Mr. Fraser's situation must be a strange ('kāfir') unbeliever not to have such a thing as a torch with him in a dark night. Had he had what he ought," he said, "I should not have lost him this time."

They passed him on the road somewhere or other almost every afternoon after this for seven days, but could never fall in with him after dark. On the eighth day, Sunday, the 22nd of March, Karim went, as usual, in the forenoon to the great mosque to say his prayers; and on his way

---

[1] For the "Bāiza Bai" see *ante*, Vol. I, p. 366. Hindoo Rāo's house became famous in 1857 as the headquarters of the British force on the Ridge, during the siege of Delhi.

back in the afternoon he purchased some plums which he was eating when he came up to Aniā, whom he found cooking his dinner. He ordered his horse to be saddled immediately, and told Aniā to make haste and eat his dinner, as he had seen Mr. Fraser at a party given by the Rājā of Kishangarh. " *When his time is come*," said Karīm, "we shall no doubt find an opportunity to kill him, if we watch him carefully." They left the groom at home that evening, and proceeded to the "dargāh" (church) near the canal. Seeing Aniā with merely a stick in his hand, Karīm bid him go back and change it for a sword, while he went in and said his evening prayers.

On being rejoined by Aniā, they took the road to cantonments, which passed by Mr. Fraser's house; and Aniā observed that the risk was hardly equal in this undertaking, he being on foot, while Karīm was on horseback; that he should be sure to be taken, while the other might have a fair chance of escape. It was now quite dark, and Karīm bid him stand by sword in hand; and if anybody attempted to seize his horse when he fired, cut him down, and be assured that while he had life, he would never suffer him, Aniā, to be taken. Karīm continued to patrol up and down on the high-road, that nobody might notice him, while Aniā stood by the road-side. At last, about eleven o'clock, they heard Mr. Fraser approach, attended by one trooper, and two "peons" on foot; and Karīm walked his horse slowly, as if he had been going from the city to the cantonments, till Mr. Fraser came up within a few paces of him, near the gate leading into his house. Karīm Khān, on leaving his house, had put one large ball into his short blunderbuss; and when confident that he should now have an opportunity of shooting Mr. Fraser, he put in two more small ones. As Mr. Fraser's horse was coming up on the left side, Karīm Khān turned round his, and, as he passed, presented his blunderbuss, fired, and all three balls passed into Mr. Fraser's breast. All three horses reared at the report and flash, and Mr. Fraser fell dead on the ground.

Karim galloped off, followed a short distance by the trooper, and the two peons went off and gave information to Major Pew and Cornet Robinson, who resided near the place. They came in all haste to the spot, and had the body taken to the deceased's own house; but no signs of life remained. They reported the murder to the magistrate, and the city gates were closed, as the assassin had been seen to enter the city by the trooper.

Aniā ran home through the Kābul gate of the city, unperceived, while Karīm entered by the Ajmīr gate, and passed first through the encampment of Hindoo Rao, to efface the traces of his horse's feet. When he reached their lodgings, he found Aniā there before him; and Rūplā, the groom, seeing his horse in a sweat, told him that he had had a narrow escape—that Mr. Fraser had been killed, and orders given for the arrest of any horseman that might be found in or near the city. He told him to hold his tongue, and take care of the horse; and calling for a light, he and Aniā tore up every letter he had received from Firōzpur, and dipped the fragments in water, to efface the ink from them. Aniā asked him what he had done with the blunderbuss, and was told that it had been thrown into a well. Aniā now concealed three flints that he kept about him in some sand in the upper story they occupied, and threw an iron ramrod and two spare bullets into a well near the mosque.

The next morning, when he heard that the city gates had been all shut to prevent any one from going out till strict search should be made, Karim became a good deal alarmed, and went to seek counsel from Moghal Beg, the friend of his master; but when in the evening he heard that they had been again opened, he recovered his spirits; and the next day he wrote a letter to the Nawāb, saying that he had purchased the *dogs* that he wanted, and would soon return with them. He then went to Mr. McPherson, and actually purchased from him for the Nawāb some dogs and pictures, and the following day sent Rūplā, the groom, with them to Firōzpur, accompanied by two bearers. A pilgrim lodged in the same place with these men, and was present when Karim came home from the murder, and gave his horse to Rūplā. In the evening, after the departure of Rūplā with the dogs, four men of the Gūjar caste came to the place, and Karim sat down and smoked a pipe with one of them,[1] who said that he had lost his bread by Mr. Fraser's death, and should be glad to see the murderer punished—-that he was known to have worn a green vest, and he hoped he would soon be discovered. The pilgrim came up to Karim shortly after these four men went away, and said that he had heard from some one that he, Karim, was himself suspected of the murder. He went again to Moghal Beg, who told him not to be alarmed, that, happily, the Regulations were now in force in the Delhi Territory, and that he had only to stick steadily to one story to be safe.

He now desired Aniā to return to Firōzpur with a letter to the Nawāb, and to assure him that he would be staunch and stick to one story, though they should seize him and confine him in prison for twelve years. He had, he said, already sent off part of his clothes, and Aniā should now take away the rest, so that nothing suspicious should be left near him.

The next morning Aniā set out on foot, accompained by Islāmullah, a servant of Moghal Beg's, who was also the bearer of a letter to the Nawāb. They hired two ponies when they became tired, but both flagged before they reached Nagina, whence Aniā proceeded to Firōzpur, on a mare belonging to the native collector, leaving Islāmullah behind. He gave his letter to the Nawāb, who desired him to describe the affair of the murder. He did so. The Nawāb seemed very much pleased, and asked him whether Karim appeared to be in any alarm. Aniā told him that he did not, and had resolved to stick to one story, though he should be

---

[1] Many of the Gūjar caste are Muhammadans.

imprisoned for twelve years. "Karim Khān," said the Nawāb, turning to the brother-in-law of the former, Wāsil Khān, and Hasan Ali, who stood near him—"Karim Khān is a very brave man, whose courage may be always relied on." He gave Aniā eighteen rupees, and told him to change his name, and keep close to Wāsil Khān. They retired together; but, while Wāsil Khān went to his house, Aniā stood on the road unperceived, but near enough to hear Hasan Ali urge the Nawāb to have him put to death immediately, as the only chance of keeping the fatal secret. He went off immediately to Wāsil Khān, and prevailed upon him to give him leave to go home for that night to see his family, promising to be back the next morning early.

He set out forthwith, but had not been long at home when he learned that Hasan Ali, and another confidential servant of the Nawāb, were come in search of him with some troopers. He concealed himself in the roof of his house, and heard them ask his wife and children where he was, saying they wanted his aid in getting out some hyænas they had traced into their dens in the neighbourhood. They were told that he had gone back to Firōzpur, and returned; but were sent back by the Nawāb to make a more careful search for him. Before they came, however, he had gone off to his friends Kamruddin and Johari, two brothers who resided in the Rāo Rājā's territory. To this place he was followed by some Mewātis, whom the Nawāb had induced, under the promise of a large reward, to undertake to kill him. One night he went to two acquaintances, Makrām and Shahāmat, in a neighbouring village, and begged them to send to some English gentleman in Delhi, and solicit for him a pardon, on condition of his disclosing all the circumstances of Mr. Fraser's murder. They promised to get everything done for him through a friend in the police at Delhi, and set out for that purpose, while Aniā returned and concealed himself in the hills. In six days they came with a paper, purporting to be a promise of pardon from the court of Delhi, and desired Kamr-ud-dīn to introduce them to Aniā. He told them to return to him in three days, and he would do so ; but he went off to Aniā in the hills, and told him that he did not think these men had really got the papers from the English gentlemen —that they appeared to him to be in the service of the Nawāb himself. Aniā was, however, introduced to them when they came back, and requested that the paper might be read to him. Seeing through their designs, he again made off to the hills, while they went out in search, they pretended, of a man to read it, but in reality to get some people who were waiting in the neighbourhood to assist in securing him, and taking him off to the Nawāb.

Finding on their return that Aniā had escaped, they offered high rewards to the two brothers if they would assist in tracing him out ; and Johari was taken to the Nawāb, who offered him a very high reward if he would bring Aniā to him, or, at least, take measures to prevent his going to the English gentlemen. This was communicated to Aniā, who went through Bharatpur to Bareilly, and from Bareilly to Secunderabad, where he heard, in the beginning of July, that bóth Karim and the Nawāb were to be tried for the murder, and that the judge, Mr. Colvin, had already arrived at Delhi to conduct the trial. He now determined to go to Delhi and give himself up. On his way he was met by Mr. Simon Fraser's man, who took him to Delhi, when he confessed his share in the crime, became king's evidence at the trial, and gave an interesting narrative of the whole affair.

Two water-carriers, in attempting to draw up the brass jug of a carpenter, which had fallen into the well the morning after the murder, pulled up the blunderbuss which Karim Khān had thrown into the same well. This was afterwards recognized by Aniā, and the man whom he pointed out as having made it for him. Two of the four Gūjars, who were mentioned as having visited Karim immediately after the murder, went to Brigadier Fast, who commanded the troops at Delhi, fearing that the native officers of the European civil functionaries might be in the interest of the Nawāb, and get them made away with.   They told him that Karīm Khān seemed to answer the description of the man named in the proclamation as the murderer of Mr. Fraser ; and he sent them with a note to the Commissioner, Mr. Metcalfe, who sent them to the Magistrate, Mr. Fraser, who accompanied them to the place, and secured Karim; with some fragments of important papers.   The two Mewātis, who had been sent to assassinate Aniā, were found, and they confessed the fact ; the brother of Aniā, Rahmat, was found, and he described the difficulty Aniā had to escape from the Nawāb's people sent to murder him.   Rūplā, the groom, deposed to all that he had seen during the time he was employed as Karīm's groom at Delhi.   Several men deposed to having met Karīm, and heard him asking after Mr. Fraser a few days before the murder.   The two peons, who were with Mr. Fraser when he was shot, deposed to the horse which he rode at the time, and which was found with him.

Karīm Khān and the Nawāb were both convicted of the crime, sentenced to death, and executed at Delhi..   I should mention that suspicion had immediately attached to Karīm Khān ; he was known for some time to have been lurking about Delhi, on the pretence of purchasing dogs ; and it was said that, had the Nawāb really wanted dogs, he would not have sent to purchase them by a man whom he admitted to his table, and treated on terms of equality.   He was suspected of having been employed on such occasions before—known to be a good shot, and a good rider, who could fire and reload very quickly while his horse was in full gallop, and called in consequence the " Bharmārū."[1] His horse, which was found in the stable by the Gūjar spies, who had before been in Mr. Fraser's service, answered the description given of the murderer's horse by Mr. Fraser's

[1] That is to say " load and fire," or " sharpshooter."

attendants; and the Nawāb was known to cherish feelings of bitter hatred against Mr. Fraser.

The Nawāb was executed some time after Karīm, on Thursday morning, the 3rd of October, 1835, close outside the north, or Kashmīr Gate, leading to the cantonments. He prepared himself for the execution in an extremely rich and beautiful dress of light green, the colour which martyrs wear; but he was made to exchange this, and he then chose one of simple white, and was too conscious of his guilt to urge strongly his claim to wear what dress he liked on such an occasion. .

The following corps were drawn up around the gallows, forming three sides of a square:—the 1st Regiment of Cavalry, the 20th, 39th, and 69th Regiments of Native Infantry, Major Pew's Light Field Battery, and a strong party of police. On ascending the scaffold, the Nawāb manifested symptoms of disgust at the approach to his person of the sweeper, who was to put the rope round his neck;[1] but he soon mastered his feelings, and submitted with a good grace to his fate. Just as he expired his body made a last turn, and left his face towards the *west*, or the *tomb of his Prophet*, which the Muhammadans of Delhi considered a miracle, indicating that he was a martyr—not as being innocent of the murder, but as being executed for the murder of an *unbeliever*. Pilgrimages were for some time made to the Nawāb's tomb,[2] but I believe they have long since ceased with the short gleam of sympathy that his fate excited. The only people that still recollect him with feelings of kindness are the prostitutes and dancing women of the city of Delhi, among whom most of his revenues were squandered.[3]   In the same manner was

[1] No one but a member of one of the "outcaste castes," if the "bull" be allowable, will act as executioner.

[2] This sinister incident shows clearly the real feeling of the Muhammadan populace towards the ruling power. That feeling is unchanged, and is not altogether confined to the populace.

[3] This remark was evidently written some time after the author's first visit to Delhi, and was probably written in the year 1839.

Wazīr Alī recollected for many years by the prostitutes and
dancing women of Benares, after the massacre of Mr.
Cherry and all the European gentlemen of that station,
save one, Mr. Davis, who bravely defended himself, wife,
and children against a host with a hog spear on the top of
his house.   No European could pass Benares for twenty
years after Wazīr Alī's arrest and confinement in the garrison of Fort William, without hearing from the windows
songs in his praise, and in praise of the massacre.[1]

[1] On the death of Āsaf-ud-daula, Wazīr Alī was, in spite of doubts
as to his legitimacy, recognized by Sir John Shore (Lord Teignmouth)
as the Nawāb Wazīr of Oudh, in 1797.   On reconsideration, the
Governor-General cancelled the recognition of Wazīr Alī, and recognized his rival Saādat Alī.   Wazīr Alī was removed from Lucknow,
but injudiciously allowed to reside at Benares.   The Marquis of Wellesley, then Earl of Mornington, took charge of the office of Governor-
General in 1798, and soon resolved that it was expedient to remove
Wazīr Alī to a greater distance from Lucknow.   Mr. Cherry, the
Agent to the Governor-General, was accordingly instructed to remove
him from Benares to Calcutta.   The outbreak alluded to in the text
occurred on the 14th January, 1799, and was the expression of Wazīr
Alī's resentment at these orders.   It is described as follows by Thornton (*History*, ch. xvii):—"A visit which Wazīr Alī made, accompanied
by his suite, to the British Agent, afforded the means of accomplishing
the meditated revenge.   He had engaged himself to breakfast with
Mr. Cherry, and the parties met in apparent amity.   The usual compliments were exchanged.   Wazīr Alī then began to expatiate on his
wrongs ; and having pursued this subject for some time, he suddenly
rose with his attendants, and put to death Mr. Cherry and Captain
Conway, an English gentleman who happened to be present.   The
assassins then rushed out, and meeting another Englishman named
Graham, they added him to the list of their victims.   They thence
proceeded to the house of Mr. Davis, judge and magistrate, who had
just time to remove his family to an upper terrace, which could only
be reached by a very narrow staircase.   At the top of this staircase,
Mr. Davis, armed with a spear, took his post, and so successfully did
he defend it, that the assailants, after several attempts to dislodge him,
were compelled to retire without effecting their object.   The benefit
derived from the resistance of this intrepid man extended beyond his
own family : the delay thereby occasioned afforded to the rest of the
English inhabitants opportunity of escaping to the place where the
troops stationed for the protection of the city were encamped.   General

It is supposed that the Nawāb Tēz Muhammad Khan of Gajper was deeply implicated in this murder, though no proof of it could be found.   He died soon after the execution of Shams-ud-dīn, and was succeeded in his fief by his eldest son, Tēz Alī Khān.[1]   This fief was bestowed on the father of the deceased, whose name was Najābat Alī Khān, by Lord Lake, on the termination of the war in 1805, for the aid he had given to the retreating army under Colonel Monson.[2]

One circumstance attending the execution of the Nawāb Shams-ud-dīn seems worthy of remark.   The magistrate, Mr. Frascott, desired his crier to go through the city the evening before the execution, and proclaim to the people

Erskine, on learning what had occurred, despatched a party to the relief of Mr. Davis, and Wazīr Alī thereupon retired to his own residence." Wazīr Alī escaped, but was ultimately given up by a chief with whom he had taken refuge, " on condition that his life should be spared, and that his limbs should not be disgraced by chains." Some of his accomplices were executed. " He was confined at Fort William, in a sort of iron cage, where he died in May, 1817, aged thirty-six, after an imprisonment of seventeen years and some odd months." (*Men whom India has Known*, art. " Vizier Ali.") It will be observed that the author was mistaken in supposing that " all the European gentlemen, except Mr. Davis and his family, were included in the massacre."

[1] These names stand in the original edition as " Tyz Mahomed Khan, of Ghujper," and " Tyz Alee Khan." Tyz may be intended for " Faiz."

[2] The disastrous retreat of Colonel Monson before Jeswant Rāo Holkār during the rainy season of 1804 is one of the few serious reverses which have interrupted the long series of British victories in India.   A considerable force under the command of Colonel Monson, sent out by General Lake at the beginning of May in pursuit of Holkār, was withdrawn too far from its base, and was compelled to retreat through Rājputāna, and fall back on Agra.   During the retreat the rains broke, and, under pressure caused by the difficulties of the march and incessant attacks of the enemy, the British troops became disorganized, and lost their guns and baggage.   The shattered remnants of the force straggled into Agra at the end of August.   The disgrace of this retreat was speedily avenged by the great victory of Dīg.

that those who might wish to be present at the execution were not to encroach upon the line of sentries that would be formed to keep clear an allotted space round the gallows, nor to carry with them any kind of arms ; but the crier, seemingly retaining in his recollection only the words *arms* and *sentries*, gave out after his " Oyes, Oyes," [1] that the sentries had orders to use their arms, and shoot any man, woman, or child that should presume to go outside the wall to look at the execution of the Nawāb. No person, in consequence, ventured out till the execution was over, when they went to see the Nawāb himself converted into smoke ; as the general impression was that as life should leave it, the body was to be blown off into the air by a general discharge of musketry and artillery. Moghal Bēg was acquitted for want of judicial proof of his guilty participation in the crime.

[1] This old Norman-French formula, if it was actually used in India in the author's time, has been long disused.

CHAPTER X[1]

Marriage of a Jāt Chief.

On the 19th[2] we came on to Balamgarh,[3] fifteen miles over a plain, better cultivated and more studded with trees than that which we had been coming over for many days before. The water was near the surface, more of the fields were irrigated, and those which were not so, looked better —[a] range of sandstone hills, ten miles off to the west, running north and south. Balamgarh is held in rent-free tenure by a young Jāt chief, now about ten years of age. He resides in a mud fort in a handsóme palace built in the European fashion. In an extensive orange garden, close outside the fort, he is building a very handsome tomb over the spot where his father's elder brother was buried. The whole is formed of white and black marble, and the firm white sandstone of Rūpbās, and so well conceived and executed as to make it evident that demand is the only thing wanted to cover India with works of art equal to any that were formed in the palmy days of the Muhammadan empire.[4] The Rājā's young sister had just been married to the son of the Jāt chief of Nābhā, who was accompanied in

[1] Chapter XVII of Vol. II of original edition.
[2] January, 1836.
[3] Also called Balabhgarh or Farīdābād (Ballamgarh, Bulubgarh, Furreedabad), twenty-nine miles south of Delhi. The estate was confiscated on account of the rebellion of the chief in 1857, and now forms part of the Delhi district. The area is stated in Thornton's *Gazetteer* to have been 190 square miles.
[4] Few observers will accept this proposition without considerable reservation.

his matrimonial visit (barāt) by the chief of Ludhaura, and the son of the Sikh chief of Patiālā,[1] with a cortége of one hundred elephants, and above fifteen thousand people.[2]

[1] Patiālā is the principal of the Cis-Satlaj Sikh Protected States. Nābhā belongs to the same group. Both states are very loyal, and supply Imperial Service troops. For a sketch of their history see chapters ii and ix of Sir Lepel Griffin's *Ranjīt Singh.*

[2] The Sikh is a military nation formed out of the Jāts (who were without a place among the castes of the Hindoos),[a] by that strong bond of union, the love of conquest and plunder. Their religious and civil codes are the Granths, books written by their reputed prophets, the last of whom was Guru Govind,[b] in whose name Ranjīt Singh stamps his gold coins with this legend :—" The sword, the *pot*, victory, and conquest were quickly found in the grace of Guru Govind

[a] It has already been observed that the author was completely mistaken in his estimate of the social position of Jāts. It is not correct to say that they " were without a place among the castes of the Hindoos." "The Jāt is in every respect the most important of the Panjāb peoples. . . The distinction between Jāt and Rājpūt is social rather than ethnic. . . Socially the Jāt occupies a position which is shared by the Rōr, the Gūjar, and the Ahīr ; all four eating and smoking together. Among the races of purely Hindoo origin I think that the Jāt stands next after the Brahman, the Rājpūt, and the Khatrī. . . There are Jāts and Jāts. . . His is the highest of the castes practising widow marriage." (Mr. Denzil Ibbetson, I.C.S., *Outlines of Panjāb Ethnography*, being extracts from the Panjāb Census Report of 1881 ; published by the Superintendent of Government Printing, India ; Calcutta, 1883, pp. 220 *seqq.*) The Jāts in the North-Western Provinces occupy much the same relative position.

[b] The Sikhs are mostly, but not all, Jāts. The organization is essentially a religious one, and a few Brahmans and many members of various other castes join it. The word Sikh means " disciple." Nānak Shāh, the founder, was born in A.D. 1469. The Adi Granth, the Sikh Bible, was composed between 1581 and 1606. It has recently been translated into English by Dr. Ernest Trumpp. The reformation in the sect effected by Guru Govind took place about 1695. Govind died in 1708. In 1764 the Sikhs finally occupied Lahore, and formed a political system. Full details will be found in *A History of the Sikhs*, 2 vols. 8vo, London, 1849, by J. D. Cunningham (of which work the article " Sikh " in Balfour's *Cyclopædia* is an abstract) ; and in Sir Lepel Griffin's excellent little book on Ranjīt Singh (1892), in the " Rulers of India " series.

The young chief of Balamgarh mustered a cortége of sixty elephants and about ten thousand men to attend him out in the " istikbāl," to meet and welcome his guests. The

Singh."[c] This prophet died insane in the end of the seventeenth century. He was the son of a priest Tēg Bahādur, who was made a martyr of by the bigoted Muhammadans of Patna in 1675. The son became a Peter the Hermit, in the same manner as Hargovind before him, when his father, Arjun Mal, was made a martyr by the fanaticism of the same people. A few more such martyrdoms would have set the Sikhs up for ever. They admit converts freely, and while they have a fair prospect of conquest and plunder they will find them ; but, when they cease, they will be swallowed up in the great ocean of Hinduism, since they have no chance of getting up an "army of martyrs" while we have the supreme power.[d] They detest us for the same reason that

---

[c] See "The Coins of the Modern Chiefs of the Panjāb," by R. C. Temple in *Indian Antiquary* for 1889, vol. xviii, p. 321 ; and "On the Coins of the Sikhs," by C. J. Rodgers in *Journal As. Soc. Bengal*, vol. i, part i (1881). The couplet is in Persian, which may be transliterated thus :—

"Dēg, tēgh, wa fath, wa nasrat be darang
Yāft az Nānak Gūrū Govind Singh."

The word *dēg*, meaning pot or cauldron, is used as a symbol of plenty.

[d] This prophecy has not been fulfilled. The annexation of the Panjāb in 1849 put an end to Sikh hopes of " conquest and plunder," and yet the sect has not been "swallowed up in the great ocean of Hinduism." At the census of 1881 its numbers were returned as 1,853,426, or nearly two millions, for all India. The corresponding figure for 1891 is 1,907,833. At the time of the first British census of 1855 the outside influences were depressing : the great Khālsa army had fallen, and Sikh fathers were slow to bring forward their sons for baptism (*pāhul*). The Mutiny, in the suppression of which the Sikhs took so great a part, worked a change. The Sikhs recovered their spirits and self-respect, and found honourable careers open in the British army and constabulary. "Thus the creed received a new impulse, and many sons of Sikhs, whose baptism had been deferred, received the *pāhul*, while new candidates from among the Jāts and lower caste Hindoos joined the faith." Some reaction then, perhaps, took place, but, on the whole, the numbers of the sect have been maintained. (Sir Lepel Griffin, *Ranjīt Singh*, p.p. 25-34.) Mr. J. A. Baines, Census Commissioner for India, informs me that the Sikhs in

bridegroom's party had to expend about six hundred thousand rupees in this visit alone. They scattered copper money all along the road from their homes to within seven miles of Balamgarh. From this point to the gate of the fort they had to scatter silver, and from this gate to the door of the palace they scattered gold and jewels of all kinds. The son of the Patiālā chief, a lad of about ten years of age, sat upon his elephant with a bag containing six hundred gold mohurs of two guineas each, mixed up with an infinite variety of gold earrings, pearls, and precious stones, which he scattered in handfuls among the crowd. The scattering of the copper and silver had been left to inferior hands. The costs of the family of the bride are always much greater than that of the bridegroom; they are obliged to entertain at their own expense all the bridegroom's guests as well as their own, as long as they remain; and over and above this, on the present occasion, the Rājā

the military followers of the other native chiefs detest us, because we say "Thus far shall you go, and no farther" in your career of conquest and plunder. As governors, they are even worse than the Marāthās— utterly detestable. They have not the slightest idea of a duty towards the people from whose industry they are provided. Such a thing was never dreamed of by a Sikh. They continue to receive in marriage the daughters of Jāts, as in this case; but they will not give their daughters to Jāts. [W. H. S.]e

the Panjāb were returned as numbering 1,716,114 in 1881, and 1,870,481 in 1891. Some decrease has occurred in Native territory. "On the whole, the increase in British territory is real; (a) because of the military value of the title of Sikh, (b) because the leaders have been preaching and gathering in converts largely in Amritsar, Lūdiāna, etc. Sweepers (Mazbi or Mazhabī) have largely increased. Possibly Hinduism has affected the ritual and ceremonial, which is less Govindī than it used to be."

e The Sikhs do not now detest us. They willingly furnish soldiers a. 1 military police of the best class, equal to the Gūrkhās, and fit to figh in line with English soldiers. The Panjāb chieftains have been among the foremost in offers of loyal assistance to the Government of India in times of danger, and in organizing the Imperial Service troops. The Sikh states are now sufficiently well-governed.

gave a rupee to every person that came, invited or uninvited. An immense concourse of people had assembled to share in this donation, and to scramble for the money scattered along the road; and ready money enough was not found in the treasury. Before a further supply could be got, thirty thousand more had collected, and every one got his rupee. They have them all put into pens like sheep. When all are in, the doors are opened at a signal given, and every person is paid his rupee as he goes out. Some European gentlemen were standing upon the top of the Rājā's palace, looking at the procession as it entered the fort, and passed underneath; and the young chief threw up some handfuls of pearls, gold, and jewels among them. Not one of them would of course condescend to stoop to take up any; but their servants showed none of the same dignified forbearance.[1]

[1] The Emperors of Delhi, from Jahāngīr onwards, used to strike special coins, generally of small size, bearing the word "nisār," which means "scattering," for the purpose of distribution among the crowd on the occasion of a wedding, or other great festivity.

CHAPTER XI[1]

Collegiate Endowment of Muhammadan Tombs and Mosques.

On the 20th[2] we came to Badarpur, twelve miles over a plain, with the range of hills on our left approaching nearer and nearer the road, and separating us from the old city of Delhi. We passed through Farīdpur, once a large town, and called after its founder, Shaikh Farīd, whose mosque is still in good order, though there is no person to read or hear prayers in it. We passed also two fine bridges, one of three, and one of four arches, both over what were once streams, but are now dry beds of sand. The whole road shows signs of having been once thickly peopled, and highly adorned with useful and ornamental works when Delhi was in its glory.

Every handsome mausoleum among Muhammadans was provided with its mosque, and endowed by the founder with the means of maintaining men of learning to read their Korān over the grave of the deceased and in his chapel ; and, as long as the endowment lasted, the tomb continued to be at the same time a college. They read the Korān morning and evening over the grave, and prayers in the chapel at the stated periods ; and the rest of their time is commonly devoted to the instruction of the youths of their neighbourhood, either gratis or for a small consideration. Apartments in the tomb were usually set aside for the purpose, and these tombs did ten times more for education in Hindustan than all the colleges formed

[1] Chapter XVIII of Vol. II of original edition.
[2] January, 1836.

especially for the purpose.[1] We might suppose that rulers
who formed and endowed such works all over the land
must have had more of the respect and the affections
of the great mass of the people than we, who, as my friend
upon the Jumna has it, "build nothing but private
dwelling-houses, factories, courts of justice, and jails," can
ever have; but this conclusion would not be altogether
just.   Though every mosque and mausoleum was a seat of
learning, that learning, instead of being a source of attrac-
tion and conciliation between the Muhammadans and
Hindoos, was, on the contrary, a source of perpetual re-
pulsion and enmity between them—it tended to keep alive
in the breasts of the Musalmāns a strong feeling of religious
indignation against the worshippers of idols; and of dread
and hatred in those of the Hindoos.

The Korān was the Book of books, spoken by God to
the angel Gabriel in parts as occasion required, and repeated by him to Muhammad; who, unable to write himself, dictated them to any one who happened to be present
when he received the divine communications;[2] it contained
all that it was worth man's while to study or know—it was
from the Deity, but at the same time coeternal with him—
it was his divine eternal spirit, inseparable from him from
the beginning, and therefore, like him, uncreated.   This
book, to read which was of itself declared to be the highest

---

[1] But the education in such schools is of very little value, being
commonly confined to the committing of the Korān to memory by
boys ignorant of Arabic.

[2] Muhammad is said to have received these communications in all
situations; sometimes when riding along the road on his camel, he
became suddenly red in the face, and greatly agitated; he made his
camel sit down immediately, and called for some one to write.   His
rhapsodies were all written at the time on leaves and thrown into a
box.   Gabriel is believed to have made him repeat over the whole
once every year during the month of Ramazān.   In the year he died
Muhammad told his followers that the angel had made him repeat
them over twice that year, and that he was sure he would not live to
receive another visit. [W. H. S.]

of all species of worship, taught war against the worshippers of idols to be of all merits the greatest in the eye of God; and no man could well rise from the perusal without the wish to serve God by some act of outrage against them. These buildings were, therefore, looked upon by the Hindoos, who composed the great mass of the people, as a kind of religious volcanos, always ready to explode and pour out their lava of intolerance and outrage upon the innocent people of the surrounding country.

If a Hindoo fancied himself injured or insulted by a Muhammadan he was apt to revenge himself upon the Muhammadans generally, and insult their religion by throwing swine's flesh, or swine's blood, into one of their tombs or churches; and the latter either flew to arms at once to revenge their God, or retaliated by throwing the flesh or the blood of the cow into the first Hindoo temple at hand, which made the Hindoos fly to arms. The guilty and the wicked commonly escaped, while numbers of the weak, the innocent and the unoffending were slaughtered. The magnificent buildings, therefore, instead of being at the time bonds of union, were commonly sources of the greatest discord among the whole community, and of the most painful humiliation to the Hindoo population. During the bigoted reign of Aurangzēb and his successors a Hindoo's presence was hardly tolerated within sight of these tombs or churches; and had he been discovered entering one of them, he would probably have been hunted down like a mad dog. The recollection of such outrages, and the humiliation to which they gave rise, associated as they always are in the minds of the Hindoos with the sight of these buildings, are perhaps the greatest source of our strength in India; because they at the same time feel that it is to us alone they owe the protection which they now enjoy from similar injuries. Many of my countrymen, full of virtuous indignation at the outrages which often occur during the processions of the Muharram, particularly when these happen to take place at the same time with some religious procession of the Hindoos, are very anxious that our government should interpose its authority to put down both. But these processions and occasional outrages are really sources of great strength to us; they show at once the necessity for the interposition of an impartial tribunal, and a disposition on the part of the rulers to interpose impartially. The Muhammadan festivals are regulated by the lunar, and those of the Hindoos by the solar year, and they cross each other every thirty or forty years, and furnish fair occasions for the local authorities to interpose effectually.[1] People who receive or imagine insults or injuries commonly postpone their revenge till these religious festivals come round, when they hope to be able to settle their accounts with impunity among the excited crowd. The mournful procession of the Muharram, when the Muhammadans are inflamed to madness by the recollection of the really affecting incidents of the massacre of the grandchildren of their prophet, and by the images of their tombs, and their sombre music,[2] crosses that of

[1] The Muhammadan year consists of twelve lunar months of 30 and 29 days alternately. The common year, therefore, consists of only 354 days. But, when intercalary days in certain years are allowed for, the mean year consists of 354$\frac{11}{30}$ days. Inasmuch as a solar year consists of about 365$\frac{1}{4}$ days, the difference amounts to nearly 11 days, and any given month in the Muhammadan year consequently goes the round of the seasons in course of time.

[2] The Muharram celebration takes its name from the first month of the Muhammadan year, during which it takes place. Ali, the cousin of Muhammad, was married to the prophet's daughter Fātima, and, according to the Shia sect, must be regarded as the lawful successor of Muhammad. But, as a matter of fact, Omar, Abū Bakr, and Othmān (Usmān) in turn succeeded to the Khalīfate, and Ali did not take possession of the office till A.D. 655. After five and a half years' reign he was assassinated in January A.D. 661, and his son Hasan, who for a few months had held the vacant office, was poisoned in A.D. 670. Husain, the younger son of Ali, strove to assert his rights by force of arms, but was slain on the tenth day of the month Muharram, (10th October, A.D. 680) in a great battle fought at Karbalā near the Euphrates. These events are commemorated yearly by noisy funeral processions. Properly, the proceedings ought to be altogether mourn-

the Holi[1] (in which the Hindoos are excited to tumultuous
and licentious joy by their bacchanalian songs and dances),
every thirty-six years; and they reign together for some
four or five days, during which the scene in every large
town is really terrific. The processions are liable to meet
in the street, and the lees of the wine of the Hindoos, or
the red powder which is substituted for them, is liable to
fall upon the tombs of the others. Hindoos pass on, for-
getting in their saturnalian joy all distinctions of age, sex,
or religion, their clothes and persons besmeared with the
red powder, which is moistened and thrown from all kinds
of machines over friend and foe; while meeting these
come the Muhammadans, clothed in their green mourning,
with gloomy downcast looks, beating their breasts, ready to
kill themselves, and too anxious for an excuse to kill anybody else. Let but one drop of the lees of joy fall upon
the image of the tomb as it passes, and a hundred swords
fly from their scabbards; many an innocent person falls;
and woe be to the town in which the magistrate is not at
hand with his police and military force. Proudly conscious
of their power, the magistrates refuse to prohibit one class
from laughing because the other happens to be weeping;
and the Hindoos on such occasions laugh the more heartily
to let the world see that they are free to do so.

A very learned Hindoo once told me in Central India
that the oracle of Mahādeo had been at the same time con-

ful, and confined to the Shīa sect, but in practice, Sunni Muhammadans,
and even Hindoos, take part in the ceremonies, which are regarded by
many of the populace as no more solemn than a Lord Mayor's show.

[1] The disgusting festival of the Holī, celebrated with drunkenness
and obscenity, takes place in March, and is supposed to be the festival
of the vernal equinox. The magistrates in India have no duty which
requires more tact, discretion, and firmness than the regulation of conflicting religious processions. The general disarmament of the people
has rendered collisions less dangerous and sanguinary than they used
to be, but, in spite of all precautions, they still occur occasionally.
The total prohibition of processions likely to cause collisions is, of
course, impracticable.

sulted at three of his greatest temples—one in the Deccan, one in Rājputāna, and one, I think, in Bengal—as to the result of the government of India by Europeans, who seemed determined to fill all the high offices of adminis- tration with their own countrymen, to the exclusion of the people of the country. A day was appointed for the answer; and when the priest came to receive it they found Mahādēo (Siva) himself with a European com- plexion, and dressed in European clothes. He told them that their European government was in reality nothing more than a multiplied incarnation of himself; and that he had come among them in this shape to prevent their cutting each other's throats as they had been doing for some centuries past; that these, his incarnations, appeared to have no religion themselves in order that they might be the more impartial arbitrators between the people of so many different creeds and sects who now inhabited the country; that they must be aware that they never had before been so impartially governed, and that they must continue to obey these their governors, without attempting to pry further into futurity or the will of the gods. Mahādēo performs a part in the great drama of the Rāmāyana, or the Rape of Sita, and he is the only figure there that is represented with a *white face*.[1]

I was one day praising the law of primogeniture among ourselves to a Muhammadan gentleman of high rank, and defending it on the ground that it prevented that rivalry and bitterness of feeling among brothers which were always found among the Muhammadans, whose law pre- scribes an equal division of property, real and personal, among the sons, and the *choice of the wisest* among them as successor to the government. "This," said he, "is no doubt the source of our weakness, but why should you condemn a law which is to you a source of so much strength? I, one day," said he, "asked Mr. Seaton, the

---

[1] *Ante*, Vol. I, p. 126.

Governor-General's representative at the court of Delhi, which of all things he had seen in India he liked best. 'You have,' replied he, smiling, 'a small species of melon called "phūt" (disunion); this is the thing we like best in your land.' There was," continued my Muhammadan friend, "an infinite deal of sound political wisdom in this one sentence. Mr. Seaton was a very good and a very wise man. Our European governors of the present day are not at all the same kind of thing. I asked Mr. B., a judge, the same question many years afterwards, and he told me that he thought the rupees were the best things he had found in India. I asked Mr. T., the Commissioner, and he told me that he thought the tobacco which he smoked in his hookah was the best thing. And pray, sir, what do you think the best thing ?"

"Why, Nawāb Sāhib, I am always very well pleased when I am free from pain, and can get my nostrils full of cool air, and my mouth full of cold water in this hot land of yours ; and I think most of my countrymen are the same. Next to these, the thing we all admire most in India, Nawāb Sāhib, is the entire exemption which you and I and every other gentleman, native or European, enjoy from the taxes which press so heavily upon them in other countries.[1] In Kāshmīr, no midwife is allowed to attend a woman in her confinement till a heavy tax has been paid to Ranjīt Singh for the infant ; and in England, a man cannot let the light of heaven into his house till he has paid a tax for the window."[2]

"Nor keep a dog, nor shoot a partridge in the jungle, I am told," said the Nawāb.

"Quite true, Nawāb Sāhib."

[1] *Tempora mutantur.* The land revenue, in the author's time, fully preserved its character of rent, and was obviously not a tax. Later legislation has obscured its real nature, and made it look like a tax. When the author wrote, the only taxes levied were indirect ones, as that on salt, which was paid unconsciously. The modern income-tax, local rates, municipal taxation, and gun licenses were all unknown.

[2] The window tax has long since been abolished.

"Hindustān, sir," said he, "is, after all, the best country in the world; the only thing wanted is a little more (rozgār) employment for the educated classes under Government."

"True, Nawāb Sāhib, we might, no doubt, greatly multiply this employment to the advantage of those who got the places, but we should have to multiply at the same time the taxes, to the great disadvantage of those who did not get them."

"True, very true, sir," said my old friend.

CHAPTER XII[1]

The Old City of Delhi.

ON the 21st we went on eight miles to the Kutb Mīnār, across the range of sandstone hills, which rise to the height of about two hundred feet, and run north and south. The rocks are for the most part naked, but here and there the soil between them is covered with *famished* grass, and a few stunted shrubs; anything more unprepossessing can hardly be conceived than the aspect of these hills, which seem to serve no other purpose than to store up heat for the people of the great city of Delhi. We passed through a cut in this range of hills, made apparently by the stream of the river Jumna at some remote period, and about one hundred yards wide at the entrance. This cut is crossed by an enormous stone wall running north and south, and intended to shut in the waters, and form a lake in the opening beyond it. Along the brow of the precipice, overlooking the northern end of the wall, is the stupendous fort of Tughlakābād, built by the Emperor Tughlak the First[2] of the sandstones of the range of hills on which it stands, cut into enormous square blocks.[3] On the brow of the opposite side of the preci-

---

[1] Chapter XIX of Vol. II of original edition.

[2] The emperor called by the author Tughlak the First, as being the first of the Tughlak dynasty, was by birth a Karaunīah Turk, named Ghāzī Bēg Tughlak. He assumed the style of Ghiyās-ud-dīn Tughlak Shāh when he seized the throne in A.D. 1320, and he reigned till A.D. 1325.

[3] This gigantic fortress is close to the village of Badarpur, about four miles due east of the Kutb Mīnār, and ten or twelve miles south of the modern city. The building of it occupied more than three years,

pice, overlooking the southern end of the wall, stands the fort of Muhammadābād, built by this Emperor's son and successor, Muhammad, and resembling in all things that built by his father.[1] These fortresses overlooked the lake, with the old city of Delhi spread out on the opposite side of it to the west. There is a third fortress upon an isolated hill, east of the great barrier wall, said to have been built in honour of his master by the Emperor Tughlak's *barber*.[2] The Emperor's tomb stands upon an isolated rock in the middle of the once lake, now plain, about a mile to the west of the barrier wall. The rock is connected with the western extremity of the northern fortress by a causeway of twenty-five arches, and about one hundred and fifty yards long. This is a fine tomb, and contains in a square centre room the remains of the Emperor Tughlak, his wife, and his son. The tomb is built of red sandstone, and surmounted by a dome of white marble. The three graves inside are built of brick covered with stucco work. The outer sides of the tomb slope slightly inwards from the base, in the form of a pyramid; but the inner walls are, of course, perpendicular.[3]

but the whole undertaking "proved eminently futile, as his son removed his Court to the old city within forty days after his accession."" (Thomas, *Chronicles*, p. 192.) The fort is described by Cunningham in *Archæol. Survey Reports*, vol. i, p. 212, and his description is copied in the guide-books.

[1] Muhammadābād is also called Adilābād. It is described in *Archæol. Surv. Rep.*, vol. i, p. 21, and in Carr Stephen's work, p. 98.

[2] "*The Barber's House*. This lies to the right of the road from Tughlakābād to Badarpur, and is close to the ruined city. It is said to have been built for Tughlak Shāh's barber about A.D. 1323. It is now a mere ruin." (Harcourt, *The New Guide to Delhi*, p. 88.)

[3] This fine tomb was built by Muhammad bin Tughlak (A.D. 1325-1351). It is described by Cunningham in *Archæol. Survey Rep.*, Vol. I, p. 213. Thomas (*Chronicles*, p. 192) and Cunningham both say that the causeway, or viaduct, has 27, not only 25, arches, as stated in the text. The causeway is 600 feet in length. The sloping walls are characteristic of the period.

The impression left on the mind after going over these stupendous fortifications is that the arts which contribute to the comforts and elegancies of life must have been in a very rude state when they were raised. Domestic architecture must have been wretched in the extreme. The buildings are all of stone, and almost all without cement, and seem to have been raised by giants, and for giants, whose arms were against everybody, and everybody's arm against them. This was indeed the state of the Pathān sovereigns in India[1]—they were the creatures of their armies ; and their armies were also employed against the people, who feared and detested them all.[1]

The Emperor Tughlak, on his return at the head of the army, which he had led into Bengal to chastise some rebellious subjects, was met at Afghānpur by his eldest son, Jūnā, whom he had left in the government of the capital. The prince had in three days raised here a palace of wood for a grand entertainment to do honour to his father's return ; and when the Emperor signified his wish to retire, all the courtiers rushed out before him to be in attendance, and among the rest, Jūnā himself. Five attendants only remained when the Emperor rose from his seat, and at that moment the building fell in and crushed them and their master. Jūnā had been sent at the head of an army into the Deccan, where he collected immense

[1] The blunder of calling the Sultāns of Delhi by the name Pathān is due to the translators of Farishta's History, and has been perpetuated by Thomas' well-known work *The Chronicles of the Pathān Kings of Delhi*, and in countless other books. The name is quite wrong. The only Pathān Sultāns were those of the Lodī dynasty, which immediately preceded Bābar. "He (*scil.* Ghiyās-ud-dīn Balban) was a *Turk* of the Ilbarī tribe, but compilers of Indian Histories and Gazetteers, and archæological experts, turn him, like many Turks, Tājzīks, Jāts, and Sayyids, into *Pathāns*, which is synonymous with Afghān, it being the vitiated Hindī equivalent of Pushtūn, the name by which the people generally known as Afghāns call themselves, in their own language. . . It is quite time to give up Dow and Briggs' Farishta." (Major Raverty, in *J. As. Soc. Bengal*, vol. lxi. part i, p. 164, *note.*)

wealth from the plunder of the palaces of princes and the temples of their priests, the only places in which much wealth was to be found in those days. This wealth he tried to conceal from his father, whose death he probably thus contrived, that he might the sooner have the free enjoyment of it with unlimited power.[1]

Only thirty years before, Alā-ud-din, returning in the same manner at the head of an army from the Deccan loaded with wealth, murdered the Emperor Fīrōz the Second, the father of his wife, and ascended the throne.[2] Jūnā ascended the throne under the name of Muhammad the Third;[3] and, after the remains of his father had been deposited in the tomb I have described, he passed in great pomp and splendour from the fortress of Tughlakābād, which his father had just then completed, to the city in which the Mīnār stands, with elephants before and behind loaded with gold and silver coins, which were scattered among the crowd, who everywhere hailed him with shouts of joy. The roads were covered with flowers, the houses adorned with the richest stuffs, and the streets resounded with music.

He was a man of great learning, and a great patron of learned men ; he was a great founder of churches, had prayers read in them at the prescribed times, and always went to prayers five times a day himself.[4]   He was rigidly

---

[1] The murder of Ghiyās-ud-dīn Tughlak by his son Fakhr-ud-dīn Jūnā, also called Ulūgh Khān, occurred in the year A.H. 725, which began on 18th December, 1324 (O.S.). The testimony of the contemporary traveller Ibn Batūtā establishes the fact that the fall of the pavilion was premeditated. (Thomas, *Chronicles*, p.p. 187, 189.) The murderer, on his accession to the throne, assumed the style of Muhammad bin Tughlak Shāh.

[2] Jalāl-ud-dīn Fīrōz Shāh Khiljī was murdered by his son-in-law and nephew Alā-ud-dīn at Karrā on the Ganges in July, 1296 A.D. The murderer reigned until A.D. 1315 under the title of Alā-ud-dīn Muhammad Shāh, Sikandar Sānī.

[3] As already noted (p. 139), his proper style is Muhammad bin Tughlak Shāh. The word "bin" means "son of."

[4] A Muhammadan must, if he can, say his prayers with the pre-

temperate himself in his habits, and discouraged all intemperance in others. These things secured him panegyrists throughout the empire during the twenty-seven years that he reigned over it, though perhaps he was the most detestable tyrant that ever filled a throne. He would take his armies out over the most populous and peaceful districts, and hunt down the innocent and unoffending people like wild beasts, and bring home their heads by thousands to hang them on the city gates for his mere amusement. He twice made the whole people of the city of Delhi emigrate with him to Daulatābād in Southern India, which he wished to make the capital, from some foolish fancy; and during the whole of his reign gave evident signs of being in an unsound state of mind.[1]

scribed forms five times in the twenty-four hours ; and on Friday, which is their sabbath, he must, if he can, say three prayers in the church *masjid*. On other days he may say them where he pleases. Every prayer must begin with the first chapter of the Korān—this is the grace to every prayer. This said, the person may put in what other prayers of the Korān he pleases, and ask for that which he most wants, as long as it does not injure other Musalmāns. This is the first chapter of the Korān :—" Praise be to God the Lord of all creatures—the most merciful—the king of the day of judgment. Thee do we worship, and of thee do we beg assistance. Direct us in the right way—in the way of those to whom thou hast been gracious : not of those against whom thou art incensed ; nor of those who go astray." [W. H. S.]   The quotation is from Sale's version. The last clause may also be rendered " The way of those to whom thou hast been gracious, against whom thou art not incensed, and who have not erred," as Sale points out in his note.

[1] This mad tyrant, among other horrible deeds, flayed his nephew alive. He attempted to invade China through the Himālayas, and for three years issued a forced currency of brass and copper, which he vainly tried to make people take as equal in value to silver. Strange to say, he was allowed to reign for nearly twenty-seven years, and to die peacefully in his bed. The hunts of the " innocent and unoffending people " were organized rather to gain the benefit of " sending infidels to hell " than for " mere amusement." Daulatābād was the name given by Muhammad bin Tughlak to the ancient fortress of Deogīr (Deogiri, Deoghur), situated about ten miles from Aurangābād, in what is now the Hyderābād State.

There was at the time of his father's death a saint at
Delhi named Nizāmuddīn Aulia, or the Saint, who was
supposed by supernatural means to have driven from Delhi
one night in a panic a large army of Moghals under Turghi,
who invaded India from Transoxiana in 1303, and laid
close siege to the city of Delhi, in which the Emperor
Alā-ud-dīn was shut up without troops to defend himself,
his armies being engaged in Southern India.[1] It is very
likely that he did strike this army with a panic by getting
some of their leaders assassinated in one night. He was
supposed to have the "dast ul ghaib," or supernatural
purse [literally, "invisible hand"], as his private expenditure is said to have been more lavish even than that of the
Emperor himself, while he had no ostensible source of
income whatever. The Emperor was either jealous of his
influence and display, or suspected him of dark crimes,
and threatened to humble him when he returned to Delhi.
As he approached the city, the friends of the saint, knowing the resolute spirit of the Emperor, urged him to quit
the capital, as he had been often heard to say, "Let me
but reach Delhi, and this proud priest shall be humbled."

The only reply that the saint would ever deign to give
from the time the imperial army left Bengal, till it was
within one stage of the capital, was "Dihlī dūr ast";
"Delhi is still far off." This is now become a proverb over
the East equivalent to our "There is many a slip between
the cup and the lip." It is probable that the saint had
some understanding with the son in his plans for the
murder of his father; it is possible that his numerous

---

[1] In the author's text the name of the Moghal leader appears in
the impossible form Turmachurn, which corresponds to the Tarmah
Shīrīn of some authors. The name Turghi is given by Mr. Thomas,
who says he invested Delhi in A.H. 703, corresponding to A.D. 1303;
and refers to an article in *J. As. Soc. Bengal*, Vol. xxxv (1816), Part i,
p. 217, entitled "Notes on the History and Topography of the
Ancient Cities of Delhi," by Mr. C. Campbell. (*Chronicles*, p. 175,
note.) The Moghals made several raids during the reign of Alā-ud-
dīn Muhammad Shāh.

wandering disciples may in reality have been murderers and robbers, and that he could at any time have procured through them the assassination of the Emperor. The Muhammadan Thugs, or assassins of India, certainly looked upon him as one of the great founders of their system, and used to make pilgrimages to his tomb as such ; and, as he came originally from Persia, and is considered by his greatest admirers to have been in his youth a robber, it is not impossible that he may have been originally one of the "assassins," or disciples of the "old man of the mountains," and that he may have set up the system of Thuggee in India and derived a great portion of his income from it.[1] Emperors now prostrate themselves, and aspire

---

[1] The tomb of Nizām-ud-dīn is further noticed in the next chapter of this work. It is situated in an enclosure which contains other notable tombs. The following extract from the author's *Ramaseeana* (p. 121) gives some additional particulars concerning this saint of questionable sanctity : "*Nizām-ud-dīn Aulia.*—A saint of the Sunnī sect of Muhammadans, said to have been a Thug of great note at some period of his life, and his tomb near Delhi is to this day visited as a place of pilgrimage by Thugs, who make votive offerings to it. He is said to have been of the Barsot class, born in the month of Safar [633], Hijrī, March A.D. 1236 ; died Rabī-ul-awwal, 725, October A.D. 1325. [The months as stated do not correspond.—*Ed.*] His tomb is visited by Muhammadan pilgrims from all parts as a place of great sanctity from containing the remains of so holy a man ; but the Thugs, both Hindoo and Muhammadan, visit it as containing the remains of the most celebrated Thug of his day. He was of the Sunnī sect, and those of the Shīa sect find no difficulty in believing that he was a Thug ; but those of his own sect will never credit it. There are perhaps no sufficient grounds to pronounce him one of the fraternity ; but there are some to suspect that he was so at some period of his life. The Thugs say he gave it up early in life, but kept others employed in it till late, and derived an income from it ; and the "dast-ul-ghaib," or supernatural purse, with which he was supposed to be endowed, gives a colour to this. His lavish expenditure so much beyond his ostensible means, gave rise to the belief that he was supplied from above with money."

The "old man of the mountains" with whom the author compares Nizām-ud-dīn (or at least the original "old man of the mountains"), was Hasan-ibn-Sabbāh (or, us-Sabbāh), known as Shaikh-ul-Jabal, who

to have their bones placed near it [*scil.* the tomb]. While wandering about the ruins, I remarked to one of the learned men of the place who attended us that it was singular Tughlak's buildings should be so rude compared with those of Iltitmish, who had reigned more than eighty years before him."[1] " Not at all singular," said he, " was he not under the curse of the holy saint Nizām-ud-dīn ? "   " And what had the Emperor done to merit the holy man's curse ? " " He had taken by force to employ upon his palaces several of the masons whom the holy man was employing upon a church," said he.

The Kutb Mīnār was, I think, more beyond my expectations than the Tāj ; first, because I had heard less of it ; and secondly, because it stands as it were alone in India— there is absolutely no other tower in this Indian empire of ours.[2]

Large pillars have been cut out of single stones, and raised in different parts of India to commemorate the conquests of Hindoo princes, whose names no one was able to discover for several centuries, till an unpretending

founded the sect of so-called Assassins in the mountains on the shores of the Caspian, and flourished from about A.D. 1089 to 1124. Hulāku the Mongol broke the power of the sect in A.D. 1256. (Balfour's *Cyclopædia*, articles " Assassin," " Ismaili," " Hulugu," etc., and Beale's *Oriental Biographical Dictionary, s.v.* " Hasan Sabba," etc.)

[1] Shams-ud-dīn Iltitmish, who had been a slave, reigned from A.D. 1210 to 1235. His Turkish name is variously written as Yulteemush, Altamsh, Alitmish, etc. The form Iltitmish is supported by the legends on the coins and certain inscriptions. His tomb is discussed *post*, p. 157.

[2] This is not quite accurate. A similar *mīnār*, or mosque tower, built in the middle of the thirteenth century, formerly existed at Koil in the Alīgarh district (*Archæol. Survey Rep.*, vol. i, 191), and two mosques at Bayāna in the Bharatpur State, have each only one *mīnār*, placed outside the courtyard (*ibid.* vol. iv, p. ix). Chitor in Rajputānā possesses two noble Hindoo towers, one about 80 feet high, erected in connection with Jain shrines, and the other, about 120 feet high, erected by Khambo Rānā as a tower or pillar of victory. (Fergusson, *Hist. Ind and E. Archit.*, p. 252, *figures* 142, 143.)

English gentleman of surprising talents and industry, Mr.
James Prinsep, lately brought them to light by mastering
the obsolete characters in which they and their deeds had
been inscribed upon them.[1] These pillars would, however,
be utterly insignificant were they composed of many stones.
The knowledge that they are cut out of single stones,
brought from a distant mountain, and raised by the united
efforts of multitudes when the mechanical arts were in a
rude state, makes us still view them with admiration. But
the single majesty of this Minār of Kutb-ud-din, so grandly
conceived, so beautifully proportioned, so chastely embellished, and so exquisitely finished, fills the mind of the
spectator with emotions of wonder and delight; without
any such aid, he feels that it is among the towers of the
earth what the Tāj is among the tombs—something unique
of its kind that must ever stand alone in his recollections.[2]

---

[1] The short life of James Prinsep extended only from the 20th
August, 1799, to the 22nd April, 1840, and practically terminated in
1838, when his brain began to fail from the undue strain caused by
incessant and varied activity. His memorable discoveries in archæology
and numismatics are recorded in the seven volumes of the *Journal of
the Asiatic Society of Bengal* for the years 1832–38.   His contributions to those volumes were edited by Mr. E. Thomas, and republished
in 1858 under the title of "Essays on Indian Antiquities."   Sir
Alexander Cunningham, who was one of Prinsep's fellow-workers sixty
years ago, gives some interesting details of the process by which the
discoveries were made, in the Introduction to the first volume of the
Reports of the Archæological Survey.   So far as the editor is aware,
no adequate account of James Prinsep's very remarkable career has
ever been published.   He was singularly modest and unassuming.   A
good summary of his life is given in Higginbotham's *Men whom India
has Known.*

[2] The monolith pillars alluded to in the text are chiefly those of the
great Emperor Piyadasi, Beloved of the Gods, also known by the name
of Asoka.   They were erected about B.C. 250, and the inscriptions on
them contain a code of moral and religious precepts.   They do not
commemorate conquests, though the Asoka pillar at Allahabad has
been utilized by later sovereigns for the recording of magniloquent
inscriptions in praise of their grandeur.   The best known of the Asoka
pillars are the two at Delhi, and the one at Allahabad.   Many scholars

It is said to have taken forty-four years in building, and formed the left of two " mīnārs " of a mosque. The other "mīnār" was never raised, but this has been preserved and repaired by the liberality of the British government.[1] It is only 242 feet high, and 106 feet in circum-

have devoted themselves to the study of the inscription of Asoka, which may be said to form the foundation of authentic Indian history. The best and most recent general work on the subject is that of M. Emile Senart, of which a translation has appeared in the *Indian Antiquary*. Certain of the Gupta emperors in the fifth century A.D. also erected monolith pillars. Some of the pillars of the Gupta period commemorate victories ; others are merely religious monuments.

" It is probably not too much to assert that the Kutb Mīnār is the most beautiful example of its class known to exist anywhere. The rival that will occur at once to most people is the campanile at Florence, built by Giotto. That is, it is true, thirty feet taller, but it is crushed by the mass of the cathedral alongside ; and, beautiful though it is, it wants that poetry of design and exquisite finish of detail which marks every moulding of the mīnār. It might have been better if the slope of the sides had been at a higher angle, but that is only apparent when seen at a distance ; when viewed from the court of the mosque its form is perfect, and, under any aspect, is preferable to the squareness of the outline of the Italian example.

" The only Muhammadan building known to be taller than this is the minaret of the mosque of Hasan, at Cairo ; but, as the pillar at old Delhi is a wholly independent building, it has a far nobler appearance, and both in design and finish far surpasses not only its Egyptian rival, but any building of its class known to me in the whole world." (Fergusson, *Hist. I. and E. Archit.*, p. 506.) On the supposed independence of the Kūtb Mīnār, see next following note.

[1] Fergusson denies that the Kutb Mīnār is related to the great mosque at the south-east corner of which it stands. According to him, " it was not designed as a place from which the muëddin should call to prayers, though its lower gallery may have been used for that purpose also, but as a Tower of Victory—a Jaya Stambha, in fact—an emblem of conquest, which the Hindus could only too easily understand and appreciate." (*Hist. of Indian and E. Archit.*, p. 506.) The great historian of architecture is certainly mistaken in this opinion. Sir A. Cunningham observes that it is distinctly called a " māzana," or muazzin's tower by the Syrian geographer, Abūlfida (A.D. 1273–1345), and that several examples are known of early mosques which have but one mīnār each. The examples cited by him are two mosques at Cairo, two at Ghaznih, one at Koil, and two at Bayāna. He further observes

ference at the base. It is circular, and fluted vertically into twenty-seven semicircular and angular divisions. There are four balconies, supported upon large stone brackets, and surrounded with battlements of richly cut stone, to enable people to walk round the tower with safety. The first is ninety feet from the base, the second fifty feet further up, the third forty further; and the fourth twenty-four feet above the third. Up to the third balcony, the tower is built of fine, but somewhat ferruginous sandstone, whose surface has become red from exposure to the oxygen of the atmosphere. Up to the first balcony, the flutings are alternately semicircular and angular; in the second story they are all semicircular, and in the third all angular. From the third balcony to the top, the building is composed chiefly of white marble; and the surface is without the deep flutings. Around the first story there are five horizontal belts of passages from the Korān, engraved in bold relief, and in the Kufic character. In the second story there are four, and in the third three. The ascent is by a spiral staircase within, of three hundred and eighty steps; and there are passages from this staircase to the balconies, with others here and there for the admission of light and air.[1]

that Alā-ud-dīn's unfinished mīnār near the Kutb Mīnār, erected about a century later, is a single column. The inscriptions also prove that the Kutb Mīnār is a māzana. (*Arch. Rep.*, vol. iv, p. ix.) It is a complete structure in itself. The author's remark that "the other mīnār was never raised" is due to the erroneous belief that a mosque must have two minarets. The unfinished mīnār of Alā-ud-dīn, if he intended it to be attached to the great Kutb mosque, was a superfluous addition. Alā-ud-dīn planned extensive additions to the mosque (*ibid.* p. 62), and it is probable that they were intended to form a separate mosque, to which the new mīnār would be attached, independent of the Kutb Mīnār.

[1] The original edition gives a coloured plate of the Kutb Mīnār. The total height stated in the text, 242 feet, is said by Fergusson (p. 505, *note*) to be that ascertained in 1794; the present height of the mīnār, since the modern pavilion on the top has been removed, is 238 feet, 1 inch, according to Cunningham. (*Arch. Rep.*, vol. i, p. 196.) Originally the building was 10, or perhaps 20, feet higher. The deep

A foolish notion has prevailed among some people, over-fond of paradox, that this tower is in reality a Hindoo building, and not, as commonly supposed, a Muhammadan one. Never was paradox supported upon more frail, I might say absurd, foundations. They are these :—*1st*, that there is only one Mīnār, whereas there ought to have been two—had the unfinished one been intended as the second, it would not have been, as it really is, larger than the first ; *2nd*, that other Mīnārs seen in the present day either do not slope inward from the base up at all, or do not slope so much as this. I tried to trace the origin of this paradox, and I think I found it in a silly old "munshī" (clerk) in the service of the Emperor. He told me that he believed it was built by a former Hindoo prince for his daughter, who wished to worship the rising-sun, and view the waters of the Jumna from the top of it every morning.[1]

---

flutings appear to have been suggested by the mīnārs of Mahmūd at Ghaznih, "which are star polygons in plan, with deeply indented angles." Three brief dated mason's inscriptions on the lower part of the building recorded in the year 1256 S., or A.D. 1199, show that work was going on in that year. (*Arch. Rep.*, vol. iv, p. v.) The Mīnār was begun by Kutb-ud-dīn Ibak, and continued by Altamash (Iltitmish). The two upper stories, which had been damaged by lightning, were rebuilt by Fīrōz Tughlak (A.D. 1351-1388). The Arabic inscriptions on the Mīnār are not exclusively passages from the Korān. They include two records giving the titles of the Sultān Muhammad bin Sām, whom Kutb-ud-dīn Ibak served as general, before he himself became Sultan (Thomas, *Chronicles*, p. 20) ; and also inscriptions of Iltitmish, Fīrōz Shah (A.D. 1368), and Sikandar Shāh (A.D. 1503). (*Arch. Rep.*, vol. i, 187.) Mr. Carr Stephen (p.p. 58-66) gives translations of most of the inscriptions, and argues that those historians were mistaken who ascribed to Alā-ud-dīn the addition of a new casing and cupola.

[1] The notion of the Hindoo origin of the Kutb Mīnār, which the author justly stigmatizes as "foolish," was taken up by Sir Sayyid Ahmad Khān, the author of an Urdū work on the antiquities of Delhi, and by Sir A. Cunningham's assistant, Mr. Beglar, who wasted a great part of Volume IV of the *Archæological Survey Reports* in trying to prove the paradox. His speculations on the subject were conclusively refuted by his chief in the Preface (p.p. v–x) of the same volume.

There is no other Hindoo building like, or of the same kind as this ;[1] the ribbons or belts of passages from the Korān are all in relief; and had they not been originally inserted as they are, the whole surface of the building must have been cut down to throw them out in bold relief. The slope is the peculiar characteristic of all the architecture of the Pathāns, by whom the church to which this tower belongs was built.[2] Nearly all the arches of the church are still standing in a more or less perfect state, and all correspond in design, proportion, and execution to the tower. The ruins of the old Hindoo temples about the place, and about every other place in India, are totally different in all three ; here they are all exceedingly paltry and insignificant, compared with the church and its tower, and it is evident that it was the intention of the founder to make them appear so to future generations of the faithful, for he has taken care to make his own great work support rather than destroy them, that they might for ever tend to enhance its grandeur.[3]

It is sufficiently clear that the unfinished mīnār was commenced upon too large a scale, and with too small a diminution of the circumference from the base upwards. It is two-fifths larger than the finished tower in circumference, and much more perpendicular. Finding these errors when they had got some thirty feet from the foundation, the founder, Shams-ud-dīn (Iltitmish), began to work anew, and had he lived a little longer, there is no doubt

Mr. Beglar was compelled to retract his opinion (p.p. xv–xvii), and it is to be hoped that the " foolish notion " will not again be heard of. The mīnār was built by Hindoo masons, and, in consequence, some of the details, notably its overlapping or corbelled arches, are Hindoo.

[1] This is quite correct. The Hindoo " towers of victory " are in a totally different style.

[2] On the misnomer " Pathāns," *see ante,* p. 141, *note.*

[3] The Kutb Mīnār mosque was constructed from the materials of twenty-seven Hindoo temples. The colonnades retain much of their Hindoo character.

that he would have raised the second tower in its proper
place, upon the same scale as the one completed. His
death was followed by several successive revolutions ; five
sovereigns succeeded each other on the throne of Delhi in
ten years.[1]   As usual on such occasions, works of peace
were suspended, and succeeding sovereigns sought renown
in military enterprise rather than in building churches.
This church was entire, with the exception of the second
minār, when Tamerlane invaded India.[2]   He took back a
model of it with him to Samarkand, together with all the
masons he could find at Delhi, and is said to have built a
church upon the same plan at that place, before he set out
for the invasion of Syria.

The west face of the quadrangle, in which the tower
stands, formed the church, which consisted of eleven large
arched alcoves, the centre and largest of which contained
the pulpit.   In size and beauty they seem to have corresponded with the Mīnār, but they are now all in ruins.[3]   In

---

[1] The author's description of the unfinished tower is far from
accurate.   The tower was not built by Shams-ud-dīn Iltitmish, but by
Alā-ud-dīn Muhammad Shāh, and is said to have been begun in the
year A.H. 711 (A.D. 1311).   It is at present about 82 feet in diameter,
and when cased with marble, as was intended, would have been at
least 85 feet in diameter, or nearly double that of the Kutb Mīnār,
which is 48 feet 4 inches.   The total height of the column as it now
stands is about 75 feet above the plinth, or 87 feet above the ground
level.   (*Archæol. Survey Rep.*, vol. i, p. 205 ; vol. iv, p. 62, Pl. vii. ;
Thomas, *Chronicles*, p. 173, citing original authorities.)   Fergusson.
(*Hist. I. and E. Arch.*, p. 506), states that this unfinished tower is
297 feet in circumference, and only about 40 feet high.   Carr Stephen
(p. 67) gives the circumference as 254 feet, and the height as about
80 feet.   Fergusson was mistaken about the height.

[2] Alā-ud-dīn's additions were never completed.   The sack of Delhi
by Taimūr Lang (Tamerlane) took place in December 1398.   The
Delhi sacked by him was the city known as Fīrōzābād.

[3] "The glory of the mosque is . . . the great range of arches
on the western side, extending north and south for about 385 feet, and
consisting of three greater and eight smaller arches ; the central one
22 feet wide, and 53 feet high ; the larger side 24 feet, 4 inches, and
about the same height as the central arch ; the smaller arches, which

the front of the centre of these alcoves stands the metal pillar of the old Hindoo sovereign of Delhi, Prithi Rāj, across whose temple all the great mosque, of which this tower forms a part, was thrown in triumph. The ruins of these temples lie scattered all round the place, and consist of colonnades of stone pillars and pedestals, richly enough carved with human figures, in attitudes rudely and obscenely conceived. The small pillar is of bronze, or a metal which resembles bronze, and is softer than brass, and of the same form precisely as that of the stone pillar at Eran, on the Binā river in Mālwā, upon which stands the figure of Krishna, with the glory around his head.[1]

are unfortunately much ruined, are about half these dimensions." The great arch "has since been carefully restored by Government under efficient superintendence, and is now as sound and complete as when first erected. The two great side arches either were never completed, or have fallen down in consequence of the false mode of construction.' (Fergusson, *Hist. of I. and E. Archit.*, 2nd ed., 1876, p.p. 503, 505.) The centre arch bears an inscription dated in A.H. 594, or A.D. 1179. (*Carr Stephen*, p. 47.)

[1] Most of the description in the text of the celebrated Iron Pillar is erroneous. The pillar has nothing to do with Prithi Rāj, who was slain by the Muhammadans in A.D. 1192 (A.H. 588). The earliest inscription on it records the victories of a Rājā Chandra, who has not been identified with certainty. Fergusson (p. 508) may possibly be right in his belief that this king was one of the Chandra Rājās of the Imperial (or Early) Gupta dynasty. The characters of the inscription indicate that it should be approximately dated A.D. 400, during the reign of Chandra Gupta II. The name Chandra was first correctly read by Dr. Bhau Dājī, and subsequently by Mr. Fleet. (*Corpus Inser. Ind.*, vol. iii, p. 139.) The pillar is by no means "small," when its material is considered; on the contrary, it is very large. That material is not " bronze, or a metal which resembles bronze," but is pure iron. "Analyses of the iron have been made both by Dr. Percy, late of the School of Mines, and Dr. Murray Thompson, of Rurki College, who have found that it consists of pure malleable iron without any alloy. It has been suggested that this pillar must have been formed by gradually welding pieces together; if so, it has been done very skilfully, since no marks of such welding are to be seen. . . . The famous iron pillar at the Kutb, near Delhi, indicates an amount of skill in the manipulation of a large mass of wrought iron, which has been

It is said that this metal pillar was put down through the earth, so as to rest upon the very head of the snake that supports the world; and that the sovereign who made it, and fixed it upon so *firm a basis*, was told by his spiritual advisers that his dynasty should last as long as the pillar remained where it was. Anxious to see that the pillar was really where the priests supposed it to be, that his posterity might be quite sure of their position, Prithī Rāj had it taken up, and he found the blood and some of the flesh of the snake's head adhering to the bottom. By this means the charm was broken, and the priests told him that he had destroyed all the hopes of his house by his want of faith in their assurances. I have never met a Hindoo that doubted either that the pillar was really upon this snake's head, or that the king lost his crown by his want of faith in the assurance of his priests. They all believe that the pillar is

the marvel of all who have endeavoured to account for it. It is not many years since the production of such a pillar would have been an impossibility in the largest foundries of the world, and even now there are comparatively few where a similar mass of metal could be-turned out. . . . The total weight must exceed 6 tons." (V. Ball, *Economic Geology of India*, p.p. 338, 339.) Mr. Fergusson observes that "it is almost equally startling to find that, after an exposure to wind and rain for fourteen centuries, it is unrusted, and the capital and inscription are as clear and sharp now as when put up fourteen centuries ago." He gives an engraving of the pillar from a photograph. An exact facsimile is set up in the Indian Museum at South Kensington. The dimensions of the pillar are as follows :—

Height above ground (total).	22 ft.
,,　below　,,	1 ft. 8 in.
Diameter at base.	16·4 in.
,,　　,, the capital.	12·05 in.
Height of capital	3½ ft.

At a distance of a few inches below the surface it expands in a bulbous form to a diameter of 2 ft. 4 in., and rests on a gridiron of iron bars, which are fastened with lead into the stone pavement. (Fergusson, p. 508, *note*; *Archæol. Surv. Rep.*, vol. iv, p. 28, Plate v.)

This last prosaic fact, established by actual excavation, destroys the basis of all the current native legends and spurious traditions.

still stuck into the head of the great snake, and that no human efforts of the present day could remove it. On my way back to my tents, I asked the old Hindoo officer of my guard, who had gone with me to see the metal pillar, what he thought of the story of the pillar?

"What the people relate about the 'kili' (pillar) having been stuck into the head of the snake that supports the world, sir, is nothing more than a simple *historical* fact known to everybody. Is it not so, my brothers?" turning to the Hindoo sipáhís and followers around us, who all declared that no fact could ever be better established.

"When the Rájá," continued the old soldier, "had got the pillar fast into the head of the snake, he was told by his chief priest that his dynasty must now reign over Hindustan for ever. 'But,' said the Rájá, 'as all seems to depend upon the pillar being on the head of the snake, we had better see that it is so with our own eyes.' He ordered it to be taken up; the clergy tried to dissuade him, but all in vain. Up it was taken—the flesh and blood of the snake were found upon it—the pillar was replaced; but a voice was heard saying—'Thy want of faith hath destroyed thee—thy reign must soon end, and with it that of thy race.'"

I asked the old soldier from whence the voice came.

He said this was a point that had not, he believed, been quite settled. Some thought it was from the serpent himself below the earth—others that it came from the high priest, or some of his clergy. "Wherever it came from," said the old man, "there is no doubt that God decreed the Rájá's fall for his want of faith; and fall he did soon after."

All our followers concurred in this opinion, and the old man seemed quite delighted to think that he had had an opportunity of delivering his sentiments upon so great a question before so respectable an audience.

The Emperor Shams-ud-din Iltitmish is said to have designed this great Muhammadan church at the suggestion of Khwaja Kutb-ud-din, a Muhammadan saint from Ush in Persia, who was his religious guide and apostle, and died some sixteen years before him.[1] His tomb is among the ruins of this old city. Pilgrims visit it from all parts of India, and go away persuaded that they shall have all they have asked, provided they have given or promised liberally in a pure spirit of faith in his influence with the Deity. The tomb of the saint is covered with gold brocade, and protected by an awning—those of the Emperors around it lie naked and exposed. Emperors and princes lie all around him; and their tombs are entirely disregarded by the hundreds that daily prostrate themselves before his, and have been doing so for the last six hundred years.[2] Among the rest I saw here the tomb of Mu'azzam, alias Bahādur Shāh, the son and successor of Aurangzēb, and that of the blind old Emperor Shāh Alam, from whom the Honourable Company got their Diwani grant.[3] The grass grows upon the slab that covers the remains of Mu'azzam, the most learned, most pious, and most amiable, I believe, of the crowned descendants of the great Akbar. These kings and princes all try to get a place as near as they can to the remains of such old saints, believing that the ground is more holy than any other, and that they may give them a lift on the day of resurrection. The heir apparent to the throne of Delhi visited the tomb the same day that I did. He was between sixty and seventy years of age.[4]

[1] This name is printed Ouse in the author's text. The saint referred to is the celebrated Kutb-ud-din Bakhtiyār Kākī, commonly called Kutb Shāh, who died on the 27th of November, A.D. 1235. Iltitmish died in April, 1236 A.D. (*Beale*.)

[2] The royal tombs are in the village of Mihraulī, close to the Kutb. See Carr Stephen, p. p. 180–184.

[3] That is to say, the revenue administration of Bengal, Bihār, and Orissa in 1765.

[4] He is now Emperor, having succeeded his father, Akbar Shāh, in 1837. [W. H. S.] He is known as Bahādur Shāh II. In consequence of his having joined the rebels in 1857, he was deposed and banished. He died at Rangoon in 1862, and with him ended the line of Emperors of Delhi. He was born on the 24th of October, 1775, and so was in

I asked some of the attendants of the tomb, on my way back, what he had come to pray for ; and was told that no one knew, but every one supposed it was for the death of the Emperor, his father, who was only fifteen years older, and was busily engaged in promoting an intrigue at the instigation of one of his wives, to oust him, and get one of her sons, Mirza Salim, acknowledged as his successor by the British government. It was the Hindoo festival of the Basant,[1] and all the avenues to the tomb of this old saint were crowded when I visited it. Why the Muhammadans crowded to the tomb on a Hindoo holiday I could not ascertain.

The Emperor Iltitmish, who died A.D. 1235, is buried close behind one end of the arched alcove, in a beautiful tomb without its cupola. He built the tomb himself, and left orders that there should be no " parda " (screen) between him and heaven ; and no dome was thrown over the building in consequence. Other great men have done the same, and their tombs look as if their domes had fallen in ; they think the way should be left clear for a start on the day of resurrection.[2] The church is stated to have

his sixty-first year when the author met him. His father was about seventy-eight (eighty lunar) years of age at his death.

[1] " Basant " means the spring. The full name of this festival of the spring time is the Basant Panchami.

[2] According to Harcourt (*The New Guide to Delhi*), the tomb of Iltitmish was erected by his children, the Sultans Rukn-ud-din and Razia, who reigned in succession after him for short periods, that is to say, Rukn-ud-din Firoz Shah for six months and twenty-eight days, and the Empress Razia for about three years, from A.D. 1236 to 1239. (See *Carr Stephen*, p. 73.) Fergusson observes that this tomb is of special interest as being the oldest Muhammadan tomb known to exist in India. He also remarks (p. 509) that the effect at present is injured by the want of a roof, which, "judging from appearance, was never completed, if ever commenced." Harcourt (p. 120) states that " Firoz Shah, who reigned from A.D. 1351 to A.D. 1385 [*sic*, 1388], is said to have placed a roof to the building, but it is doubtful if there ever was one, as there are no traces of the same. Cunningham and Carr Stephen (p. 74) both find sufficient evidence remaining to satisfy them that a dome once existed. The interior, a square of twenty-nine

been added to it by the Emperor Balban, and the Mīnār finished.[1] About the end of the seventeenth century, it was so shaken by an earthquake that the two upper stories fell down. Our government, when the country came into our possession, undertook to repair these two stories, and entrusted the work to Captain Smith, who built up one of stone, and the other of wood, and completed the repairs in three years. The one was struck by lightning eight or nine years after, and came down. If it was anything like the one that is left, the lightning did well to remove it.[2]

About five years ago, while the Emperor was on a visit to the tomb of Kutb-ud-dīn, a madman got into his private apartments. The servants were ordered to turn him out. On passing the Mīnār he ran in, ascended to the top, stood a few moments on the verge, laughing at those who were

and a half feet, is beautifully and elaborately decorated, and in wonderful preservation considering its age and the exposure to which it has been subjected. The walls are over seven feet thick, the principal entrance being to the east. The tomb is built of red sandstone and marble ; the sarcophagus is in the centre, and is of pale marble."

[1] Ghiyās-ud-dīn Balban (who was known as Ulūgh Khān before his accession), reigned from February, A.D. 1266 to 1286, I cannot discover any authority for the statement that he finished the Kutb Mīnār, or "added the church." It is not clear which "church," or mosque, the author refers to. For a notice of Balban's tomb and buildings, see Carr Stephen, p.p. 79–81. He certainly did not finish the Kutb Mīnār.

[2] See *Archæol. Survey Reports*, vol. i, p. 199. "*Top of the Kutb Mīnār.*—This octagonal stone pavilion was put up over the Mīnār by Major Smith, of the Engineers, who had the superintendence of the repairs of the Kutb, but it was taken down by the order of Government. It is now placed on a raised plot of ground in front of the long colonnade which runs from the pillar to the east. It is not in the least ornamental, but it would be more expense than it is worth to remove it and clear the ground on which it stands, so it will probably remain where it is, as useless as it is unsightly. Built in A.D. 1826." (Harcourt, *The New Guide to Delhi*, p. 123.) This "grotesque ornament" was removed in 1848 by order of Lord Hardinge, and bereft of its wooden pavilion, which had carried a flag-staff. (*Carr Stephen*, p. 64.)

running after him, and made a spring that enabled him to reach the bottom, without touching the sides. An eye-witness told me that he kept his erect position till about half-way down, when he turned over, and continued to turn till he got to the bottom, when his fall made a report like a gun. He was of course dashed to pieces. About five months ago another fell over by accident, and was dashed to pieces against the sides. A new road has been here cut through the tomb of the Emperor Alā-ud-dīn, who mur-dered his father-in-law,—the first Muhammadan conqueror of Southern India, and his remains have been scattered to the winds.[1]

A very pretty marble tomb, to the west of the alcoves,

---

[1] This alleged outrage does not appear to have really occurred. "*Alā-ud-dīn's Palace.*—This lies to the south-west of the arches in the Kutb grounds, and though termed above a palace, it may have been anything. The walls are of enormous thickness, but much injured, and there is not a roof left to any of the many adjacent rooms. The Emperor Alā-ud-dīn commenced to govern in A.D. 1295, and had a long and splendid reign, though he himself was a most ignorant and brutal tyrant. Popular report gives this as his last resting-place, as also to its being his palace while alive ; but there is no proof that he was interred on this spot ; as there is no trace of any sarcophagus to be found anywhere. One story has it that he built this structure as a tomb for himself in A.D. 1307." (Harcourt, *The New Guide to Delhi*, p. 121.) "The remains of Hazār Sutūn, as already noticed, exist close outside Siri, exactly where, according to history, they ought to exist ; and Alā-ud-dīn's tomb, instead of being in the great ruined mass facing Iltitmish's tomb in the Kutb, ought, according to history, to be in Hazār Sutūn . . . . and in the ruins of Hazār Sutūn, at the end near the tank, exists a fine marble tombstone, yellow with age and exposure, of which the people have no traditions, but which can be no other than Alā-ud-dīn's tomb. At any rate, Alā-ud-dīn's tomb has never yet been found, and Sayyid Ahmad himself says no tombstone exists in what he calls Alā-ud-dīn's tomb ; certainly none exists now, and the disposition of the great structure is quite different to that of a tomb, and, further, is inconsistent with what is recorded in history, that Alā-ud-dīn was buried in Hazār Sutūn." (Mr. Beglar, in *Archæol. Survey Reports*, vol. iv, p. 77.) But Mr. Beglar and the author were both in error. The tomb still exists, and is in front of the great mosque. (*Carr Stephen*, p. 88.)

covers the remains of Imām Mashhadī, the religious guide of the Emperor Akbar ; and a magnificent tomb of free-stone covers those of his four foster-brothers. This was long occupied as a dwelling-house by the late Mr. Blake, of the Bengal Civil Service, who was lately barbarously murdered at Jaipur. To make room for his dining-tables he removed the marble slab, which covered the remains of the dead, from the centre of the building, against the urgent remonstrance of the people, and threw it carelessly on one side against the wall, where it now lies. The people appealed in vain, it is said, to Mr. Fraser, the Governor-General's representative, who was soon after assassinated ; and a good many attribute the death of both to this outrage upon the remains of the dead foster-brother of Akbar. Those of Alā-ud-dīn were, no doubt, older and less sensitive. Tombs equally magnificent cover the remains of the other three foster-brothers of Akbar, but I did not enter them.[1]

[1] The tomb desecrated by Mr. Blake is on the right of the road leading from the Kutb Mīnār to the village of Mihraulī, and is that of Adham Khān, whom Akbar put to death in A.D. 1562 for the murder of Shams-ud-dīn Muhammad Atgah Khān, one of the Emperor's foster-fathers. The best-known of the "kokahs," or foster-brothers, of Akbar is Azīz, the son of Shams-ud-dīn above mentioned. Azīz received the title of Khān-i-Azam. One of his daughters was married to Murād, Akbar's drunken son, and another to the unhappy Khusrū, son of Salīm (Jahāngīr). (Von Noer, *The Emperor Akbar*, tr. by Beveridge ; vol. i, p.p. 78, 95 ; vol. ii, p.p. 212, 387, etc. ; and Bloch-mann's *Aīn-i-Akbarī*, vol. i, p.p. 321, 323, etc.) The family of Shams-ud-dīn is often called in histories *Atgah Khail*, "the foster-father battalion." The young chief of Jaipur died in 1834, and in the course of disturbances which followed, the Political Agent was wounded, and Mr. Blake, his assistant, was killed. (D. Boulger, *Lord William Bentinck*, p. 143.) I can find no mention in any authority of Imām Mashhadī, though it is well known that Akbar sent to Persia for a Parsee priest named Ardshēr. (*Blochmann*, p. 210.) Mr. Fraser's murder has been fully described *ante* p.p. 106–125.

CHAPTER XIII[1]

New Delhi, or Shāhjahānābād.

ON the 22nd of January, 1836, we went on twelve miles to the new city of Delhi, built by the Emperor Shāhjahān, and called after him Shāhjahānābād; and took up our quarters in the palace of the Bēgam Samrū, a fine building, agreeably situated in a garden opening into the great street, with a branch of the great canal running through it, and as quiet as if it had been in a wilderness.[2] We had obtained from the Bēgam permission to occupy this palace during our stay. It was elegantly furnished, the servants were all exceedingly attentive, and we were very happy.

The Kutb Mīnār stands upon the back of the sandstone range of low hills, and the road descends over the north-eastern face of this range for half a mile, and then passes over a level plain all the way to the new city, which lies on the right bank of the river Jumna. The whole plain is literally covered with the remains of splendid Muhammadan mosques and mausoleums. These Muhammadans seem as if they had always in their thoughts the saying of Christ which Akbar has inscribed on the gateway at Fathpur Sīkrī :—"Life is a bridge which you are to pass over, and not to build your dwellings upon."[3] The buildings which they have left behind them have almost all a refer-

---

[1] Chapter XX of Vol. II of original edition.

[2] Chapter XX *post* is devoted to the history of the Bēgam Samrū (Sumroo). The "great street" is the celebrated Chandnī Chauk, a very wide thoroughfare. The branch of the canal which runs down the middle of it is now covered over.

[3] *Ante,* Vol. I, p. 427.

ence to a future state—they laid out their means in a
church, in which the Deity might be propitiated; in a
tomb where learned and pious men might chant their
Korān over their remains, and youth be instructed in their
duties; in a serai, a bridge, a canal built gratuitously for
the public good, that those who enjoyed these advantages
from generation to generation might pray for the repose of
their souls. How could it be otherwise where the land
was the property of government, where capital was never
concentrated or safe, when the only aristocracy was that of
office, while the Emperor was the sole recognized heir of
all his public officers?

The only thing that he could not inherit were his tombs,
his temples, his bridges, his canals, his caravanserais. I
was acquainted with the history of most of the great men
whose tombs and temples I visited along the road; but I
asked in vain for a sight of the palaces they occupied in
their day of pride and power. They all had, no doubt,
good houses agreeably situated, like that of the Bēgam
Samrū, in the midst of well-watered gardens and shrub-
beries, delightful in their season; but they cared less about
them—they knew that the Emperor was heir to every
member of the great body to which they belonged, the
aristrocracy of office; and might transfer all their wealth to
his treasury, and all their palaces to their successors, the
moment the breath should be out of their bodies.[1] If
their sons got office, it would neither be in the same grades,
nor in the same places as those of their fathers.

How different it is in Europe, where our aristocracy is
formed upon a different basis; no one knows where to find
the tombs in which the remains of great men who have

---

[1] The Emperors were not in the least ashamed of this practice,
and robbed the families of rich merchants as well as those of officials.
In fact they levied in a rough way the high " death duties " so much
admired by Radicals with small expectations. Some remarkable
cases are related in detail by Bernier. (Constable's *Bernier*, p.p. 163–
167.)

passed away repose; or the churches and colleges they have founded; or the serāis, the bridges, the canals they formed gratuitously for the public good; but everybody knows where to find their " proud palaces ; " life is not to them "a bridge over which they are to pass, and not build their dwellings upon." The eldest sons enjoy all the patrimonial estates, and employ them as best they may to get their younger brothers into situations in the church, the army, the navy, and other public establishments, in which they may be honourably and liberally provided for out of the public purse.

About half-way between the great tower and the new city, on the left-hand side of the road, stands the tomb of Mansūr Alī Khān, the great-grandfather of the present King of Oudh. Of all the tombs to be seen in this immense extent of splendid ruins, this is perhaps the only one raised over a subject, the family of whose inmates are now in a condition even to keep it in repair. It is a very beautiful mausoleum, built after the model of the Tāj at Agra ; with this difference, that the external wall around the quadrangle of the Tāj is here, as it were, thrown back, and closed in upon the tomb. The beautiful gateway at the entrance of the gardens of the Tāj forms each of the four sides of the tomb of Mansūr Alī Khān, with all its chaste beauty of design, proportion, and ornament.[1] The quadrangle in which this mausoleum stands is about three hundred and fifty yards square, surrounded by a stone wall, with handsome gateways, and filled in the same manner as that of the Tāj at Agra, with cisterns and fruit-trees. Three kinds of stones are used—white marble, red sandstone, and the fine white and flesh-coloured sandstone of Rupbās. The dome is of white marble, and exactly of the same form as that of the Tāj ; but it stands on a neck or base of sandstone with twelve sides, and the marble is of a quality very inferior to that of the Tāj. It is of coarse

---

[1] The meaning of this sentence is obscure.

dolomite, and has become a good deal discoloured by time, so as to give it the appearance, which Bishop Heber noticed, of *potted meat.* The neck is not quite so long as that of the Tāj, and is better covered by the marble cupolas that stand above each face of the building. The four noble minarets are, however, wanting. The apartments are all in number and form exactly like those of the Tāj, but they are somewhat less in size. In the centre of the first floor lies the beautiful marble slab that bears the date of this small pillar of *a tottering state,* A.H. 1167 ;[1] and in a vault underneath repose his remains by the side of those of one of his grand-daughters. The graves that cover these remains are of plain earth strewed with fresh flowers, and covered with plain cloth. About two miles from this tomb to the east stands that of the father of Akbar, Humāyūn, a large and magnificent building. As I rode towards this building to see the slab that covers the head of poor Dārā Shikoh, I frequently cast a lingering look behind to view, as often as I could, this very pretty imitation of the most beautiful of all the tombs of the earth.[2]

[1] Corresponding to A.D. 1753-54. In the original edition the date is misprinted A.D. 1167.

[2] The tomb of Mansūr Alī Khān is better known as that of Safdar Jang, which was the honorary title of the noble over whom the edifice was raised. He was the wazīr, or chief minister, of the Emperor Ahmad Shāh from 1748 to 1752, and he was practically King of Oudh, where he had succeeded to the power of his father-in-law, the well-known Saādat Alī Khān : Safdar Jang died in A.D. 1753, and was succeeded in Oudh by Shujā-ud-daula.

The author's praise of the beauty of Safdar Jang's tomb will seem extravagant to most critics. In the editor's judgment the building is a very poor attempt to imitate the inimitable Tāj. Fergusson (p. 604) gives its the qualified praise that " it looks grand and imposing at a distance, but it will not bear close inspection." Lieutenant Harcourt (*The New Guide to Delhi*, p. 95) justly remarks that it is much smaller than the Tāj, and " for beauty is not to be compared " with it.

In the original edition a coloured plate of this mausoleum is given. The buildings are now in bad repair. Mr. Carr Stephen (*Archæology of Delhi*, p. 278) says that " this mausoleum is in some respects not

On my way I turned in to see the tomb of the celebrated saint, Nizām-ud-dīn Auliā, the defeater of the Transoxianian army under Tarmah Shīrīn in 1303, to which pilgrimages are still made from all parts of India.[1] It is a small building, surmounted by a white marble dome, and kept very clean and neat.[2] By its side is that of the poet Khusrū,

unlike that of Humāyūn, and is believed to have been intended as a duplicate of that superb building." There is, of course, a general resemblance between the main building of the Tāj and the tomb of Humāyūn.

[1] Nizām-ud-dīn was the disciple of Farīd-ud-dīn Ganj Shakar, so called from his look being sufficient to convert *clods of earth into lumps of sugar.* Farīd was the disciple of Kutb-ud-dīn of Old Delhi, who was the disciple of Mūin-ud-dīn of Ajmīr, the greatest of all their saints. [W. H. S.] Mūin-ud-dīn died A.D. 1236. For further particulars of the three saints see Beale's *Oriental Biographical Dictionary.*

[2] For the personal history of Nizām-ud-dīn see the last preceding chapter, p.p. 144-146. His tomb is situated in a kind of cemetery, which also contains the tombs of the poet Khusrū, the Princess Jahānārā, and the Emperor Muhammad Shāh, which will be presently noticed. Nizāmud-dīn's tomb " has a very graceful appearance, and is surrounded by a verandah of white marble, while a cut screen encloses the sarcophagus, which is always covered with a cloth. Round the gravestone runs a carved wooden guard, and from the four corners rise stone pillars draped with cloth, which support an angular wooden frame-work, and which has something the appearance of a canopy to a bed. Below this wooden canopy there is stretched a cloth of green and red, much the worse for wear. The interior of the tomb is covered with painted figures in Arabic, and at the head of the grave is a stand with a Korān. The marble screen is very richly cut, and the roof of the arcade-like verandah is finely painted in a flower pattern. Altogether there is a quaint look about the building, which cannot fail to strike any one. A good deal of money has at various times been spent on this tomb ; the dome was added to the roof in Akbar's time by Muhammad Imām-ud-dīn Hasan, and in the reign of Shāh Jahān (A.D. 1628 [*sic., leg.* 1627]-58) the whole building was put into thorough repair. . . . The tomb is in the village of Ghyāspur, and is reached after passing through the "Chaunsath Khambā." (Harcourt, *The New Guide to Delhi,* p. 107.)

In the original edition a small coloured illustration of this tomb, from a miniature, is given on Plate 24. Mr. Carr Stephen (p.p. 102–107) gives a good and full account of Nizām-ud-dīn and his tomb.

his contemporary and friend, who moved about where he pleased through the palace of the Emperor Tughlak Shāh the First, five hundred years ago, and sang extempore to his lyre while the greatest and the fairest watched his lips to catch the expressions as they came warm from his soul. His popular songs are still the most popular ; and he is one of the favoured few who live through ages in the every-day thoughts and feelings of many millions, while the crowned heads that patronized them in their brief day of pomp and power are forgotten, or remembered merely as they happened to be connected with them.   His tomb has also a dome, and the grave is covered with rich brocade,[1] and attended with as much reverence and devotion as that of the great saint himself, while those of the emperors, kings, and princes that have been crowded around them are entirely disregarded.   A number of people are employed to read the Korān over the grave of the old saint [scil. Nizām-ud-dīn], who died A.H. 725 [A.D. 1324–1325], and are paid by contributions from the present Emperor, and the members of his family, who occasionally come in their hour of need to entreat his intercession with the Deity in their favour, and by the humble pilgrims who flock from all parts for the same purpose.   A great many boys are here educated by these readers of their sacred volume.   All my attendants bowed their heads to the dust before the shrine of the saint, but they seemed especially indifferent to those of the royal family, which are all open to the sky.   Respect

[1] According to Harcourt (p. 108) the tomb of Khusrū was erected about A.D. 1350, but this is a mistake.   The poet, whose proper name was Abūl Hasan, and is often called Amīr Khusrū, was of Turkish origin.   He was born A.D. 1253, and died in September, 1325.   His works are very numerous. (*Beale.*) The grave, and wooden railing round it, were built in 937 A.H. (1530 A.D.) . . . . The present tomb was built in 1014 A.H. (1605 A.D.) by Amād-ud-dīn Hasan, in the reign of Jahāngīr, and this date occurs in an inscription under the dome and over the red sandstone screens. (*Carr Stephen,* p. 115.) In the original edition a small coloured illustration of this tomb, from a miniature, is given on Plate 24.

shown or neglect towards them could bring neither good nor evil, while any slight to the tomb of the *crusty old saint* might be of serious consequence.

In an enclosure formed by marble screens beautifully carved is the tomb of the favourite son of the present Emperor,[1] Mirzā Jahāngīr, whom I knew intimately at Allahabad in 1816,[2] when he was killing himself as fast as he could with Hoffman's cherry brandy. " This," he would say to me, "is really the only liquor that you Englishmen have worth drinking, and its only fault is that it makes one drunk too soon." To prolong his pleasure, he used to limit himself to one large glass every hour, till he got dead drunk. Two or three sets of dancing women and musicians used to relieve each other in amusing him during this interval. He died, of course, soon, and the poor old Emperor was persuaded by his mother, the favourite sultana, that he had fallen a victim to sighing and grief at the treatment of the English, who would not permit him to remain at Delhi, where he was continually employed in attempts to assassinate his eldest brother, the heir apparent, and to stir up insurrections among the people. He was not in confinement at Allahabad, but merely prohibited from returning to Delhi. He had a splendid dwelling, a good income, and all the honours due to his rank.[3]

---

[1] Akbar II., who died in 1837.

[2] When the author was with his regiment, after the close of the Nepalese war.

[3] Harcourt (p. 109) truly observes that this tomb "is a most exquisite piece of workmanship. The tomb itself, raised some few feet from the ground, is entered by steps, and is enclosed in a beautiful cut marble screen, the sarcophagus being covered with a very artistic representation of leaves and flowers carved in marble. Mirzā Jahāngīr was the son of Akbar II., and the tomb was built in A.D. 1832."

"He was, in consequence of having fired a pistol at Mr. Seton, the Resident at Delhi, sent as a State prisoner to Allahabad, where he resided in the garden of Sultān Khusro for several years, and died there in 1821 A.D. (1236 A.H.), aged thirty-one years; a salute of thirty-one guns was fired from the ramparts of the fort of Allahabad at

In another enclosure of the same kind are the Emperor Muhammad Shāh,[1]—who reigned when Nādir Shāh invaded Delhi—his mother, wife, and daughter; and in another close by is the tomb which interested me most, that of Jahānārā Bēgam, the favourite sister of poor Dārā Shikoh, and daughter of Shāh Jahān.[2] It stands in the same enclosure, with the brother of the present Emperor on one side, and his daughter on the other. Her remains are covered with a marble slab hollow at the top, and exposed to the sky—the hollow is filled with earth covered with green grass. Upon her tomb is the following inscription, the three first lin · of which are said to have been written by herself :—

the time of his burial. He was at first interred in the same garden, and subsequently his remains were transferred to Delhi, and buried in the court-yard of the mausoleum of Nizām-ud-dīn Auliā." (Beale's *Dictionary.*) Th young man's " overt act of rebellion " occurred in 1808, and his body was removed to Delhi in 1832. The form of the monument is that ordinarily used for a woman, " but it was put over the remains of the Prince on a dispensation being granted for the purpose by Muhammadan lawyers." (*Carr Stephen*, p. 111.)

[1] Muhammad Shāh feebly reigned from September, 1719, to April, 1748. " He is the last of the Mughals who enjoyed even the semblance of power, and has been called 'the seal of the house of Bābar,' for ' after his demise everything went to wreck.' " (*Lane-Poole*, p. xxxviii.) Nādir Shāh occupied Delhi in 1738, and is said to have massacred 120,000 people. The tomb is described by Carr Stephen, p. 110.

[2] Jahānārā Bēgam, or the Bēgam Sāhib, was the elder daughter of Shāhjahān, a very able intriguer, the partisan of Dārā, and the opponent of Aurangzēb during the struggle for the throne. She was closely confined in Agra till her father's death in 1666. After that event she was removed to Delhi, where she died, not without suspicion of poison. (Ball's *Tavernier*, Vol. I, p. 345.) She built the Bēgam Sarāi at Delhi. Her amours, real or supposed, furnished Bernier with some very scandalous and sensational stories. (Constable's *Bernier*, p.p. 11–14.) Some writers credit her with all the virtues, *e.g.*, Beale in his *Oriental Biographical Dictionary*. The author has omitted the last line of the inscription—" May God illuminate his intentions. In the year 1093," corresponding to A.D. 1682. The first line is, " Let nothing but the green [grass] conceal my grave." (*Carr Stephen*, p. 109.)

"Let no rich canopy cover my grave.
This grass is the best covering for the tombs of the poor in spirit.
The humble, the transitory Jahānārā,
The disciple of the holy men of Chisht,
The daughter of the Emperor Shāh Jahān."

I went over the magnificent tomb of Humāyūn, which was raised over his remains by the Emperor Akbar. It stands in the centre of a quadrangle of about four hundred yards square, with a cloistered wall all round; but I must not describe any more tombs.[1] Here, under a marble slab, lies the head of poor Dārā Shikoh, who, but for a little infirmity of temper, had perhaps changed the destinies of India, by changing the character of education among the aristocracy of the countries under his rule, and preventing the birth of the Marāthā powers by leaving untouched the independent kingdoms of the Deccan, upon whose ruins, under his bigoted brother, the former rose. Secular and and religious education were always inseparably combined among the Muhammadans, and invited to India from Persia by the public offices, civil and military, which men of education and courtly manners could alone obtain. These offices had long been exclusively filled by such men,

[1] The tomb of Humāyūn, according to Lieutenant Harcourt (p. 103), was erected by the emperor's widow, Hājī Bēgam, and not by Akbar. Mr. Carr Stephen (p. 203) says that the mausoleum was completed in A.D. 1565, or, according to some, in A.D. 1569, at a cost of fifteen lākhs of rupees. It is of special interest as being the earliest specimen of the architecture of the Moghal dynasty. The massive dome of white marble is a conspicuous landmark for many miles round. The body of the building is built of red sandstone with marble decorations. It stands on two noble terraces. Humāyūn rests in the central hall under an elaborately carved marble sarcophagus. The head of Dārā and the bodies of many members of the royal family are interred in the side rooms. After the fall of Delhi in September, 1857, the rebel princes took refuge in this mausoleum. The story of their execution by Hodson on the road to Delhi is well known, and has been the occasion of much controversy.

In the original edition a small coloured illustration of this tomb, from a miniature, is given on Plate 24.

who flocked in crowds to India from Khorāsān and Persia.
Every man qualified by secular instruction to make his way
at court and fill such offices was disposed by his religious
instruction to assert the supremacy of his creed, and to
exclude the followers of every other from the employments
over which he had any control. The aristocracy of office
was the ocean to which this stream of Muhammadan
education flowed from the west, and spread all over India;
and had Dārā subdued his brothers and ascended the
throne, he would probably have arrested the flood by
closing the public offices against these Persian adventurers,
and filling them with Christians and Hindoos. This would
have changed the character of the aristocracy and the
education of the people.[1]

While looking upon the slab under which his head
reposes, I thought of the slight "accidents by flood and
field," the still slighter thought of the brain and feeling of
the heart, on which the destinies of nations and of empires
often depend—on the discovery of the great diamond in
the mines of Golconda—on the accident which gave it into
the hands of an ambitious Persian adventurer—on the

[1] The tragic history of Dārā, the elder brother, and unsuccessful
rival, of Aurangzēb, is very fully given by Bernier. The notes in
Constable's edition of that traveller's work give many additional particulars. Dārā was executed by Aurangzēb in 1659, and with a horrid
refinement of cruelty, the emperor, acting on the advice of his sister,
Roshanārā Bēgam, caused the head to be embalmed and sent packed
in a box as a present to the old ex-emperor, Shāh Jahān, the father of
the three, in his prison at Agra. Dārā died invoking the aid of Jesus,
and was favourably disposed towards Christianity. He was also
attracted by the doctrines of Sūfism, or heretical Muhammadan
mysticism, and by those of the Hindoo Upanishads. In fact, his
religious attitude seems to have much resembled that of his great-
grandfather Akbar. The "Broad Church" principles and practice of
Akbar failed to leave any permanent mark on Muhammadan institutions or the education of the people, and if Dārā had been victorious
in the contest for the throne, it is not probable that he would have
been able to effect lasting reforms which were beyond the power of
his illustrious ancestor.

thought which suggested the advantage of presenting it to Shāh Jahān—on the feeling which made Dārā get off, and Aurangzēb sit on his elephant at the battle of Samūgarh, on which depended the fate of India, and perhaps the advancement of the Christian religion and European literature and science over India.[1] But for the accident which gave Charles Martel the victory over the Saracens at Tours,[2] Arabic and Persian had perhaps been the classical languages, and Islamism the religion of Europe ; and where we have cathedrals and colleges we might have had mosques and mausoleums ; and America and the Cape, the compass and the press, the steam-engine, the telescope, and the Copernican system, might have remained still undiscovered ; and but for the accident which turned Hannibal's face from Rome after the battle of Cannæ, or that which intercepted his brother Asdrubal's letter, we might now all be speaking the languages of Tyre and Sidon, and roasting our own children in offerings to Siva or Saturn, instead of saving

[1] The "great diamond" alluded to is the Kohinūr, presented by the "Persian adventurer," Amīr Jumla, to Shāh Jahān, who was advised to attack and conquer the country which produced such gems. (*Ante*, Vol. I, Ch. XLVIII.) The decisive battle between Dārā, on the one side, and Aurangzēb, supported by his brother and dupe, Murād, on the other, was fought on the 28th May, 1658 [O. S.], at the small village of Samūgarh (Samogar), four miles from Agra. Dārā was winning the battle, when a traitor persuaded him to come down from his conspicuous seat on an elephant and mount a horse. The report quickly spread that the prince had been killed. "In a few minutes," says Bernier, "the army seemed disbanded, and (strange and sudden reverse !) the conqueror became the vanquished. Aurangzēb remained during a quarter of an hour steadily on his elephant, and was rewarded with the crown of Hindustān ; Dārā left his own elephant a few minutes too soon, and was hurled from the pinnacle of glory, to be numbered among the most miserable of Princes ; so short-sighted is man, and so mighty are the consequences which sometimes flow from the most trivial incident."

According to another account Dārā's change from the elephant to the horse was due to want of personal courage, and not to treacherous advice. (Constable's *Bernier*, p. 54.)

[2] Battle fought between Tours and Poitiers, A.D. 732.

those of the Hindoos.   Poor Dārā ! but for thy little
jealousy of thy father and thy son, thy desire to do all thy
work without their aid, and those occasional ebullitions of
passion which alienated from thee the most powerful of all
the Hindoo princes, whom it was so much thy wish and
thy interest to cherish, thy generous heart and enlightened
mind had reigned over this vast empire, and made it, per-
chance, the garden it deserves to be made.

I visited the celebrated mosque known by the name of
Jāmi (Jumma) Masjid, a fine building raised by Shāh Jahān,
and finished in six years, A.H. 1060, at a cost of ten lākhs of
rupees, or one hundred thousand pounds.   Money compared
to man's labour and subsistence is still four times more
valuable in India than in England ; and a similar building in
England would cost at least four hundred thousand pounds.
It is, like all the buildings raised by this Emperor, in the
best taste and style.[1]   I was attended by three well-dressed
and modest Hindoos, and a Muhammadan servant of the
Emperor.   My attention was so much taken up with the
edifice that I did not perceive, till I was about to return,
that the doorkeepers had stopped my three Hindoos.   I

---

[1] The principal mosque of every town is known as the Jāmi Masjid,
and is filled by large congregations on Fridays.   The great mosque of
Delhi stands on a natural rocky eminence, which is completely covered
by the building, and is approached on three sides by magnificent
flights of steps, which give it peculiar dignity.   It is, perhaps, the
finest mosque in the world, and certainly has few rivals.   It differs
from most mosques in that its exterior is more magnificent than its
interior.   The two minarets are each about 130 feet high.   The year
A.H. 1060 corresponds to A.D. 1650.   Carr Stephen (p. 250) says that
the mosque, according to all native authorities, was begun in that year,
and finished six years later.   This mosque is close to the palace, and
seems to have been designed to serve as the mosque for the palace, as
well as the city, for which reason no place of worship was included in
the palace by Shāh Jahān.   The pretty little Motī Masjid in the private
apartments of the palace was added by Aurangzēb.   Fergusson (p.
601) gives a view of the great mosque.   Carr Stephen (p.p. 250-256)
gives approximate measurements, translations of the inscriptions, and
many details.

found that they had offered to leave their shoes behind, and submit to anything to be permitted to follow me; but the porters had, they said, strict orders to admit no *worshippers of idols;* for their master was a *man of the book,* and had, therefore, got a little of the *truth* in him, though unhappily not much, since his heart had not been opened to that of the Korān. Nathū could have told him that he also had a *book,* which he and some fourscore millions more thought as good as his or better; but he was afraid to descant upon the merits of his "shāstras," and the miracles of Kishan Jī [Krishna], among such fierce, cut-throat-looking people; he looked, however, as if he could have eaten the porter, Korān and all, when I came to their rescue. The only volumes which Muhammadans designate by the name of the *book* are the Old and New Testaments, and the Korān.

I visited also the palace, which was built by the same Emperor. It stands on the right bank of the Jumna, and occupies a quadrangle surrounded by a high wall built of red sandstone, about one mile in circumference; one side looks down into the clear stream of the Jumna, while the others are surrounded by the streets of the city.[1] The entrance is by a noble gateway to the west;[2] and facing this gateway on the inside, a hundred and twenty yards distant is the Dīwān-i-Am, or the common hall of audience. This is a large hall, the roof of which is supported upon four colonnades of pillars of red sandstone, now white-washed, but once covered with stucco work and gilded. On one of these pillars is shown the mark of the dagger of a Hindoo prince of Chitōr, who, in the presence of the

[1] Since the Mutiny multitudes of houses between the palace and the great mosque have been cleared away.

[2] "Entering within its deeply recessed portal, you find yourself beneath the vaulted hall, the sides of which are in two storeys, and with an octagonal break in the centre. This hall, which is 375 feet in length over all, has very much the effect of the nave of a gigantic Gothic cathedral, and forms the noblest entrance known to belong to any existing palace." (*Fergusson,* p. 591.) This is the Lahore Gate.

Emperor, stabbed to the heart one of the Muhammadan
ministers who made use of some disrespectful language
towards him.   On being asked how he presumed to do this
in the presence of his sovereign he answered in the very
words almost of Roderic Dhu,

> " I right my wrongs where they are given,
> Though it were in the court of Heaven." [1]

The throne projects into the hall from the back in front of
the large central arch ; it is raised ten feet above the floor,
and is about ten feet wide, and covered by a marble canopy,
all beautifully inlaid with mosaic work exquisitely finished,
but now much dilapidated.   The room or recess in which
the throne stands is open to the front, and about fifteen feet
wide and six deep.   There is a door at the back by which
the Emperor entered from his private apartments, and one
on his left, from which his prime minister or chief officer of
state approached the throne by a flight of steps leading into
the hall.   In front of the throne, and raised some three
feet above the floor, is a fine large slab of white marble, on
which one of the secretaries stood during the hours of
audience to hand up to the throne any petitions that were
presented, and to receive and convey commands.   As the
people approached over the intervening one hundred and
twenty yards between the gateway and the hall of audience
they were made to bow down lower and lower to the figure
of the Emperor, as he sat upon his throne, without deign-
ing to show by any motion of limb or muscle that he was
really made of flesh and blood, and not cut out of the
marble he sat upon.

The marble walls on three sides of this recess are inlaid
with precious stones representing some of the most beautiful birds and flowers of India, according to the boundaries

[1] " What recked the Chieftain if he stood
On Highland heath, or Holy-rood ?
He rights such wrong where it is given,
If it were in the court of heaven."
—(Scott, *Lady of the Lake*, Canto V, stanza 6.)

of the country when Shāh Jahān built this palace, which
included Kābul and Kāshmīr, afterwards severed from it on
the invasion of Nādir Shāh.[1]

On the upper part of the back wall is represented, in
the same precious stones, and in a graceful attitude, an
European in a kind of Spanish costume, playing upon his
guitar, and in the character of Orpheus charming the birds
and beasts which he first taught the people of India so well
to represent in this manner. This I have no doubt was
intended by Austin de Bordeaux for himself. The man
from Shīrāz, Amānat Khān, who designed all the noble
Tughra characters in which the passages from the Korān
are inscribed upon different parts of the Tāj at Agra, was
permitted to place his own name in the same bold characters on the right-hand side as we enter the tomb of the
Emperor and his queen. It is inscribed after the date,
thus, A.H. 1048 [A.D. 1638–39], "The humble fakīr Amānat
Khān of Shīrāz." Austin was a still greater favourite than
Amānat Khān; and the Emperor Shāh Jahān, no doubt,
readily acceded to his wishes to have himself represented
in what appeared to him and his courtiers so beautiful a
picture.[2]

[1] The foundation-stone of the palace was laid on the 12th of May,
1639 (N.S.—9 Muharrum, A.H. 1049.) (Dowson's *Elliot*, Vol. VII,
p. 86), and the work continued for nine years, three months, and some
days. Nādir Shāh's invasion took place in 1738. Kāshmīr was
annexed by Akbar in 1587. Kābul had been more or less closely
united with the empire since Bābar's time.

[2] "In front, at the entrance, was the Naubat Khāna, or music hall,
beneath which the visitor entered the second or great court of the palace,
measuring 550 feet north and south. by 385 feet east and west. In the
centre of this stood the Dīwān-i-Am, or great audience hall of the
palace, very similar in design to that at Agra, but more magnificent.
Its dimensions are, as nearly as I can ascertain, 200 feet by 100 feet
over all. In its centre is a highly ornamental niche, in which on a
platform of marble richly inlaid with precious stones, and directly
facing the entrance, once stood the celebrated peacock throne, the
most gorgeous example of its class that perhaps even the East could
ever boast of. Behind this again was a garden-court; on its eastern

The Dīwān-i-Khās, or hall of private audience, is a much
more splendid building than the other from its richer
materials, being all built of white marble beautifully
ornamented. The roof is supported upon colonnades of
marble pillars. The throne stands in the centre of this
hall, and is ascended by steps, and covered by a canopy,
with four artificial peacocks on the four corners.[1] Here,
thought I, as I entered this apartment, sat Aurangzēb when
he ordered the assassination of his brothers Dārā and
Murād, and the imprisonment and destruction by slow

side was the Rang Mahal, or painted hall, containing a bath and other
apartments."

The inlaid pictures have been carried off, and were sold by the
spoiler to Government, set as table tops. They are now in the Indian
Museum. The representation of Orpheus "is a bad copy from
Raphael's picture of Orpheus charming the beasts." (*Fergusson*, p.
592.) Austin de Bordeaux has already been noticed, Vol. I, p. 385. It is
stated in Beresford's *Guide to Delhi* (1856 ; quoted by Harcourt, p. 75)
that Austin, "after defrauding several of the Princes of Europe by
means of false gems, which he fabricated with great skill, sought refuge
at the court of Shāh Jahān, where he made his fortune, and was in high
favour with the Emperor." But this statement is copied from Bernier
(*Constable's ed.*, p. 269), who does not mention the "Frenchman's"
name. According to one writer the "Frenchman" who made the
peacock throne was named La Grange.

The peacock throne and the six other thrones in the palace are fully
described by Tavernier. (*Ball's edition*, Vol. I, p.p. 381-387.) Further
details will be found in Carr Stephen's *Archæology of Delhi*, p.p. 220 -227.

[1] The throne here referred to was a makeshift arrangement used by
the later emperors. Nādir Shāh in 1738 cleared the palace of the
peacock throne, and almost everything portable of value. The little
that was left the Marāthās took. Their chief prize was the silver
filagree ceiling of the Dīwān-i-Khās. This hall was, "if not the most
beautiful, certainly the most highly ornamented of all Shāh Jahān's
buildings. It is larger certainly, and far richer in ornament than that
of Agra, though hardly so elegant in design ; but nothing can exceed
the beauty of the inlay of precious stones with which it is adorned, or
the general poetry of the design. It is round the roof of this hall that
the famous inscription runs : 'If there is a heaven on earth, it is this,
it is this,' which may safely be rendered into the sober English assertion that no palace now existing in the world possesses an apartment
of such singular elegance as this." (*Fergusson*, p. 593.)

poison of his son Muhammad, who had so often fought bravely by his side in battle. Here also, but a few months before, sat the great Shāh Jahān to receive the insolent commands of this same grandson Muhammad when flushed with victory, and to offer him the throne, merely to disappoint the hopes of the youth's father, Aurangzēb.. Here stood in chains the graceful Sulaimān, to receive his sentence of death by slow poison with his poor young brother Sipihr Shikoh, who had shared all his father's toils and dangers, and witnessed his brutal murder.[1] Here sat Muhammad Shāh, bandying compliments with his ferocious conqueror, Nādir Shāh, who had destroyed his armies, plundered his treasury, stripped his throne, and ordered the murder of a hundred thousand of the helpless inhabitants of his capital, men, women, and children, in a general massacre. The bodies of these people lay in the streets tainting the air, while the two sovereigns sat here sipping their coffee, and swearing to the most deliberate lies in the name of their God, Prophet, and Korān ;—all are now dust ; that of the oppressor undistinguishable from that of the oppressed.[2]

[1] All the events alluded to are related in detail by Bernier. Sulaimān and Sipihr Shikoh were the sons of Dārā. The author makes a slip in saying that Shāh Jahān sat in the palace at Delhi to negotiate with his grandson. During that negotiation Shāh Jahān was at Agra.

[2] It is related that the coffee was delivered to the two sovereigns in this room upon a gold salver by the most polished gentleman of the court. His motions, as he entered the gorgeous apartment, amidst the splendid train of the two Emperors, were watched with great anxiety ; if he presented the coffee first to his own master, the furious conqueror, before whom the sovereign of India and all his courtiers trembled, might order him to instant execution ; if he presented it to Nādir first, he would insult his own sovereign out of fear of the stranger. To the astonishment of all, he walked up with a steady step direct to his own master. "I cannot," said he, "aspire to the honour of presenting the cup to the king of kings, your majesty's honoured guest, nor would your majesty wish that any hand but your own should do so." The Emperor took the cup from the golden salver, and presented it to Nādir Shāh, who said with a smile as he took it,

Within this apartment and over the side arches at one end is inscribed in black letters the celebrated couplet, "If there be a paradise on the face of the earth, it is this— it is this—it is this."[1]   Anything more unlike paradise than this place now is can hardly be conceived. Here are crowded together twelve hundred *kings* and *queens* (for all the descendants of the Emperors assume the title of Salātīn, the plural of Sultān) literally eating each other up.[2]

"Had all your officers known and done their duty like this man, you had never, my good cousin, seen me and my Kizil Bāshis at Delhi ; take care of him for your own sake, and get round you as many like him as you can." [W. II. S.]

[1] "The famous inscription of Saād-Ullah Khān, supposed to be in the handwriting of Rashīd, the greatest caligraphist of his time : *Agar Firdaus bar rūe zamīn ast—hamīn ast, to hamīn ast, to hamīn ast.*" (*Carr Stephen*, p. 229.)

[2] All these people were cleared out by the events of 1857, and the few beautiful fragments of the palace which have retained anything of their original magnificence are now clean and in good order. The elaborate decorations of the Dīwān-i-Khās have been partially restored, and the interior of this building is still extremely rich and elegant.

"Of the public parts of the palace all that now remains is the entrance hall, the Naubat Khāna, Dīwān-i-Am and Khās, and the Rang Mahal—now used as a mess-room, and one or two small pavilions. They are the gems of the palace it is true, but without the courts and corridors connecting them they lose all their meaning and more than half their beauty. Being now situated in the middle of a British barrack-yard, they look like precious stones torn from their settings in some exquisite piece of Oriental jeweller's work and set at random in a bed of the commonest plaster." (*Fergusson*, p. 594.)

The books about Delhi are nearly as tantalizing and unsatisfactory as those which deal with Agra. Mr. Beglar's contribution to Volume IV of the *Archæological Survey Reports* is a little, but very little, better than Mr. Carlleyle's disquisition on Agra in the same volume. Sir A. Cunningham's observations in the first and twentieth volumes of the same series are of much greater value, but are fragmentary and imperfect, and scarcely notice at all the city of Shāhjahān. Fergusson's criticisms, so far as they go, are of the highest value, though the scheme of his work did not allow him to treat in detail of any particular section. Guide-books by Beresford Cooper, Harcourt, and Keene exist, of which Keene's is the latest, and, consequently, in

Government, from motives of benevolence, has here attempted to apportion out the pension they assign to the Emperor, to the different members of his great family circle who are to be subsisted upon it, instead of leaving it to his own discretion. This has perhaps tended to prevent the family from throwing off its useless members to mix with the common herd, and to make the population press against the means of subsistence within these walls. Kings and queens of the house of Taimūr are to be found lying about in scores, like broods of vermin, without food to eat or clothes to cover their nakedness. It has been proposed by some to establish colleges for them in the palace to fit them by education for high offices under our government. Were this done, this pensioned family, which never can possibly feel well affected towards our government or any government but their own, would alone send out men enough to fill all the civil offices open to the natives of the country, to the exclusion of the members of the humbler but better affected families of Muhammadans and Hindoos. If they obtained the offices they would be educated for, the evil to government and to society would be very great; and if they did not get them, the evil would be great to themselves, since they would be encouraged to entertain hopes that could not be realized. Better let them shift for themselves and quietly sink among the crowd. They would only become rallying points for the dissatisfaction and multiplied sources of disaffection;

some respects the best, but all are extremely unsatisfactory. The late Mr. Carr Stephen, a resident of Delhi, wrote a valuable book on the Archæology of the city, but it has no illustrations, except a few plans on a small scale. It was published in India in 1876, and is not very widely known, though much the best book on the subject. A good critical, comprehensive, well illustrated description of the remains of the thirteen cities, which are all grouped together by European writers under the name of Delhi, does not exist, and it is very unlikely that the Panjāb Government will cause the blank to be filled. No government in India has such great opportunities, or has done so little, to elucidate the history of the country, as the government of the Panjāb.

everywhere doing mischief, and nowhere doing good. Let
loose upon society, they everywhere disgust people by their
insolence and knavery, against which we are every day
required to protect the people by our interference ; the
prestige of their name will by degrees diminish, and they
will sink by-and-by into utter insignificance. During his
stay at Jubbulpore, Kāmbaksh, the nephew of the Emperor,
whom I have already mentioned as the most sensible
member of the family,[1] did an infinite deal of good by
cheating almost all the tradesmen of the town. Till he
came down among them with all his ragamuffins from
Delhi, men thought the Pādshāhs and their progeny must
be something superhuman, something not to be spoken of,
much less approached, without reverence. During the
latter part of his stay my court was crowded with complaints ; and no one has ever since heard a scion of the
house of Taimūr spoken of but as a thing to be avoided—a
person more prone than others to take in his neighbours.
One of these *kings*, who has not more than ten shillings a
month to subsist himself and family upon will, in writing
to the representative of the British government, address
him as " Fidwī Khās," " Your particular slave ; " and be
addressed in reply with " Your majesty's commands have
been received by your slave."[2]

I visited the college which is in the mausoleum of
Ghāzī-ud-dīn, a fine building, with its usual accompani-
ment of a mosque and a college. The slab that covers
the grave, and the marble screens that surround the ground
that contains it are amongst the most richly cut things that
I have seen. The learned and pious Muhammadans in the
institution told me in my morning visit that there should

---

[1] *Ante*, Vol. I, p. 409.

[2] These epistolary formulas mean no more than the similar official
phrases in English, " Your most obedient humble servant," and the
like. The " fortunate occurrence " of the Mutiny—for such it was,
in spite of all the blood and suffering—cut out many plague-spots from
the body politic of India. Among these the reeking palace swarm of
Delhi was not the least malignant.

always be a small hollow in the top of marble slabs, like that on Jahānārā's, whenever any of them were placed over graves, in order to admit water, earth, and grass ; but that, strictly speaking, no slab should be allowed to cover the grave, as it could not fail to be in the way of the dead when summoned to get up by the trumpet of Azrail on the day of the resurrection."[1] "Earthly pride," said they, "has .violated this rule; and now everybody that can afford it gets a marble slab put over his grave. But it is not only in this that men have been falling off from the letter and spirit of the law; for we now hear drums beating and trumpets sounding even among the tombs of the saints, a thing that our forefathers would not have considered possible. In former days it was only a prophet like Moses, Jesus, or Muhammad, that was suffered to have a stone placed over his head." I asked them how it was that the people crowded to the tombs of their saints, as I saw them at that of Kutb Shāh in old Delhi, on the Basant, a Hindoo festival. "It only shows," said they, "that the end of the world is approaching. Are we not divided into seventy-two sects among ourselves, all falling off into Hinduism, and everyday committing greater and greater follies? These are the manifest signs long ago pointed out by wise and holy men as indicating the approach of the *last day*."[2]

A man might make a curious book out of the indications of the end of the world according to the notions of different people or different individuals. The Hindoos have had many different worlds or ages ; and the change from the good to the bad, or the golden to the iron age, is considered to have been indicated by a thousand

---

[1] Azrail is the angel of death, whose duty it is to separate the souls from the bodies of men. Isrāfil is entrusted with the task of blowing the last trump.

[2] The resurrection, and the signs foretelling it, are described in the Mishkāt-ul-Masābih, book xxiii, chapters iii to xi. (*Matthews*, vol. ii, p.p. 556–620.)

curious incidents.[1] I one day asked an old Hindoo priest, a very worthy man, what made the five heroes of the Mahābhārata, the demigod brothers of Indian story, leave the plains and bury themselves no one knew where, in the eternal snows of the Himālaya mountains. "Why, sir," said he, "there is no question about that. Yudhisthhira, the eldest, who reigned quietly at Delhi after the long war, one day sat down to dinner with his four brothers and their single wife, Draupadī; for you know, sir, they had only one among them all. The king said grace and the covers were removed, when, to their utter consternation, a full-grown fly was seen seated upon the dish of rice that stood before his majesty. Yudhisthhira rose in consternation. 'When flies begin to blow upon men's dinners,' said his majesty, 'you may be sure, my brothers, that the end of the world is near—the golden age is gone— the iron one has commenced, and we must all be off; the plains of India are no longer a fit abode for gentlemen.' Without taking one morsel of food," added the priest, "they set out, and were never after seen or heard of. They were, however, traced by manifest supernatural signs up through the valley of the Ganges to the snow tops of the Himālaya, in which they no doubt left their mortal coils." They seem to feel a singular attachment for the birthplace of their great progenitrix, for no place in the world is, I suppose, more infested by them than Delhi, at present; and there a dish of rice without a fly would, in the iron, be as rare a thing as a dish with one in the golden, age.

Muhammadans in India sigh for the restoration of the old Muhammadan régime, not from any particular attachment to the descendants of Taimūr, but with precisely the same feelings that Whigs and Tories sigh for the return to power of their respective parties in England;

[1] The Hindoo "ages" are (1) Krita, or Satya, (2) Treta, (3) Dwāpara, (4) Kālī, the present evil age. The long periods assigned to these are merely the result of the calculations of astronomers, who preferred integral to fractional numbers.

it would give them all the offices in a country where office
is everything. Among them, as among ourselves, every
man is disposed to rate his own abilities highly, and to
have a good deal of confidence in his own good luck ;
and all think that if the field were once opened to them
by such a change, they should very soon be able to find
good places for themselves and their children in it.
Perhaps there are few communities in the world among
whom education is more generally diffused than among
Muhammadans in India. He who holds an office worth
twenty rupees a month commonly gives his sons an
education equal to that of a prime minister. They learn,
through the medium of the Arabic and Persian languages,
what young men in our colleges learn through those of the
Greek and Latin—that is, grammar, rhetoric, and logic.
After his seven years of study, the young Muhammadan
binds his turban upon a head almost as well filled with the
things which appertain to these branches of knowledge as
the young man raw from Oxford—he will talk as fluently
about Socrates and Aristotle, Plato and Hippocrates, Galen
and Avicenna ; (*alias* Sokrāt, Aristotalis, Aflātūn, Bokrāt,
Jālinus, and Bū Ali Sena) ; and, what is much to his advantage in India, the languages in which he has learnt what he
knows are those which he most requires through life.[1] He
therefore thinks himself as well fitted to fill the high
offices which are now filled exclusively by Europeans,
and naturally enough wishes the establishments of that
power would open them to him. On the faculties and
operations of the human mind, on man's passions and
affections, and his duties in all relations of life, the
works of Imām Muhammad Ghazāli[2] and Nāsir-ud-dīn

[1] This kind of education does not now pay, and is, consequently,
going out of fashion. The Muhammadans are slowly, and very
unwillingly, yielding to the pressure of necessity and beginning to
accept English education.

[2] Imām Muhammad Ghazzāli, who is also entitled Hujjat-ul-Islām,
is the surname of Abū Hāmid Muhammad Zain-ud-dīn Tūsī, one of

Tūsī[1] hardly yield to those of Plato and Aristotle, or to those of any other authors who have written on the same subjects in any country. These works, the Ihya-ul-ulūm, epitomized into the Kīmiā-i-Saādat, and the Akhlāk-i-Nāsiri, with the didactic poems of Sādī,[2] are the great " Pierian spring " of moral instruction from which the Muhammadan delights to " drink deep " from infancy to old age ; and a better spring it would be difficult to find in the works of any other three men.

It is not only the desire for office that makes the educated Muhammadans cherish the recollection of the old régime in Hindustan : they say, " We pray every night for the Emperor and his family, because our forefathers ate the salt of his forefathers ; "—that is, our ancestors were in the service of his ancestors ; and, consequently, were the *aristocracy* of the country. Whether they really were so matters not ; they persuade themselves or their children that they were. This is a very common and a very innocent sort of vanity. We often find Englishmen in India, and I suppose in all the rest of our foreign settlements, sporting high Tory opinions and feelings, merely with a view to have it supposed that their families are, or at some time were, among the aristocracy of the land. To express a wish for Conservative predominance is the same thing with them as to express a wish for the promotion in the army, navy, or church of some of their near relations ; and thus to indicate that they are among the privileged

---

the greatest and most celebrated Musalmān doctors, who was born A.D. 1058, and died A.D. IIII. (Beale, *The Oriental Biographical Dictionary, s.v.* " Ghazzāli.") The length of these Muhammadan names is terrible. They are much mangled in the original edition. See *ante,* Vol. I, p. 411, note 3, and Blockmann (Aīn.) p.p. 103, 182.

[1] Khwāja Nāsir-ud-dīn Tūsī, the famous philosopher and astronomer, the most universal scholar that Persia ever produced. Born A.D. 1201, died A.D. 1274. (*Beale.*) See *ante, loc. cit.*

[2] Especially the Būstān and Gulistān. Beale gives a list of Sādī's works. See *ante,* Vol. I, p. 93, note.

class whose wishes the Tories would be obliged to consult were they in power.[1]

Man is indeed "fearfully and wonderfully made;" to be fitted himself for action in the world, or for directing ably the actions of others, it is indispensably necessary that he should mix freely from his youth up with his fellow-men. I have elsewhere mentioned that the state of imbecility to which a man of naturally average powers of intellect may be reduced when brought up with his mother in the seraglio is inconceivable to those who have not had opportunities of observing it.[2] The poor old Emperor of Delhi, to whom so many millions look up, is an instance. A more venerable-looking man it is difficult to conceive, and had he been educated and brought up with his fellow-men, he would no doubt have had a mind worthy of his person.[3] As it is, he has never been anything but a baby. Rājā Jivan Rām, an excellent portrait painter, and a very honest and agreeable person, was lately employed to take the Emperor's portrait. After the first few sittings, the portrait was taken into the seraglio to the ladies. The next time he came, the Emperor requested him to remove the great blotch from under the nose. "May it please your majesty, it is impossible to draw any person without *a shadow;* and I hope many millions will long continue to repose under that of your majesty." "True, Rājā," said his majesty, "men must have shadows; but there is surely no necessity for placing them immediately under their noses. The ladies will not allow mine to be put there; they say it looks as if I had been taking snuff all my life, and it certainly has a most filthy appearance; besides, it is all awry, as I told you when you began upon it." The Rājā

---

[1] This is a very cynical and inadequate explanation of the prevalence of Conservative opinions among Englishmen in the East.

[2] *Ante,* Vol. I, p. 310.

[3] In the original edition the portrait of Akbar II. is twice given, namely, in the frontispiece of Volume I. as a full-page plate, and again as a miniature, dated 1836, in the frontispiece of Volume II.

was obliged to remove from under the imperial, and certainly very noble, nose, the shadow which he had thought worth all the rest of the picture. Queen Elizabeth is said, by an edict, to have commanded all artists who should paint her likeness, "to place her in a garden with a full light upon her, and the painter to put *any shadow* in her face at his peril." The next time the Rājā came, the Emperor took the opportunity of consulting him upon a subject that had given him a good deal of anxiety for many months, the dismissal of one of his personal servants who had become negligent and disrespectful. He first took care that no one should be within hearing, and then whispered in the artist's ear that he wished to dismiss this man. The Rājā said carelessly, as he looked from the imperial head to the canvas, "Why does your majesty not discharge the man if he displeases you?"

"Why do I not discharge him? I wish to do so, of course, and have wished to do so for many months, but *kuchchh tadbir chāhiye*, some plan of operations must be devised." "If your majesty dislikes the man, you have only to order him outside the gates of the palace, and you are relieved from his presence at once." "True, man, I am relieved from his presence, but his enchantments may still reach me; it is them that I most dread—he keeps me in a continual state of alarm; and I would give anything to get him away in a good humour."

When the Rājā returned to Meerut, he received a visit from one of the Emperor's sons or nephews, who wanted to see the place. His tents were pitched upon the plain not far from the theatre; he arrived in the evening, and there happened to be a play that night. Several times during the night he got a message from the prince to say that the ground near his tents was haunted by all manner of devils. The Rājā sent to assure him that this could not possibly be the case. At last a man came about midnight to say that the prince could stand it no longer, and had given orders to prepare for his immediate return to Delhi; for the devils were increasing so rapidly that they must all be inevitably devoured before daybreak if they remained. The Rājā now went to the prince's camp, where he found him and his followers in a state of utter consternation, looking towards the theatre. The last carriages were leaving the theatre, and going across the plain ; and these silly people had taken them all for devils.[1]

The present pensioned imperial family of Delhi are commonly considered to be of the house of Taimūr lang (the Lame), because Bābar, the real founder of the dynasty, was descended from him in the seventh stage.[2] Taimūr merely made a predatory inroad into India, to kill a few million of unbelievers,[3] plunder the country of all the moveable valuables he and his soldiers could collect, and take back into slavery all the best artificers of all kinds that they could lay their hands upon. He left no one to represent him in India, he claimed no sovereignty, and founded no dynasty there. There is no doubt much in the prestige of a name ; and though six generations had passed away, the people of Northern India still trembled at that of the lame monster. Bābar wished to impress upon the minds of the people the notion that he had at his back the same army of demons that Taimūr had commanded ; and he boasted his descent from him for the same motive that Alexander boasted his from the horned and cloven-footed god of the Egyptian desert, as something to sanctify all enterprises, justify the use of all means, and carry before him the belief in his invincibility.

Bābar was an admirable chief—a fit founder of a great dynasty—a very proper object for the imagination of future generations to dwell upon, though not quite so good as his grandson, the great Akbar. Taimūr was a ferocious mon-

[1] The most secluded native prince of the present day could not be guilty of this absurdity.

[2] Bābar was sixth in descent from Taimūr, not seventh. Bābar's grandfather, Abū Sayyid, was great-grandson of Taimūr.

[3] This is probably an exaggeration. The actual facts are sufficiently horrible.

ster, who knew how to organize and command the set of
demons who composed his army, and how best to direct
them for the destruction of the civilized portion of mankind
and their works ; but who knew nothing else.   In his
invasion of India he caused the people of the towns and
villages through which he passed to be all massacred without
regard to religion, age, or sex.   If the soldiers in the town
resisted, the people were all murdered because they did so ;
if they did not, the people were considered to have forfeited
their lives to the conqueror for being conquered ; and told
to purchase them by the surrender of all their property, the
value of which was estimated by commissaries appointed
for the purpose.   The price was always more than they
could pay ; and after torturing a certain number to death in
the attempt to screw the sum out of them, the troops were
let in to murder the rest ; so that no city, town, or village
escaped ; and the very grain collected for the army, over
and above what they could consume at any stage, was
burned, lest it might relieve some hungry infidel of the
country who had escaped from the general carnage.

All the soldiers, high and low, were murdered when
taken prisoners, as a matter of course ; but the officers and
soldiers of Taimūr's army, after taking all the valuable
moveables, thought they might be able to find a market for
the artificers by whom they were made, and for their
families ; and they collected together an immense number
of men, women, and children.   All who asked for mercy
pretended to be able to make something that these Tartars
had taken a liking to.   On coming before Delhi, Taimūr's
army encamped on the opposite or left bank of the river
Jumna ; and here he learned that his soldiers had collected
together above one hundred thousand of these artificers,
besides their women and children.   There were no soldiers
among them ; but Taimūr thought it might be troublesome
either to keep them or to turn them away without their
women and children ; and still more so to make his soldiers
send away these women and children immediately.   He

asked whether the prisoners were not for the most part unbelievers in his prophet Muhammad; and being told that the majority were Hindoos, he gave orders that every man should be put to death; and that any officer or soldier who refused to kill or have killed all such men, should suffer death. "As soon as this order was made known," says Taimūr's historian and great eulogist, "the officers and soldiers began to put it in execution; and, in less than one hour, one hundred thousand prisoners, according to the smallest computation, were put to death, and their bodies thrown into the river Jumna. Among the rest, Mulānā Nasir-ud-din Amr, one of the most venerable doctors of the court, who would never consent so much as to kill a single sheep, was constrained to order fifteen slaves, whom he had in his tents, to be slain. Taimūr then gave orders that one-tenth of his soldiers should keep watch over the Indian women, children, and camels taken in the pillage."

The city was soon after taken, and the people commanded, as usual, to purchase their lives by the surrender of their property—troops were sent in to take it—numbers were tortured to death—and then the usual pillage and massacre of the whole people followed without regard to religion, age, or sex; and about a hundred thousand more of innocent and unoffending people were murdered. The troops next massacred the inhabitants of the old city, which had become crowded with fugitives from the new;[1] the last remnant took refuge in a mosque, where two of Taimūr's most distinguished generals rushed in upon them at the head of five hundred soldiers; and, as the amiable historian tells us, "sent to the abyss of hell the souls of these infidels, of whose heads they erected towers, and gave their bodies for food to birds and beasts of prey." Being at last tired of slaughter, the soldiers made slaves of the survivors, and

---

[1] The "old city" was that of Kutb-ud-din and Iltitmish; the "new city" was that of Fīröz Shāh, which partly coincided with the existing city, and partly lay to the south, outside the Delhi gate.

drove them out in chains; and, as they passed, the officers
were allowed to select any they liked except the masons,
whom Taimūr required to build for him at Samarkand a
church similar to that of Iltitmish in old Delhi.

He now set out to take Meerut, which was at that time a
fortified town of much note. The people determined to
defend themselves, and happened to say that Tarmah Shirīn,
who invaded India at the head of a similar body of Tartars
a century before[1] had been unable to take the place. This
so incensed Taimūr that he brought all his forces to bear on
Meerut, took the place, and having had all the Hindoo
men found in it *skinned alive*, he distributed their wives
and children among his soldiers as slaves. He now sent
out a division of his army to murder unbelievers, and
collect plunder, over the cultivated plains between the
Ganges and Jumna, while he led the main body on the
same *pious duty* along the hills from Hardwār[2] on the
Ganges to the west. Having massacred a few thousands of
the hill people, Taimūr read the noon prayer, and returned
thanks to God for the victories he had gained, and the
numbers he had murdered through his goodness; and told
his admiring army that a religious war like this produced
two great advantages; it secured eternal happiness in
heaven, and a good store of valuable spoils on earth—that
his design in all the fatigues and labours which he had
undertaken was solely to render himself *pleasing to God*,
treasure up *good works* for his eternal happiness, and get
riches to bestow upon his soldiers and the poor. The historian makes a grave remark upon this invasion:—"The
Korān declares that the highest glory man can attain in this
world is unquestionably waging a successful war in person
against the enemies of his religion (no matter whether those
against whom it is waged happen ever to have heard of this
religion or not). Muhammad inculcated the same doctrine
in his discourses with his friends; and, in consequence, the

---

[1] In A.D. 1303.   [2] Now in the Sahāranpur district.

great Taimūr always strove to exterminate all the unbelievers, with a view to acquire that glory, and to spread the renown of his conquests. My name," said he, "has spread terror through the universe, and the least motion I make is capable of shaking the whole earth."

Taimūr returned to his capital of Samarkand in Transoxiania in May 1399. His army, besides other things which they brought from India, had an immense number of men, women, and children, whom they had reduced to slavery, and driven along like flocks of sheep to forage for their subsistence in the countries through which they passed, or perish. After the murder on the banks of the Jumna of part of the multitude they had collected before taking the capital, amounting to one hundred thousand men, Taimūr was obliged to assign one-tenth of his army to guard what were left, the women and children. "After the murder in the capital of Delhi," says the historian, an eye-witness, "there were some soldiers who had a hundred and fifty slaves, men, women, and children, whom they drove out of the city before them; and some soldiers' boys had twenty slaves to their own share." On reaching Samarkand, they employed these slaves as best they could; and Taimūr employed his, the masons, in raising his great church from the quarries of the neighbouring hills.[1]

In October following, Taimūr led this army of demons over the rich and polished countries of Syria, Anatolia, and Georgia, levelling all the cities, towns, and villages, and massacring the inhabitants without any regard to age or sex, with the same *amiable view* of correcting the notions of people regarding his creed, propitiating the Deity, and rewarding his soldiers. He sent to the Christian inhabitants of Smyrna, then one of the first commercial cities in the world, to request that they would at once embrace Muhammadanism, in the *beauties* of which the general and his soldiers had orders generously and diligently to instruct them. They refused, and Taimūr repaired immediately to

[1] This is a repetition of the statement made above.

the spot, that he might "share in the merit of sending their souls to the abyss of hell." Bajazet, the Turkish emperor of Anatolia, had recently terminated an unavailing siege of seven years. Taimūr took the city in fourteen days, December 1402 ;[1] had every man, woman, and child that he found in it murdered ; and caused some of the heads of the Christians to be thrown by his balistas or catapultas into the ships that had come from different European nations to their succour. All other Christian communities found within the wide range of this dreadful tempest were swept off in the same manner, nor did Muhammadan communities fare better. After the taking of Baghdad, every Tartar soldier was ordered to cut off and bring away the head of one or more prisoners, because some of the Tartar soldiers had been killed in the attack ; " and they spared," says the historian, " neither old men of fourscore, nor young children of eight years of age ; no quarter was given either to rich or poor, and the number of dead was so great that they could not be counted ; towers were made of their heads to serve as an example to posterity." Ninety thousand were murdered in cold blood, and one hundred and twenty pyramids were made of the heads for trophies. Damascus, Nice, Aleppo, Sabaste, and all the other rich and populous cities of Palestine, Syria, Asia Minor, and Georgia, then the most civilized region of the world, shared in the same fate ; all were reduced to ruins, and their people, without regard to religion, age, or sex, barbarously and brutally murdered.

In the beginning of 1405, this man recollected that, among the many millions of unbelieving Christians and Hindoos "whose souls he had sent to the abyss of hell," there were many Muhammadans, who had no doubt what-

---

[1] Bajazet, or more accurately Bayezīd I., was defeated by Taimūr at the battle of Angora in 1402, and died the following year. The story of his confinement in an iron cage is discredited by modern critics, though Gibbon (Chap. LXV) shows that it is supported by much good evidence. Anatolia is a synonym for Asia Minor. It is a vague term, the Greek equivalent of " the Levant."

ever in the divine origin or co-eternal existence of the Korān; and, as their death might, perhaps, not have been altogether pleasing to his God and his prophet, he determined to appease them both by undertaking the murder of some two hundred millions of industrious and unoffending Chinese; among whom there was little chance of finding one man who had ever even *heard of the Korān*—much less believed in its divinity and co-eternity—or of its interpreter, Muhammad. At the head of between two and three hundred thousand well-mounted Tartars and their followers, he departed from his capital of Samarkand on the 8th of January, 1405, and crossed the Jaxartes[1] on the ice. In the words of his *judicious* historian, "he thus *generously* undertook the conquest of China, which was inhabited only by unbelievers, that by so good a work he might atone for what had been done amiss in other wars, in which the blood of so many of the faithful had been shed."

"As all my vast conquests," said Taimūr-himself,[2] "have caused the destruction of a good many of the faithful, I am resolved to perform some good action, to atone for the crimes of my past life; and to make war upon the infidels, and exterminate the idolaters of China, which cannot be done without very great strength and power. It is therefore fitting, my dear companions in arms, that those very soldiers, who were the instruments whereby those my faults were committed, should be the means by which I work out my repentance, and that they should march into China, to acquire for themselves and their Emperor the merit of that holy war, in demolishing the temples of those unbelievers and erecting good Muhammadan mosques in their places. By this means we shall obtain pardon for all our sins, for the holy Korān assures us that good works efface the sins

---

[1] Otherwise called Sihōn, or Syr Daryā.

[2] Taimūr left behind him two works, the "Memoirs" (*Malfūzāt*) and the "Institutes" (*Tuzukāt*). These have been translated into English by Major Stewart.

of this world." At the close of the Emperor's speech, the
princes of the blood and other officers of rank besought
God to bless his generous undertaking, unanimously
applauding his sentiments, and loading him with praises.
"Let the Emperor but display his standard, and we will
follow him to the end of the world."

Taimūr died soon after crossing the Jaxartes, on the 1st
of April, 1405, and China was saved from this dreadful
scourge. But, as the *philosophical* historian, Sharf-ud-dīn,[1]
profoundly observes, "The Korān remarks that if any one
in his pilgrimage to Mecca should be surprised by death,
the merit of the good work is still written in heaven in his
name, as surely as if he had had the good fortune to
accomplish it. It is the same with regard to the ' ghaza '
(holy war), where an eternal merit is acquired by troubles,
fatigues, and dangers ; and he who dies during the enterprise, at whatever stage, is deemed to have completed his
design." Thus Taimūr the Lame had the merit, beyond all
question of doubt, of sending to the abyss of hell two hundred millions of men, women, and children, for not believing in a certain book of which they had never heard or
read ; for the Tartars had not become Muhammadans
when they conquered China in the beginning of the
thirteenth century. Indeed, the *amiable* and *profound* historian is of opinion, after the most mature deliberation, that
" God himself must have arranged all this in favour of so
great and good a prince ; and knowing that his end was
nigh, inspired him with the idea of undertaking this enterprise, that he might have the merit of having completed it ;
otherwise, how should he have thought of leading out his
army in the dead of winter to cross countries covered with
ice and snow ? "

[1] Alī Yazdī, commonly called Sharf-ud-dīn, author of the "Zafar-
nāma " in Persian ; which was translated into French by Petis de La
Croix in 1722, and translated into English from the French by J. Darby
in the following year. Ibn Arabshāh, in an Arabic work, describes
Taimūr from a hostile point of view. (*Encyclo. Brit.*, 9th ed., *s.v.*
"Timūr.")

The heir to the throne, the Prince Pir Muhammad, was absent when Taimūr died ; but his wives, who had accompanied him, were all anxious to share in the merit of the holy undertaking ; and in a council of the chiefs held after his death, the opinions of these amiable princesses prevailed that the two hundred million of Chinese ought still to be sent to " the abyss of hell," since it had been the earnest wish of their deceased husband, and must undoubtedly have been the will of God, to send them thither without delay.   Fortunately quarrels soon arose among his sons and grandsons about the succession, and the army recrossed the Jaxartes, still over the ice, in the beginning of April, and China was saved from this scourge. Such was Taimūr the Lame, the man whose greatness and goodness are to live in the hearts of the people of India, nine-tenths of whom are Hindoos, and to fill them with overflowing love and gratitude towards his descendants.

In this brief sketch will perhaps be found the true history of the origin of the gipsies, the tide of whose immigration began to flow over all parts of Europe immediately after the return of Taimūr from India.   The hundreds of thousands of slaves which his army brought from India in men, women, and children, were cast away when they got as many as they liked from the more beautiful and polished inhabitants of the cities of Palestine, Syria, Asia Minor, and Georgia, which were all, one after the other, treated in the same manner as Delhi had been.   The Tartar soldiers had no time to settle down and employ them as they intended for their convenience ; they were marched off to ravage Western Asia in October, 1399, about three months after their return from India.   Taimūr reached Samarkand in the middle of May, but he had gone on in advance of his army, which did not arrive for some time after.   Being cast off, the slaves from India spread over those countries which were most likely to afford them the means of subsistence as beggars ; for they knew nothing of the manners, the arts, or the language of those among whom they were

thrown ; and as Arabia, Palestine, Syria, Anatolia, Georgia,
Circassia, and Russia, had been, or were being, desolated
by the army of this Tartar chief, they passed into Egypt and
Bulgaria, whence they spread over all other countries.
Scattered over the face of these countries, they found small
parties of vagrants who were from the same region as themselves, who spoke the same language, and who had in all
probability been drawn away by the same means of armies
returning from the invasion of India. Chingiz Khān
invaded India two centuries before ; his descendant, Tarmah
Shirin, invaded India in 1303, and must have taken back
with him multitudes of captives. The unhappy prisoners
of Taimūr the Lame gathered round these nuclei as the
only people who could understand or sympathize with them.
From his sixth expedition into India Mahmūd is said to
have carried back with him to Ghaznih two hundred
thousand Hindoo captives in a state of slavery, A.D. 1011.
From his seventh expedition in 1017, his army of one
hundred and forty thousand fighting men returned
" laden with Hindoo captives, who became so cheap, that
a Hindoo slave was valued at less than two rupees."
Mahmūd made several expeditions to the west immediately
after his return from India, in the same manner as Taimūr
did after him, and he may in the same manner have
scattered his Indian captives. They adopted the habits of
their new friends, which are indeed those of all the vagrant
tribes of India, and they have continued to preserve them
to the present day. I have compared their vocabularies
with those of India, and find so many of the words the
same that I think a native of India would, even in the
present day, be able without much difficulty to make himself understood by a gang of gipsies in any part of
Europe.[1]

---

[1] It is impossible within the limits of a note to discuss the problem
of the origin of the gipsies. Much has been written about it, though
nothing quite satisfactory. The gipsy, or Romany, language is certainly closely related to, though not derived from, the existing languages

A good Christian may not be able exactly to understand the nature of the merit which Tamerlane expected to acquire from sending so many unoffending Chinese to the abyss of hell. According to the Muhammadan creed, God has vowed " to fill hell chock full of men and genii." Hence his reasons for *hardening* their hearts against that faith in the Korān which might send them to heaven, and which would, they think, necessarily follow an impartial examination of the evidence of its divinity and certainty. Taimūr thought, no doubt, that it would be very meritorious on his part to assist God in this his labour of filling the great abyss by throwing into it all the existing population of China : while he spread over their land in pastoral tribes the goodly seed of Muhammadanism, which would give him a rich supply of recruits for paradise.

The following dialogue took place one day between me and the " muftī," or head Muhammadan law officer, of one of our regulation courts.[1]

" Does it not seem to you strange, Muftī Sahib, that your prophet, who, according to your notions, must have been so well acquainted with the universe and the laws that govern it, should not have revealed to his followers some great truths hitherto unknown regarding these laws, which might have commanded their belief, and that of all future generations, in his divine mission ? "

of Northern India. Some of the forms are very archaic. A vocabulary of it has been published by Mr. and Mrs. Grierson in the *Indian Antiquary.* The author's theory does not tally with all the facts. Gipsies existed in Persia and Europe long before Taimūr's time. They certainly did not come through Egypt. The article in the 9th edition of the *Encyclopædia Britannica* gives a readable summary of the various opinions on their origin.

[1] Before the Codes were passed (1859–1861) the criminal law administered in India was, in the main, that of the Muhammadans, and each judge's court had a Muhammadan law officer attached, who pronounced a " fatwa," or decision, intimating the law applicable to the case, and the penalty which might be inflicted. Several examples of these " fatwas " will be found among the papers bound up with the author's " Ramaseeana."

" Not at all," said the Mufti; "they would probably not have understood him ; and if they had, those who did not believe in what he did actually reveal to them, would not have believed in him had he revealed *all* the laws that govern the universe."

" And why should they not have believed in him ? "

" Because what he revealed was sufficient to convince all men whose hearts had not been hardened in unbelief. God said, ' As for the unbelievers, it is the same with them whether you admonish them or do not admonish them ; they will not believe. God hath sealed up their hearts, their ears, and their eyes ; and a grievous punishment awaits them.' "[1]

" And why were the hearts of any men thus hardened to unbelief, when by unbelief they were to incur such dreadful penalties ? "

" Because they were otherwise wicked men."

" But you think, of course, that there was really much of good in the revelations of your prophet ? "

" Of course we do."

" And that those who believed in it were likely to become better men for their faith ? "

" Assuredly."

" Then why harden the hearts of even bad men against a faith that might make them good ? "

" Has not God said, ' If we had pleased, we had certainly given unto every soul its direction ; but the word which hath proceeded from me must necessarily be fulfilled when I said, *Verily, I will fill hell with men and genii altogether.*[2] And again, ' Had it pleased the Lord he would have made all men of one religion ; but they shall not cease to differ among them, unless those on whom the Lord shall have mercy ; and unto this hath he created

---

[1] See Korān, chap. ii. [W. H. S.]   The passage is the second sentence in chap. ii.   The wording, as quoted, differs slightly from Sale's version.

[2] See Korān, chap. xxxii. [W. H. S.]

them; for the word of thy Lord shall be fulfilled when he said, *Verily, I will fill hell altogether with genii and men.*"[1]

"You all believe that the devil, like all the angels, was made of fire?"

"Yes."

"And that he was doomed to hell because he would not fall down and worship Adam, who was made of clay?"

"Yes, God commanded him to bow down to Adam; and when he did not do as he was bid, God said, 'Why, Iblīs, what hindered thee from bowing down to Adam as the other angels did?' He replied, 'It is not fit that I should worship man, whom thou hast formed of dried clay, or black mud.' God said, 'Get thee, therefore, hence, for thou shalt be pelted with stones; and a curse shall be upon thee till the day of judgment.' The devil said, 'O Lord, give me respite unto the day of resurrection.' God said, 'Verily, thou shalt be respited until the appointed time.'"[2]

"And does it not appear to you, Muftī Sāhib, that in respiting the devil Iblīs till the day of resurrection, some injustice was done to the children of Adam?"

"How?"

"Because he replies, 'O Lord, because thou hast seduced me, I will surely tempt men to disobedience in the earth.'"

"No, sir, because he could only tempt those who were *predestined* to go astray, for he adds, 'I will seduce all, except such of them as shall be *thy chosen servants.*' God said, 'This is the right way with me. Verily, as to my servants, thou shalt have no power over them; but over those only who shall be seduced, and who shall follow thee; and hell is surely denounced to them all.'"[3]

---

[1] *Ibid.* chap. xi. [W. H. S.] Sale's version, with trifling verbal differences. The "muftī's" reasoning has been heard in Europe.

[2] See Korān, chap. xv. [W. H. S.] Sale's version, with modifications.

[3] "This is a revelation of the most mighty, the merciful God; that

"Then you think, Mufti Sāhib, that the devil could seduce only such as were predestined to go astray, and who would have gone astray whether he, the devil, had been respited or not?"

"Certainly I do."

"Does it not then appear to you that it is as unjust to predestine men to do that for which they are to be sent to hell, as it would be to leave them all unguided to the temptations of the devil?"

"These are difficult questions," replied the Mufti, "which we cannot venture to ask even ourselves. All that we can do is to endeavour to understand what is written in the holy book, and act according to it. God made us all, and he has the right to do what he pleases with what he has made; the potter makes two vessels, he dashes the one on the ground, but the other he sells to stand in the palaces of princes."

"But a pot has no soul, Mufti Sāhib, to be roasted to all eternity in hell!"

"True, sir; these are questions beyond the reach of human understanding."

"How often do you read over the Korān?"

"I read the whole over about three times a month," replied the Mufti.[1]

I mentioned this conversation one day to the Nawāb Ali-ud-dīn,[2] a most estimable old gentleman of seventy years

thou mayest warn a people whose fathers were not warned, and who live in negligence. Our sentence hath justly been pronounced against the greater part of them, wherefore they shall not believe. It shall be equal unto them whether thou preach unto them, or do not preach unto them; they shall not believe." Korān, chap. xxxvi. [W. H. S.] From beginning of the chapter. Sale's version; a sentence being omitted between "believe" and "It shall."

[1] I have never met another man so thoroughly master of the Korān as the Mufti, and yet he had the reputation of being a very corrupt man in his office. [W. H. S.]

[2] Aleeoodeen; an unusual name; perhaps a misprint for Alā-ud-dīn.

of age, who resides at Murādābād, and asked him whether he did not think it a singular omission on the part of Muhammad, after his journey to heaven, not to tell mankind some of the truths that have since been discovered regarding the nature of the bodies that fill these heavens, and the laws that govern their motions. Mankind could not, either from the Korān, or from the traditions, perceive that he was at all aware of the errors of the system of astronomy that prevailed in his day, and among his people."

"Not at all," replied the Nawāb; "the prophets had, no doubt, abundant opportunities of becoming acquainted with the heavenly bodies, and the laws which govern them, particularly those who, like Muhammad, had been up through the seven heavens; but their thoughts were so entirely taken up with the Deity that they probably never noticed the objects by which he was surrounded; and if they had noticed them, they would not, perhaps, have thought it necessary to say anything about them. Their object was to direct men's thoughts towards God and his commandments, and to instruct them in their duties towards him and towards each other."

"Suppose," continued the Nawāb, "you were to be invited to see and converse with even your earthly sovereign, would not your thoughts be too much taken up with him to admit of your giving, on your return, an account of the things you saw about him? I have been several times to see you, and I declare that I have been so much taken up with the conversations which have passed, that I have never noticed the many articles I now see around me, nor could I have told any one on my return home what I had seen in your room—the wall-shades, the pictures, the sofas, the tables, the book-cases," continued he, casting his eyes round the room, "all escaped my notice, and might have escaped it had my eyes been younger and stronger than they are. What then must have been the state of mind of those great prophets, who were admitted to see and converse with

the great Creator of the universe, and were sent by him to
instruct mankind ? "

I told my old friend that I thought his answer the best
that could be given ; but still, that we could not help thinking that if Muhammad had really been acquainted with the
nature of the heavenly bodies, and the laws which govern
them, he would have taken advantage of his knowledge to
secure more firmly their faith in his mission, and have
explained to them the real state of the case, instead of
talking about the stars as merely made to be thrown at
devils, to give light to men upon this little globe of ours,
and to guide them in their wanderings upon it by sea
and land.

"But what," said the Nawāb, "are the great truths
that you would have had our holy prophet to teach
mankind ? "

"Why, Nawāb Sāhib, I would have had him tell us,
amongst other things, of that law which makes this our
globe and the other planets revolve round the sun, and
their moons around them. I would have had him
teach us something of the nature of the things we
call comets, or stars with large tails, and of that of
the fixed stars, which we suppose to be suns, like
our sun, with planets revolving round them like ours,
since it is clear that they do not borrow their light
from our sun, nor from anything that we can discover in
the heavens. I would also have had him tell us the
nature of that white belt which crosses the sky, which
you call the ovarious belt, 'Khatt-i-abyāz,' and we the
milky way, and which we consider to be a collection of
self-lighted stars; while many orthodox but unlettered
Musalmāns think it the marks made in the sky by
'Borak,' the rough-shod donkey, on which your prophet
rode from Jerusalem to heaven. And you think, Nawāb
Sāhib, that there was quite evidence enough to satisfy any
person whose heart had not been hardened to unbelief ?
and that no description of the heavenly bodies, or of the

laws which govern their motion, could have had any influence on the minds of such people ? " [1]

"Assuredly I do, sir ! Has not God said, ' If we should
open a gate in the heavens above them, and they should
ascend thereto all the day long, they would surely say, our
eyes are only dazzled, or rather we are a people deluded by
enchantments.' [2]   Do you think, sir, that anything which
his majesty Moses could have said about the planets, and
the comets, and the milky way, would have tended so much
to persuade the children of Israel of his divine mission as
did the single stroke of his rod, which brought a river of
delicious water gushing from a dry rock when they were all
dying from thirst ?   When our holy prophet," continued
the Nawāb (placing the points of the four fingers of his
right hand on the table), placed his blessed hand thus on
the ground, and caused four streams to gush out from the
dug plain, and supply with fresh water the whole army
which was perishing from thirst ; and when out of only *five
small dates* he afterwards feasted this immense army till
they could eat no more, he surely did more to convince his
followers of his divine mission than he could have done by
any discourse about the planets, and the milky way (Khatt-
i-abyāz)."

"No doubt, Nawāb Sāhib, these were very powerful
arguments for those who saw them, or believed them to
have been seen ; and those who doubt the divinity of your

---

[1] The 17th chapter of the Korān opens with the words, " Praise be
unto him who transported his servant by night from the sacred
temple of Mecca to the farther temple of Jerusalem," "from whence,"
as Sale observes, "he was carried through the seven heavens to the
presence of God, and brought back again to Mecca the same night."
The commentators dispute whether the journey to heaven was cor-
poreally performed, or merely in a vision.   "But the received opinion
is that it was no vision, but that he was actually transported in the
body to his journey's end ; and if any impossibility be objected, they
think it a sufficient answer to say that it might easily be effected by an
omnipotent agent."

[2] See Korān, chap. xv. [W. H. S.]

prophet's mission are those who doubt their ever having been seen."

"The whole army saw and attested them, sir, and that is evidence enough for us; and those who saw them, and were not satisfied, must have had their hearts hardened to unbelief."

"And you think, Nawāb Sāhib, that a man is not master of his own belief or disbelief in religious matters; though he is rewarded by an eternity of bliss in paradise for the one, and punished by an eternity of scorching in hell for the other?"

"I do, sir, faith is a matter of feeling; and over our feelings we have no control. All that we can do is to prevent their influencing our actions, when these actions would be mischievous. I have a desire to stretch out this arm, and crush that fly on the table. I can control the act, and do so; but the desire is not under my control."

"True, Nawāb Sāhib; and in this life we punish men not for their feelings, which are beyond their control, but for their acts, over which they have control; and we are apt to think that the Deity will do the same."

"There are, sir," continued the Nawāb, "three kinds of certainty—the moral certainty, the mathematical, and the religious certainty, which we hold to be the greatest of al —the one in which the mind feels entire repose. This repose I feel in everything that is written in the Korān, in the Bible, and, with the few known exceptions, in the New Testament.[1] We do not believe that Christ was the son of God, though we believe him to have been a great prophet sent down to enlighten mankind; nor do we believe that he was crucified. We believe that the wicked Jews got hold of a thief, and crucified him in the belief that he was the Christ; but the real Christ was, we think, taken up into heaven, and not suffered to be crucified."

---

[1] The Muhammadans believe that the Christians have tampered with the Scriptures.

" But, Nawāb Sāhib, the Sikhs have their book, in which they have the same faith."

" True, sir, but the Sikhs are unlettered, ignorant brutes ; and you do not, I hope, call their ' Granth ' a book—a thing written only the other day, and full of nonsense.   No ' book ' has appeared since the Korān came down from heaven ; nor will any other come till the day of judgment.   And how," said the Nawāb, " have people in modern days made all the discoveries you speak of in astronomy ? "

" Chiefly, Nawāb Sāhib, by means of the telescope, which is an instrument of modern invention."

" And do you suppose, sir, that I would put the evidence of your ' dūrbins ' (telescopes) in opposition to that of the holy prophet ?   No, sir, depend upon it that there is much fallacy in a telescope—it is not to be relied upon.   I have conversed with many excellent European gentlemen, and their great fault appears to me to lie in the implicit faith they put in these *telescopes*—they hold their evidence above that of the prophets, Moses, Abraham, and Elijah.   It is dreadful to think how much mischief these telescopes may do.   No, sir, let us hold fast by the prophets ; what they tell us is the truth, and the only truth that we can entirely rely upon in this life.   I would not hold the evidence of all the telescopes in the world as anything against one word uttered by the humblest of the prophets named in the Old or New Testament, or the holy Korān.   The prophets, sir, keep to the prophets, and throw aside your telescopes— there is no truth in them ; some of them turn people upside down, and make them walk upon their heads ; and yet you put their evidence against that of the prophets."[1]

Nothing that I could say would, after this, convince the Nawāb that there was any virtue in telescopes ; his religious

[1] It would be difficult to give more vivid expression to the eternal conflict between the theological and the scientific spirit.   Compare the remarks *ante*, Vol. I, p. 215*n.*, on the attitude of Hindoos towards modern science.

feeling had been greatly excited against them; and had
Galileo, Tycho Brahe, Kepler, Newton, Laplace, and the
Herschels, all been present to defend them, they would not
have altered his opinion of their demerits. The old man has, I
believe, a shrewd suspicion that they are inventions of the
devil to lead men from the right way; and were he told all
that these great men have discovered through their means,
he would be very much disposed to believe that they were
incarnations of his satanic majesty playing over again with
" dūrbins ". (telescopes) the same game which the serpent
played with the apple in the garden of Eden.

> Solicit not thy thoughts with matters hid ;
> Leave them to God above : him serve and fear ;
> Of other creatures, as him pleases best,
> Wherever placed, let him dispose : joy thou
> In what he gives to thee, this Paradise
> And thy fair Eve : heaven is for thee too high
> To know what passes there : be lowly wise :
> Think only what concerns thee, and thy being :
> Dream not of other worlds, what creatures there
> Live, in what state, condition, or degree :
> Contented that thus far hath been revealed,
> Not of earth only, but of highest heaven."[1]

[1] *Paradise Lost*, Book viii. [W. H. S.]   Line 167 ; from Raphael's
address to Adam.

CHAPTER XIV[1]

Indian Police—Its Defects—and their Cause and Remedy.

On the 26th[2] we crossed the river Jumna, over a bridge of boats, kept up by the King of Oudh for the use of the public, though his majesty is now connected with Delhi only by the tomb of his ancestor ;[3] and his territories are separated from the imperial city by the two great rivers, Ganges and Jumna.

We proceeded to Farrukhnagar, about twelve miles over an execrable road running over a flat but rugged surface of unproductive soil.[4] India is, perhaps, the only civilized country in the world where a great city could be approached by such a road from the largest military station in the empire,[5] not more than three stages distant. After breakfast the head native police officer of the division came to pay his respects. He talked of the dreadful murders which used to be perpetrated in this neighbourhood by miscreants,

[1] Chapter XXI of Vol. II of original edition.

[2] January, 1836.

[3] The tomb of Safdar Jang, or Mansūr Ali Khān, described *ante,* Vol. II, p. 163. The bridges over the Jumna are now, of course maintained by Government and the railway companies.

[4] The main highways approaching Delhi are now excellent metalled roads.

[5] By the term "the largest military station in the empire," the author means Meerut. At present the largest military station in Northern India is, I believe, Rāwal Pindi, and the combined cantonments of Secunderābād and Bolarum in the Nizam's dominions constitute the largest military station in the empire.

who found shelter in the territories of the Bēgam Samrū,[1] whither his followers dared not hunt for them; and mentioned a case of nine persons who had been murdered just within the boundary of our territories about seven years before, and thrown into a dry well. He was present at the inquest held on their bodies, and described their appearance; and I found that they were the bodies of a news writer from Lahore, who, with his eight companions, had been murdered by Thugs on his way back to Rohilkhand. I had long before been made acquainted with the circumstances of this murder, and the perpetrators had all been secured, but we wanted this link in the chain of evidence. It had been described to me as having taken place within the boundary of the Bēgam's territory, and I applied to her for a report on the inquest. She declared that no bodies had been discovered about the time mentioned; and I concluded that the ignorance of the people of the neighbourhood was pretended, as usual in such cases, with a view to avoid a summons to give evidence in our courts. I referred forthwith to the magistrate of the district, and found the report that I wanted, and thereby completed the ~~chain~~ of evidence upon a very important case. The Thānadār seemed much surprised to find that I was so well acquainted with the circumstances of this murder, but still more that the perpetrators were not the poor old Bēgam's subjects, but our own.

The police officers employed on our borders find it very convenient to trace the perpetrators of all murders and gang robberies into the territories of native chiefs, whose subjects they accuse often when they know that the crimes have been committed by our own. They are, on the one hand, afraid to seize or accuse the real offenders, lest they should avenge themselves by some personal violence, or by thefts or robberies, which they often commit with a view to

---

[1] Comprising parts of the Meerut and Muzaffarnagar districts of the North-Western Provinces. The Bēgam's history will be discussed in Chapter XX, *post.*

get them turned out of office as inefficient; and, on the other, they are tempted to conceal the real offenders by a liberal share of the spoil, and a promise of not offending again within *their beat.* Their tenure of office is far too insecure, and their salaries are far too small. They are often dismissed summarily by the magistrate if they send him in no prisoners; and also if they send in to him prisoners who are not ultimately convicted, because a magistrate's merits are too often estimated by the proportion that his convictions bear to his acquittals among the prisoners committed for trial to the Sessions. Men are often ultimately acquitted for want of judicial proof, when there is abundance of that moral proof on which a police officer or magistrate has to act in the discharge of his duties; and in a country where gangs of professional and hereditary robbers and murderers extend their depredations into very remote parts, and seldom commit them in the districts in which they reside, the most vigilant police officer must often fail to discover the perpetrators of heavy crimes that take place within his range.[1]

When they cannot find them, the native officers either seize innocent persons, and frighten them into confession, or else they try to conceal the crime, and in this they are seconded by the sufferers in the robbery, who will always avoid, if they can, a prosecution in our courts, and by their neighbours, who dread being summoned to give evidence as a serious calamity. The man who has been robbed, instead of being an object of compassion among his neighbours, often incurs their resentment for subjecting them to this calamity; and they not only pay largely themselves, but make him pay largely to have his losses concealed from the magistrate. Formerly, when a district

---

[1] The members of the reformed police force, constituted under Act V. of 1861, generally on the model of the Royal Irish Constabulary, have no reason to complain of insecurity of tenure. It is now very difficult to obtain sanction to the dismissal of a corrupt or inefficient officer, unless he has been judicially convicted of a statutory offence.

was visited by a judge of circuit to hold his sessions only
once or twice a year, and men were constantly bound over
to prosecute and appear as evidence from sessions to
sessions, till they were wearied and worried to death, this
evil was much greater than at present, when every district
is provided with its judge of sessions, who is, or ought to
be, always ready to take up the cases committed for trial by
the magistrate.[1] This was one of the best measures of
Lord W. Bentinck's admirable, though much abused,
administration of the government of India.[2] Still, however, the inconvenience and delay of prosecution in our
courts are so great, and the chance of the ultimate conviction of great offenders is so small that strong temptations
are held out to the police to conceal or misrepresent the
character of crimes ; and they must have a great feeling of
security in their tenure of office, and more adequate

---

[1] Ordinarily there is for each district, or administrative unit, a separate
Sessions and District Judge, who tries both civil and criminal cases of
the more serious kind. Occasionally two or three districts have only
one judge between them, who is then usually very much in arrear with
his work. Sessions for the trial of serious criminal cases are held
monthly, bimonthly, or quarterly, according to circumstances. In
some districts, and for some classes of cases, the jury system has been
introduced, but, as a rule, in Northern India the responsibility rests
with the judge alone, who receives some slight aid from assessors.
Capital sentences passed by a Sessions Judge must be confirmed by two
Judges of a High Court.

[2] The historian Thornton (chapter xxvii) went so far as to declare
that Lord William Bentinck has "done less for the interest of
India, and for his own reputation, than any who had occupied his
place since the commencement of the nineteenth century, with the
single exception of Sir George Barlow." The abolition of widow-
burning is the only act of the Bentinck administration which this
writer could praise. Such a criticism is manifestly unjust, the out-
come of contemporary anger and prejudice. The inscription written
by Macaulay, the friend and coadjutor of Lord William, and placed
on the statue of the reforming Governor-General in Calcutta, does not
give undeserved praise to the much-abused statesman. Sir William
Sleeman so much admired Lord William Bentinck, and formed such a
favourable estimate of the merits of his government, that it may be

salaries, better chances of rising, and better supervision over them, before they will resist such temptation. These Thānadārs, and all the public officers under them, are all so very inadequately paid that corruption among them excites no feeling of odium or indignation in the minds of those among whom they live and serve. Such feelings are rather directed against the government that places them in such situations of so much labour and responsibility with salaries so inadequate; and thereby confers upon them virtually a license to pay themselves by preying upon those whom they are employed ostensibly to protect. They know that with such salaries they can never have the reputation of being honest, however faithfully they may discharge their duties; and it is too hard to expect that men will long submit to the necessity of being thought corrupt, without reaping some of the advantages of cor-

well to support his opinion by that of Macaulay. The text of the inscription is :—

TO

WILLIAM CAVENDISH BENTINCK,

who during seven years ruled India with eminent prudence, integrity,
and benevolence;
who, placed at the head of a great Empire, never laid aside the simplicity and moderation of a private citizen;
who infused into Oriental despotism the spirit of British freedom; who
never forgot that the end of Government is
the happiness of the governed;
who abolished cruel rites;
who effaced humiliating distinctions;
who gave liberty to the expression of public opinion;
whose constant study it was to elevate the intellectual and
moral character of the nation committed to his charge,

THIS MONUMENT

was erected by men
who, differing in race, in manners, in language, and in religion,
cherish with equal veneration and gratitude
the memory of his wise, reforming, and paternal administration.

(*Lord William Bentinck*, by D. Boulger, p. 203; "Rulers of India" series.)

ruption.   Let the Thānadārs have everywhere such salaries as will enable them to maintain their families in comfort, and keep up that appearance of respectability which their station in society demands ; and over every three or four Thānadārs' jurisdiction let there be an officer appointed upon a higher scale of salary, to supervise and control their proceedings, and armed with powers to decide minor offences.   To these higher stations the Thānadārs will be able to look forward as their reward for a faithful and zealous discharge of their duties.[1]

He who can suppose that men so inadequately paid, who have no promotion to look forward to, and feel no security in their tenure of office, and consequently no hope of a provision for old age,[2] will be zealous and honest in the discharge of their duties, must be very imperfectly acquainted with human nature, and with the motives by which men are influenced in all quarters of the world ; but we are none of us so ignorant, for we all know that the same motives actuate public servants in India as elsewhere. We have acted successfully upon this knowledge in the scale of salaries and gradation of rank assigned to European civil functionaries, and to all native functionaries employed in the judicial and revenue branches of the public service ; and why not act upon it in that of the salaries assigned to the native officers employed in the police ?   The magistrate of a district gets a salary of from two thousand to two thousand five hundred rupees a month.[3]

---

[1] An European District Superintendent of Police, under the general supervision of the Magistrate of the District, now commands the police of each district, and frequently has one or two European Assistants.   He is also aided by well-paid Inspectors, who are for the most part natives.   Measures have recently been taken, especially in the North-Western Provinces and Oudh, to improve the pay, training, and position of the police force, European and native.

[2] Police officers and men now obtain pensions, like public servants in other departments.

[3] In some provinces the highest salaries of magistrates are very much lower than the rates stated by the author, which are the highest paid

The native officer next under him is the Thānadār, or head native police officer of a subdivision of his district, containing many towns and villages, with a population of a hundred thousand souls. This officer gets a salary of twenty-five rupees a month. He cannot possibly do his duty unless he keeps one or two horses ; indeed, he is told by the magistrate that he cannot ; and that he must have one or two horses, or resign his post. The people, seeing how much we expect from the Thānadār, and how little we give him, submit to his demands for contributions without murmuring, and consider almost any demand trivial from a man so employed and so paid. They are confounded at our inconsistency, and say, " We see you giving high salaries, and high prospects of advancement to men who have nothing to do but collect your rents, and decide our disputes about pounds, shillings, and pence, which we used to decide much better ourselves, when we had no other court but that of our elders—while those who are to protect life and property, to keep peace over the land, and enable the industrious to work in security, maintain their families, and pay the government revenue, are left with hardly any pay at all."

There is really nothing in our rule in India which strikes the people so much as this inconsistency, the evil effects of which are so great and manifest ; the only way to remedy the evil is to give a greater feeling of security in the tenure of office, a higher rate of salary, the hope of a provision for old age, and, above all, the gradation of rank, by interposing the officers I speak of between the Thānadārs and the magistrate.[1] This has all been done in the establish-

to the most senior officers in certain provinces ; and, in all provinces, officiating incumbents, who form a large proportion of the officers employed, draw only a part of the full salary. The fall in exchange has enormously reduced the real value of all Indian salaries.

[1] Another popular view of this subject, and, I think, the one more commonly taken, is expressed in the anecdote told *ante*, p. 58 of this volume. Well-paid Inspectors of Police drawing salaries of 150 to 200 rupees a month are often extremely corrupt, and retire with large

ments for the collection of the revenue, and administration of civil justice.

Hobbes, in his *Leviathan*, says, " And seeing that the end of punishment is not revenge and discharge of choler, but correction, either of the offender, or of others by his example, the severest punishments are to be inflicted for those crimes that are of most danger to the public; such as are those which proceed from malice to the government established; those that spring from contempt of justice; those that provoke indignation in the multitude; and those which, unpunished, seem authorized, as when they are committed by sons, servants, or favourites of men in authority.[1] For indignation carrieth men, not only against the actors and authors of injustice, but against all power that is likely to protect them; as in the case of Tarquin, when, for the insolent act of one of his sons, he was driven out of Rome, and the monarchy itself dissolved." (Para. 2, chap. xxx.) Almost every one of our Thānadārs is, in his way, a little Tarquin, exciting the indignation of the people against his rulers; and no time should be lost in converting him into something better.

By the obstacles which are still everywhere opposed to the conviction of offenders, in the distance of our courts, the forms of procedure, and other causes of "the law's delay," we render the duties of our police establishment everywhere " more honoured in the breach than the observance," by the mass of the people among whom they are placed. We must, as I have before said, remove some of these obstacles to the successful prosecution of offenders in our criminal courts, which tend so much to deprive the government of all popular aid and support in the administration of justice; and to convert all our police establishments into instruments of oppression, instead of what they

fortunes. I know many cases, but could never obtain judicial proof of one.

[1] When "sons, servants, or favourites of men in authority," in India, no longer oppress their fellows, the millennium will have arrived.

should be, the efficient means of protection to the persons, property, and character of the innocent. Crimes multiply from the assurance the guilty are everywhere apt to feel of impunity to crime; and the more crimes multiply, the greater is the aversion the people everywhere feel to aid the government in the arrest and conviction of criminals; because they see more and more the innocent punished by attendance upon distant courts at great cost and inconvenience, to give evidence upon points, which seem to them unimportant, while the guilty escape owing to technical difficulties which they can never understand.[1]

The best way to remove these obstacles is to interpose officers between the Thānadār and the magistrate, and arm them with judicial powers to try minor cases, leaving an appeal open to the magistrate and to extend the final jurisdiction of the magistrate to a greater range of crimes, though it should involve the necessity of reducing the measure of punishment annexed to them.[2] Beccaria has justly observed that "Crimes are more effectually prevented by the certainty than by the severity of punishment. The certainty of a small punishment will

[1] It is some slight satisfaction to a zealous magistrate of the present day, when he sees a great and influential criminal escape his just doom, to think that even the best magistrates sixty years ago had to submit to similar painful experiences. India cannot truly be described as an uncivilized or barbarous country, but, side by side with elements of the highest civilization, it contains many elements of primitive and savage barbarism. The savagery of India cannot be dealt with by barristers or moral text-books.

[2] The number of subordinate magistates, paid and unpaid, has of late years been enormously increased, and courts are, consequently, much more numerous than they used to be. The vast increase in facility of communication has also diminished the inconveniences which the author deplores. In Oudh, and some other provinces, which used to be called Non-Regulation, the chief Magistrate of the District has power to try and adequately punish all offences, except capital ones. The power is useful, when the district officer has time to exercise it, which is not always the case. The Government of the North-Western Provinces has lately proposed to confer this power on all the chief magistrates of Districts within its jurisdiction.

make a stronger impression than the fear of one more severe, if attended with the hope of escaping ; for it is the nature of mankind to be terrified at the approach of the smallest inevitable evil ; whilst hope, the best gift of Heaven, has the power of dispelling the apprehensions of a greater, especially if supported by examples of impunity, which weakness or avarice too frequently affords."

I ought to have mentioned that the police of a district, in our Bengal territories, consists of a magistrate, and his assistant, who are European gentlemen of the Civil Service ; and a certain number of Thānadārs, from twelve to sixteen, who preside over the different sub-divisions of the district in which they reside with their establishments. These Thānadārs get twenty-five rupees a month, have under them four or five Jemadārs upon eight rupees, and thirty or forty Barkandāzes upon four rupees a month. The Jemadārs are, most of them, placed in charge of " nākas," or sub-divisions of the Thānadār's jurisdiction, the rest are kept at their headquarters, ready to move to any point where their services may be required. These are all paid by government ; but there is in each village one watchman, and in larger villages more than one, who are appointed by the heads of villages, and paid by the communities, and required daily or periodically to report all the police matters of their villages to the Thānadārs.[1]

The distance between the magistrates and Thānadārs is at present immeasurable ; and an infinite deal of mischief is done by the latter and those under them, of which the

[1] There is a Superintendent of Police for the Province of Bengal ; but in the North-Western Provinces his duties are divided among the Commissioners of Revenue. [W. H. S.] By " Superintendent of Police " the author means the high officer now called the Inspector-General of Police. Under the present system each Local Government or Administration has one of these officers, who is aided by one or more staff officers as Assistant-Inspectors-General. The Commissioners in the North-Western Provinces have been relieved of police duties. The organization of police stations has been much modified since the author's time.

magistrates know nothing whatever. In the first place, they levy a fee of one rupee from every village at the festival of the Holi in February, and another at that of the Dasehra in October, and in each Thānadār's jurisdiction there are from one to two hundred villages. These and numerous other unauthorized exactions they share with those under them, and with the native officers about the person of the magistrate, who, if not conciliated, can always manage to make them appear unfit for their places.[1]

A robbery affords a rich harvest. Some article of stolen property is found in one man's house, and by a little legerdemain it is conveyed to that of another, both of whom are made to pay liberally; the man robbed also pays, and all the members of the village community are made to do the same. They are all called to the court of the Thānadār to give evidence, as to what they have seen or heard regarding either the fact, or the persons in the remotest degree connected with it—as to the arrests of the supposed offenders— the search of their house—the character of their grandmothers and grandfathers—and they are told that they are to be sent to the magistrate a hundred miles distant, and then made to stand at the door among a hundred and fifty pairs of shoes, till *his excellency* the Nāzir, the under-sheriff of the court, may be pleased to announce them to his highness the magistrate, which, of course, he will not do without a *consideration*. To escape all these threatened evils, they pay handsomely and depart in peace. The Thānadār reports that an attempt to rob a house by persons unknown had been defeated by his exertions, and the *good fortune* of the magistrate; and sends a liberal share of spoil to those who are to read his report to that

[1] All these practices are still carried on; and experienced magistrates are well aware of their existence, though powerless to stop them. People will often give private information of malpractices, but will hardly ever come into court, and speak out openly, and a magistrate cannot take action on statements which the makers will not submit to cross-examination.

functionary.[1] This goes on more or less in every district,
but more especially in those where the magistrate happens
to be a man of violent temper, who is always surrounded
by knaves, because men who have any regard for their
character will not approach him—or a weak, good-natured
man, easily made to believe anything, and managed by
favourites—or one too fond of field-sports, or of music,
painting, European languages, literature, and sciences, or
lastly, of his own ease.[2] Some magistrates think they can
put down crime by dismissing the Thānadār; but this

---

[1] This is still a favourite trick. Every year Inspectors-General of
Police and Secretaries to Government make the same sarcastic remarks about the wonderful number of "attempts at burglary," and the
apparent contentment of the criminal classes with the small results of
their labours. But the Thānadār is too much for even Inspectors-
General and Secretaries to Government. No amount of reorganiza-
tion changes him.

[2] Mr. R., when appointed magistrate of the district of Fathpur on
the Ganges, had a wish to translate the "Henriade," and, in order to
secure leisure, he issued a proclamation to all the Thānadārs of his
district to put down crime, declaring that he would hold them responsible for what might be committed, and dismiss from his situation
every one who should suffer any to be committed within his charge.
This district lying on the borders of Oudh, had been noted for the
number and atrocious character of its crimes. From that day all the
periodical returns went up to the superior court blank—not a crime
was reported. Astonished at this sudden result of the change of
magistrates, the superior court of Calcutta (the Sadr Nizāmat Adālat)
requested one of the judges, who was about to pass through the district on his way down, to inquire into the nature of the system which
seemed to work so well, with a view to its adoption in other districts.
He found crimes were more abundant than ever ; and the Thānadārs
showed him the proclamation, which had been understood, as all such
proclamations are, not as enjoining vigilance in the prosecution of
crime, but as prohibiting all *report* of them, so as to *save the magistrate
trouble*, and get him a good name with his superiors. [W. H. S.]

Great caution should always be used by local officers in making com-
ments on statistics. The native subordinate cares nothing for the facts.
When a superior objects that the birth-rate is too low, and the death-rate
too high in any police circle, the practical conclusion drawn by the police
is that the figures of the next return must be made more palatable, and

tends only to prevent crimes being reported to him ; for in such cases the feelings of the people are in exact accordance with the interests of the Thānadārs ; and crimes augment by the assurance of impunnity thereby given to criminals. The only remedy for all this evil is to fill up the great gulf between the magistrate and Thānadār by officers who shall be to him what I have described the patrol officers to be to the collectors of customs, at once the *tapis* of Prince Husain, and the *telescope* of Prince Ali —a medium that will enable him to be everywhere, and see everything.[1]   And why is this remedy not applied ? Simply and solely because such appointments would be given to the uncovenanted, and might tend indirectly to diminish the appointments open to the covenanted servants of the company.   Young gentlemen of the Civil Service are supposed to be doing the duties which would be assigned to such officers, while they are at school as assistants to magistrates and collectors ; and were this great gulf filled up by efficient uncovenanted officers, they would have no school to go to.   There is no doubt some truth in this ; but the welfare of a whole people should not be sacrificed to keep this school or play-ground open exclusively for them ; let them act for a time as they would unwillingly do with the uncovenanted, and they will learn much more

they are cooked accordingly. So, if burglaries are too numerous, they cease to be reported, and so forth.

The old Supreme Court was known as the Sadr Nizāmat Adālat, on the criminal, and as the Sadr Dīwānī Adālat, on the civil side. These courts have now been replaced by the High Courts.   In the author's time the High Court for the North-Western Provinces had not yet been established.   Its seat is now at Allahabad, but was formerly at Agra.

[1] The gap has been filled up by numbers of Deputy Magistrates, Tahsīldārs, etc., invested with magisterial powers, Honorary Magistrates, District Superintendents, and Inspectors, and yet all the old games still go on merrily.   The reason is that the character of the people has not changed.   The police must have the power to arrest, and this power, when wielded by unscrupulous hands, must always be formidable.

than if they occupied the ground exclusively and acted alone—they will be always with people ready and willing to tell them the real state of things ; whereas, at present, they are always with those who studiously conceal it from them.[1]

It is a common practice with Thānadārs all over the country to connive at the residence within their jurisdiction of gangs of robbers, on the condition that they shall not rob within those limits, and shall give them a share of what they bring back from their distant expeditions.

They [scil. the gangs] go out ostensibly in search of service, on the termination of the rains of one season in October, and return before the commencement of the next in June ; but their vocation is always well known to the police, and to all the people of their neighbourhood, and very often to the magistrates themselves, who could, if they would, secure them on their return with their booty ; but this would not secure their conviction unless the proprietors could be discovered, which they scarcely ever could. Were the police-officers to seize them, they would be all finally acquitted and released by the judges—the magistrate would get into disrepute with his superiors, by the number of acquittals compared with convictions exhibited in his monthly tables ; and he would vent his spleen upon the poor Thānadār, who would at the same time have incurred the resentment of the robbers ; and between both, he would have no possible chance of escape. He therefore consults his own interest and his own ease by leaving them to carry on their trade of robbery or murder unmolested ; and his master, the magistrate, is well pleased not to be pestered with charges against men whom he has no chance of getting ultimately convicted. It was in this way that so many hundred families of assassins by profession were able for so many generations to reside in the most cultivated and populous

---

[1] A magistrate who can find in his district even one man, official or unofficial, who will tell him " the real state of things," and not merely repeat scandal and malignant gossip, is unusually fortunate.

parts of our territories, and extend their depredations into the remotest parts of India, before our system of operations was brought to bear upon them in 1830. Their profession was perfectly well known to the people of the districts in which they resided, and to the greater part of the police; they murdered not within their own district, and the police of that district cared nothing about what they might do beyond it.[1]

The most respectable native gentleman in the city and district told me one day an amusing instance of the proceedings of a native officer of that district, which occurred about five years ago. " In a village which he had purchased and let in farms, a shopkeeper was one day superintending the cutting of some sugar-cane which he had purchased from a cultivator as it stood. His name was Girdhāri, I think, and the boy who was cutting it for him was the son of a poor man called Madāri. Girdhāri wanted to have the cane cut down as near as he could to the ground, while the boy, to save himself the trouble of stooping, would persist in cutting it a good deal too high up. After admonishing him several times, the shopkeeper gave him a smart clout on the head. The boy, to prevent a repetition, called out, 'Murder! Girdhāri has killed me—Girdhāri has killed me!' His old father, who was at work carrying away the cane at a little distance out of sight, ran off to the village watchman, and, in his anger, told him that Girdhāri had murdered his son. The watchman went as fast as he could to the Thānadār, or head police officer of the division,

1 The Thugs were suppressed because a special organization was devised and directed for the purpose. The ordinary law and methods of procedure are of very little effect against the secret societies known as "criminal tribes." These criminal tribes number hundreds of thousands of persons, and present a problem almost unknown to European experience. The gipsies, who are largely of Indian origin, are, perhaps, the only European example of an hereditary criminal tribe. But they are not sheltered and abetted by the landowners as their brethren in India are. A Bill for dealing with habitual criminals is now pending (April, 1893) before the Indian Legislative Council.

who resided some miles distant.   The Thānadār ordered
off his subordinate officer, the Jemadār, with half a dozen
policemen, to arrange everything for an inquest on the
body, by the time he should reach the place, with all due
pomp.   The Jemadār went to the house of the murderer,
and dismounting, ordered all the shopkeepers of the village,
who were many and respectable, to be forthwith seized, and
bound hand and feet.   'So,' said the Jemadār, 'you have
all been aiding and abetting your friend in the murder of
poor Madāri's only son.'   'May it please your excellency,
we have never heard of any murder.'   'Impudent scoundrels,' roared the Jemadār, 'does not the poor boy lie dead
in the sugar-cane field, and is not his highness the Thānadār
coming to hold an inquest upon it ? and do you take us for
fools enough to believe that any scoundrel among you
would venture to commit a deliberate murder without being
aided and abetted by all the rest ? '   The village watchman
began to feel some apprehension that he had been too
precipitate ; and entreated the Jemadār to go first and see
the body of the boy.   'What do you take us for,' said the
Jemadār, 'a thing without a stomach ?   Do you suppose
that government servants can live and labour on air ?   Are
we to go and examine bodies upon empty stomachs ?   Let
his father take care of the body, and let these murdering
shopkeepers provide us something to eat.'   Nine rupees
worth of sweetmeats, and materials for a feast were forthwith
collected at the expense of the shopkeepers, who stood
bound, and waiting the arrival of his highness the Thānadār,
who was soon after seen approaching majestically upon a
richly caparisoned horse.   'What,' said the Jemadār, 'is
there nobody to go and receive his highness in due form ? '
One of the shopkeepers was untied, and presented with
fifteen rupees by his family, and those of the other shopkeepers.   These he took up and presented to his highness,
who deigned to receive them through one of his train, and
then dismounted and partook of the feast that had been
provided.   'Now,' said his highness, 'we will go and hold

an inquest on the body of the poor boy;' and off moved all the great functionaries of government to the sugar-cane field, with the village watchman leading the way. The father of the boy met them as they entered, and was pointed out by the village watchman. 'Where,' said the Thānadār, 'is your poor boy?' 'There,' said Madārī, 'cutting the canes.' 'How! cutting the canes? Was he not murdered by the shopkeepers?' 'No,' said Madārī, 'he was beaten by Girdhārī, and richly deserved it! I find.' Girdhāri and the boy were called up, and the little urchin said that he called out murder merely to prevent Girdhārī from giving him another clout on the side of the head. His father was then fined nine rupees for giving a false alarm, and Girdhārī fifteen for so unmercifully beating the boy; and they were made to pay on the instant, under the penalty of all being sent off forty miles to the magistrate. Having thus settled this very important affair, his highness the Thānadār walked back to the shop, ordered all the shopkeepers to be set at liberty, smoked his pipe, mounted his horse, and rode home, followed by all his police officers, and well pleased with his day's work."

The farmer of the village soon after made his way to the city, and communicated the circumstances to my old friend, who happened to be on intimate terms with the magistrate.[1] He wrote a polite note to the Thānadār to say that he should never get any rents from his estate if the occupants were liable to such fines as these, and that he should take the earliest opportunity of mentioning them to his friend the magistrate. The Thānadār ascertained that he was really in the habit of visiting the magistrate, and communicating with him freely; and hushed up the matter by causing all, save the expenses of the feast, to be paid back. These are things of daily occurrence in all parts of our dominions, and the Thānadārs are not afraid to play such "fantastic tricks" because all those under and all those

---

[1] The magistrate, of course, was the author.

above them share more or less in the spoil, and are bound
in honour to conceal them from the European magistrate,
whom it is the interest of all to keep in the dark.   They
know that the people will hardly ever complain, from the
great dislike they all have to appear in our courts, particularly, when it is against any of the officers of those courts,
or their friends and creatures in the district police.[1]

When our operations commenced in 1830, these assassins
[*scil.* the Thugs] revelled over every road in India in gangs
of hundreds, without the fear of punishment from divine or
human laws ; but there is not now, I believe, a road in India
infested by them.   That our government has still defects,
and great ones, must be obvious to every one who has
travelled much over India with the requisite qualifications
and disposition to observe ; but I believe that in spite of
all the defects I have noticed above in our police system,
the life, property, and character of the innocent are now
more secure, and, all their advantages more freely enjoyed,
than they ever were under any former government with
whose history we are acquainted, or than they now are
under any native government in India.[2]

Those who think they are not so almost always refer to
the reign of Shāh Jahān, when men like Tavernier
travelled so securely all over India with their bags of diamonds ; but I would ask them whether they think that
the life, property, and character of the innocent could be
anywhere very secure, or their advantages very freely
enjoyed, in a country where a man could do openly with
impunity what the traveller describes to have been done by

[1] These motives all retain their full force, and are unaffected by
Police Commissions and re-organization schemes.   Some people think
that the character of the police will be raised by the employment as
officers of young natives of good family.   I am sorry to say that I have
found these young men to be the worst offenders.   They are more
daring in their misdeeds than the ordinary policeman, and no better in
their morals.

[2] This is quite true ; and it is also true that our police administration
is the weakest part of our system.

the Persian physician of the governor of Allahabad? This governor, being sickly, had in attendance upon him *eleven physicians,* one of whom was a European gentleman of education, Claudius Maille of Bourges.[1] The chief favourite of the eleven was, however, a Persian ; " who one day threw his wife from the top of a battlement to the ground in a fit of jealousy. He thought the fall would kill her, but she had only a few ribs broken ; whereupon the kindred of the woman came and demanded justice at the feet of the governor. The governor, sending for the physician, commanded him to be gone, resolving to retain him no longer in his service. The physician obeyed ; and putting his poor maimed wife in a palankeen, he set forward upon the road with all his family. But he had not gone above three or four days' journey from the city, when the governor, finding himself worse than he was wont to be, sent to recall him ; which the physician perceiving, stabbed his wife, his four children, and thirteen female slaves, and returned again to the governor, who said not a word to him; but entertained him again in his service." This occurred within Tavernier's own knowledge and about the time he visited Allahabad ; and is related as by no means a very extraordinary circumstance.[2]

[1] " M. Claude Maille of Bourges. As we shall see in Book I, chap. xviii, a man of this name, who had escaped from the Dutch service, was, in the year 1652, a not very successful amateur gunfounder for Mīr Jumla ; he had, after his escape, set up as a surgeon to the Nawāb, with an equipment consisting of a case of instruments and a box of ointments which he had stolen from M. Cheteur, the Dutch Ambassador to Golconda. Tavernier throws no light upon his identity with this physician." (Ball's *Tavernier,* vol. i, p. 116, *note.*)

[2] Mr. Ball's version of this horrible story,(vol. i, p. 117) does not differ materially from that quoted in the text. Tavernier does not mention the name of the governor, though he observes that he was " one of the greatest nobles in India." Tavernier visited Allahabad in December, 1665, and then heard the story, the governor concerned being at the time in the fort. I have no doubt that in the reign of Shāh Jahān ordinary offences committed by ordinary criminals were

ruthlessly punished, and to a large extent suppressed.   But, under the best native governments, great men and their dependents have always been able to do pretty much what they pleased.   The English government has the merit of refusing to give formal recognition to difference of rank in criminals, and of often trying to punish influential offenders, though seldom succeeding in the attempt.   From time to time a conspicuous example, like that of the Nawāb Shams-ud-dīn, is made, and a few such examples, combined with the greater vigilance and more complete organization of the English executive, prevent the occurrence of atrocities so great as that described, without a word of comment, by the French traveller.   I have not the slightest doubt, nor has any magistrate of long experience any doubt, that women are frequently made away with quietly in the recesses of the "zanāna."   I have known several such cases, which were notorious, though incapable of judicial proof.   The amount of serious secret crime which occurs in India, and never comes to light, is very considerable.

CHAPTER XV[1]

Rent-free Tenures—Right of Government to Resume such Grants.

ON the 27th[2] we went on fifteen miles to Bēgamābād, over a sandy and level country. All the peasantry along the roads were busy watering their fields ; and the singing of the man who stood at the well to tell the other who guides the bullocks when to pull, after the leather bucket had been filled at the bottom, and when to stop as it reached the top, was extremely pleasing. It is said that Tānsēn of Delhi, the most celebrated singer they have ever had in India, used to spend a great part of his time in these fields, listening to the simple melodies of these water-drawers, which he learned to imitate and apply to his more finished vocal music. Popular belief ascribes to Tānsēn the power of stopping the river Jumna in its course. His contemporary and rival, Brij Baula (?),[3] who, according to popular belief, could split a rock with a single note, is said to have learned his bass from the noise of the stone mills which the women use in grinding the corn for their families. Tānsēn waś a Brahman from Patna, who entered the service of the Emperor Akbar, became a Musalmān, and after the service of twenty-seven years, during which he was much beloved by the Emperor and all his court, he died at Gwālior in the thirty-fourth year of the Emperor's reign. His tomb is still to be seen at

[1] Chap. XXII of Vol. II of original edition.
[2] January, 1836.
[3] Brij Bowla in the original edition. The editor has been unable to obtain any information concerning this man.

Gwālior. All his descendants are said to have a talent for music, and they have all Sēn added to their names.[1]

While Mādhoji Sindhia, the Gwālior chief, was prime minister, he made the émperor assign to his daughter the Bālā Bāī in jāgīr, or rent-free tenure, ninety-five villages, rated in the imperial "sanads" [deeds of grant] at three lākhs of rupees a year. When the Emperor had been released from the "durance vile" in which he was kept by Daulat Rāo Sindhia, the adopted son of this chief,[2] by Lord Lake in 1803, and the countries, in which these villages were situated, taken possession of, she was permitted to retain them on condition that they were to escheat to us on her death. She died in 1834, and we took possession of the villages, which now yield, it is said, four lākhs of rupees a year. Bēgamābād was one of them. It paid to the Bālā Bāī only six hundred rupees a year, but it pays now to us six hundred and twenty rupees ; but the farmers and cultivators do not pay a farthing more—the difference was taken by the favourite to whom she assigned

---

[1] The more correct statement appears to be that Tānsēn died at Lahore, his body being removed by Akbar's orders to Gwālior for burial. The dancing girls believe that chewing the leaves of the tamarind-tree which grows over his grave greatly improves the voice. (Forbes' *Oriental Memoirs*, London, 1813, vol. iii, p. 32.)

"Rām Chand [Rājā of Rīwā] was the patron of the renowned musician and singer, Tānsēn. His fame had reached Akbar ; and in the seventh year the Emperor sent Jalāluddīn Qūrchi to Bhat'h to induce Tānsēn to come to Agra. Rām Chand, feeling himself powerless to refuse Akbar's request, sent his favourite with his musical instruments and many presents to Agra, and the first time that Tānsēn performed at Court the Emperor made him a present of two lākhs of rupees [more than £20,000]. Tānsēn remained with Akbar. Most of his compositions are written in Akbar's name, and his melodies are even now-a-days everywhere repeated by the people of Hindustān." (Blochmann, *Aīn-i-Akbarī*, p. 406.)

[2] The Emperor Shāh Alam is the sovereign alluded to. Mādhojī (Mādhava Rāo) Sindhia died, and was probably murdered, in February, 1794. His successor, Daulat Rāo, was then a boy of fifteen. (See Mr. Keene's book, *Mādhavo Rāo Sindhia, otherwise called Madhoji* ; Oxford, 1891 ; in "Rulers of India" series.

the duties of collection, and who always took as much as he could get from them, and paid as little as he could to her.[1] The tomb of the old collector stood near my tents, and his son, who came to visit it, told me that he had heard from Gwālior that a new Governor-General was about to arrive,[2] who would probably order the villages to be given back, when he should be made collector of the village, as his father had been.

Had our government acted by all the rent-free lands in our territories on the same principle, they would have saved themselves a vast deal of expense, trouble and odium. The justice of declaring all lands liable to resumption on the death of the present incumbents when not given by competent autority for, and actually applied to, the maintenance of religious, charitable, educational, or other establishments of manifest public utility, would never have been for a moment questioned by the people of India, because they would have all known that it was in accordance with the customs of the country. If, at the same time that we declared all land liable to resumption, when not assigned by such authority for such purposes and actually applied to them, we had declared that all grants by competent authority registered in due form before the death of the present incumbents should be liable on their death to the payment to government of only a quarter or half the rent arising from them, it would have been universally hailed as an act of great liberality, highly calculated to make our reign popular. As it is, we have admitted the right of former rulers of all descriptions to alienate in perpetuity the land, the principal source of the revenue of the state, in favour of their relatives, friends, and favourites,

---

[1] This observation is a good illustration of the tendency of administrators in a country so poor as India to take notice of the infinitely little. In Europe no one would take the trouble to notice the difference between £60 and £62 rental.

[2] Lord Auckland, in March, 1836, relieved Sir Charles Metcalfe, who had succeeded Lord William Bentinck as temporary Governor-General.

leaving upon the holders the burthen of proving, at a ruinous cost in fees and bribes, through court after court, that these alienations had been made by the authorities we declare competent, before the time prescribed; and we have thus given rise to an infinite deal of fraud, perjury, and forgery, and to the opinion, I fear, very generally prevalent, that we are anxious to take advantage of unavoidable flaws in the proof required, to trick them out of their lands by tedious judicial proceedings, while we profess to be desirous that they should retain them. In this we have done ourselves great injustice.[1]

Though these lands were often held for many generations under former governments, and for the exclusive benefit of the holders, it was almost always, when they were of any value, in collusion with the local authorities, who concealed the circumstances from their sovereign for a certain stipulated sum or share of the rents while they held office. This of course the holders were always willing to pay, knowing that no sovereign would hesitate much to resume their lands, should the circumstance of their holding them for their private use alone be ever brought to his notice. The local authorities were, no doubt, always willing to take a moderate share of the rent, knowing that they would get nothing should the lands be resumed by the sovereign. Sometimes the lands granted were either at the time the grant was made, or became soon after, waste and depopulated, in consequence of invasion or internal disorders; and remaining in this state for many generations, the intervening sovereigns either knew nothing or cared nothing

---

[1] The resumption, that is to say, assessment, of revenue-free lands was a burning question in the author's day. It has long since got settled. The author was quite right in his opinion. All native governments freely exercised the right of resumption, and did not care in the least what phrases were used in the deed of grant. The old Hindoo deeds commonly directed that the grant should last "as long as the sun and moon shall endure," and invoked awful curses on the head of the resumer. But this was only formal legal phraseology, meaning nothing. No native ruler was bound by his predecessor's acts.

about the grants. Under our rule they became by degrees again cultivated and peopled, and in consequence valuable, not by the exertions of the rent-free holders, for they were seldom known to do anything but collect the rents, but by those of the farmers and cultivators who pay them.

When Saādat Ali Khān, the sovereign of Oudh, ceded Rohilkhand and other districts to the Honourable Company in lieu of tribute in 1801, he resumed every inch of land held in rent-free tenure within the territories that remained with him, without condescending to assign any other reason than state necessity. The measure created a good deal of distress, particularly among the educated classes; but not so much as a similar measure would have created within our territories, because all his revenues are expended in the maintenance of establishments formed exclusively out of the members of Oudh families, and retained within the country, while ours are sent to pay establishments formed and maintained at a distance; and those whose lands are resumed always find it exceedingly difficult to get employment suitable to their condition.

The face of the country between Delhi and Meerut is sadly denuded of its groves; not a grove or an avenue is to be seen anywhere, and but few fine solitary trees.[1] I asked the people of the cause, and was told by the old men of the village that they remembered well when the Sikh chiefs who now bask under the sunshine of our protection used to come over at the head of " dalas " (bodies) of ten or twelve horse each, and plunder and lay waste with fire and sword, at every returning harvest, the fine country which I now saw covered with rich sheets of cultivation, and which they had rendered a desolate waste, " without a man to make, or a man to grant, a petition," when Lord Lake came among them.[2] They were, they say, looking on

---

[1] This is not now the case.

[2] " It is difficult to realize that the dignified, sober, and orderly men who now fill our regiments are of the same stock as the savage free-booters whose name, a hundred years ago, was the terror of Northern

at a distance when he fought the battle of Delhi, and drove the Marāthās, who were almost as bad as the Sikhs, into the Jumna river, where ten thousand of them were drowned. The people of all classes in Upper India feel the same reverence as our native soldiery for the name of this admirable soldier and most worthy man, who did so much to promote our interests and sustain our reputation in this country.[1]

The most beautiful trees in India are the " bar " (banyan), the " pīpal," and the tamarind.[2] The two first are of the fig tribe, and their greatest enemies are the elephants and camels of our public establishments and public servants, who prey upon them wherever they can find them when under the protection of their masters or keepers, who, when appealed to, generally evince a very philosophical disregard to the feeling of either property or piety involved in

India. But the change has been wrought by strong and kindly government and by strict military discipline under sympathetic officers whom the troops love and respect." (Sir Lepel Griffin, *Ranjīt Singh*, p. 37.)

[1] Gerard Lake was born on the 27th July, 1744, and entered the army at the age of fourteen. He served in the Seven Years' War in Germany, in the American war, in the French campaign of 1793, and against the Irish rebels in 1798. In the year 1801 he became Commander-in-Chief in India, and proceeded to Cawnpore, then our frontier station. Two years later the second Marāthā war began, and gave General Lake the opportunity of winning a series of brilliant victories. In rapid succession he defeated the enemy at Kōil, Alīgarh, the Jehna Nāla, near Delhi (the battle alluded to in the text), Agra, and Laswārī. Next year, 1804, the glorious record was marred by the disaster to Colonel Monson's force, but this was quickly avenged by the decisive victories of Dīg and Farrukhābād, which shattered Holkār's power. The year 1805 saw General Lake's one personal failure, the unsuccessful siege of Bharatpur. The Commander-in-Chief then resumed the pursuit of Holkār, and forced him to surrender. He sailed for England in February, 1807, and on his arrival at home was created a Viscount, and appointed Governor of Plymouth. On the 21st of February, 1808, he died. (*Men whom India has Known.*)

[2] The banyan is the *Ficus Indica*, or *Urostigma Bengalense ;* the "pīpal " is *Ficus religiosa,* or *Urostigma religiosum ;* and the tamarind is the *Tamarindus Indica,* or *occidentalis,* or *officinalis.*

the trespass. It is consequently in the driest and hottest parts of the country where the shade of these trees is most wanted that it is least to be found; because it is there that camels thrive best, and are most kept, and it is most difficult to save such trees from their depredations.

In the evening a trooper passed our tents on his way in great haste from Meerut to Delhi, to announce the death of the poor old Bēgam Samrū, which had taken place the day before at her little capital of Sardhana. For five-and-twenty-years had I been looking forward to the opportunity of seeing this very extraordinary woman, whose history had interested me more than that of any other character in India during my time; and I was sadly disappointed to hear of her death when within two or three stages of her capital.[1]

[1] The history of the Bēgam is given in Chapter XX, *post*.

CHAPTER XVI[1]

The Station of Meerut—"Atālīs" who Dance and Sing gratuitously for the Benefit of the Poor.

On the 30th,[2] we went on twelve miles to Meerut, and encamped close to the Sūraj Kund, so called after Sūraj-mal, the Jāt chief of Dīg, whose tomb I have described at Govardhan.[3] He built here a very large tank, at the recommendation of the *spirit* of a Hindoo saint, Manohar Nāth, whose remains had been burned here more than two hundred years before, and whose spirit appeared to the Jāt chief in a dream, as he was encamped here with his army during one of his *kingdom-taking* expeditions. This is a noble work, with a fine sheet of water, and flights of steps of "pakkā" masonry from the top to its edge all round. The whole is kept in repair by our government.[4] About

---

[1] Chap. XXIII of Vol. II of original edition.
[2] January 1836. The date is misprinted 20th in the original edition.
[3] *Ante*, p. 9 of this volume.
[4] "Amongst the remains of former times in and around Meerut may be noticed the Sūraj kund, commonly called by Europeans 'the monkey tank.' It was constructed by Jawāhir Mal, a wealthy merchant of Lāwār, in 1714. It was intended to keep it full of water from the Abū Nāla, but at present the tank is nearly dry in May and June. There are numerous small temples, 'dharmsālās' [*i. e.* rest-houses], and 'satī' pillars on its banks, but none of any note. The largest of the temples is dedicated to Manohar Nāth, and is said to have been built in the reign of Shāh-Jahan. Lāwār, a large village. . . . . is distant 12 miles north of the civil station. . . . There is a fine house here called Mahal Sarāi, built about 1700 A.D. by Jawāhir Singh, Mahājan, who constructed the Sūraj kund near

half a mile to the north-west of the tank stands the tomb of
Shāh Pīr, a Muhammadan saint, who is said to have
descended from the mountains with the Hindoo, and to
have been his bosom friend up to the day of his death.
Both are said to have worked many wonderful miracles
among the people of the surrounding country, who used to
see them, according to popular belief, quietly taking their
morning ride together upon the backs of two enormous
tigers who came every morning at the appointed hour
from the distant jungle.   The Hindoo is said to have been
very fond of music ; and though he has been now dead
some three centuries, a crowd of amateurs (atālis) assemble
every Sunday afternoon at his shrine, on the bank of the
tank, and sing gratis, and in a very pleasing style, to an
immense concourse of people, who assemble to hear them,
and to solicit the spirit of the old saint, softened by their
melodies.   At the tomb of the Muhammadan saint a
number of professional dancers and singers assemble every
Thursday afternoon, and dance, sing, and play gratis to a
large concourse of people, who make offerings of food to
the poor, and implore the intercession of the old man with
the Deity in return.

   The Muhammadan's tomb is large and handsome, and
built of red sandstone, inlaid with marble, but without any
cupola, that there may be no *curtain* between him and
heaven when he gets out of his " last long sleep " at the
resurrection.[1]   Not far from his tomb is another, over the
bones of a pilgrim they call Ganjishan, or the granary of

Meerut." (*N. W. P. Gazetteer*, vol. iii, p.p. 406, 400.) This information, supplied by the local officials, is more to be depended on than
the author's statement.
   [1] " The 'dargāh ' [*i.e.*, shrine] of Shāh Pīr is a fine structure of red
sandstone, erected about 1620 A.D. by Nūr Jahān, the wife of the
Emperor Jahāngīr, in memory of a pious fakīr named Shāh Pīr. An
' urs,' or religious assembly, is held here every year in the month of
Ramazān. The 'dargāh ' is supported from the proceeds of the
revenue-free village of Bhagwānpur." (*N. W. P. Gazetteer*, vol. iii,
p. 406.)

science. Professional singers and dancers attend it every Friday afternoon, and display their talents gratis to a large concourse, who bestow what they can in charity to the poor, who assemble on all these occasions to take what they can get. Another much frequented tomb lies over a Muhammadan saint, who has not been dead more than three years, named Gohar Sāh. He owes his canonization to a few circumstances of recent occurrence, which are, however, universally believed. Mr. Smith, an enterprising merchant of Meerut, who had raised a large windmill for grinding corn in the Sadr Bāzār, is said to have abused the old man as he was one day passing by, and looked with some contempt on his method of grinding, which was to take the bread from the mouths of so many old widows. " My child," said the old saint, " amuse thyself with this toy of thine, for it has but a few days to run." In four days from that time the machine stopped. Poor Mr. Smith could not afford to set it going again, and it went to ruin. The whole native population of Meerut considered this a miracle of Gohar Sāh. Just before his death the country round Meerut was under water, and a great many houses fell from incessant rain. The old man took up his residence during this time in a large sarāi in the town, but finding his end approach, he desired those who had taken shelter with him to have him taken to the jungle where he now reposes. They did so, and the instant they left the building it fell to the ground. Many who saw it told me they had no doubt that the virtues of the old man had sustained it while he was there, and prevented its crushing all who were in it. The tomb was built over his remains by a Hindoo officer of the court, who had been long out of employment and in great affliction. He had no sooner completed the tomb, and implored the aid of the old man than he got into excellent service, and has been ever since a happy man. He makes regular offerings to his shrine, as a grateful return for the saint's kindness to him in his hour of need. Professional singers and dancers display their talents here gratis, as at the other tombs, every Wednesday afternoon.

The ground all round these tombs is becoming crowded with the graves of people, who in their last moments request to be buried (*zēr-i-sāya*) under the shadow of these saints, who in their lifetime are all said to have despised the pomps and vanities of this life, and to have taken nothing from their disciples and worshippers but what was indispensably necessary to support existence—food being the only thing offered and accepted, and that taken only when they happened to be very hungry. Happy indeed was the man whose dish was put forward when the saint's appetite happened to be sharp. The death of the poor old Bēgam has, it is said, just canonized another saint, Shākir Shāh, who lies buried at Sardhana, but is claimed by the people of Meerut, among whom he lived till about five years ago, when he desired to be taken to Sardhana, where he found the old lady very dangerously ill and not expected to live. He was himself very old and ill when he set out from Meerut; and the journey is said to have shaken him so much that he found his end approaching, and sent a messenger to the princess in these words :—" Ayā torē, chale ham "; that is, " Death came for thee, but I go in thy place "; and he told those around him that she had precisely five years more to live. She is said to have caused a tomb to be built over him, and is believed by the people to have died that day five years.

All these things I learned as I wandered among the tombs of the old saints the first few evenings after my arrival at Meerut. I was interested in their history from the circumstance that amateur singers and professional dancers and musicians should display their talents at their shrines gratis, for the sake of getting alms for the poor of the place, given in their name—a thing I had never before heard of—though the custom prevails no doubt in other places ; and that Musalmāns and Hindoos should join promiscuously in their devotions and charities at all these

shrines.   Manohar Nāth's shrine, though he was a Hindoo,
is attended by as many Musalmān as Hindoo pilgrims. He
is said to have taken the *samādh*, that is, to have buried
himself alive in this place as an offering to the Deity.
Men who are afflicted with leprosy or any other incurable
disease in India often take the samādh, that is, bury or
drown themselves with due ceremonies, by which they are
considered as acceptable sacrifices to the Deity.   I once
knew a Hindoo gentleman of great wealth and respectability,
and of high rank under the government of Nāgpur, who
came to the river Nerbudda, two hundred miles, attended
by a large retinue, to *take the samādh* in due form, from a
painful disease which the doctors pronounced incurable.
After taking an affectionate leave of all his family and
friends, he embarked on board the boat, which took him
into the deepest part of the river.   He then loaded himself with sand, as a sportsman who is required to carry
weights in a race loads himself with shot, and stepping into
the water disappeared.   The funeral ceremonies were then
performed, and his family, friends, and followers returned
to Nāgpur, conscious that they had all done what they had
been taught to consider their duty.   Many poor men do
the same every year when afflicted by any painful disease
that they consider incurable.[1]   The only way to prevent
this is to carry out the plan now in progress of giving to
India in an accessible shape the medical science of Europe,
—a plan first adopted under Lord W. Bentinck, prosecuted
by Lord Auckland, and superintended by two able and
excellent men, Doctors Goodeve and O'Shaughnessy.   It
will be one of the greatest blessings that India has ever
received from England.[2]

[1] An interesting collection of modern cases of a similar kind is given
in Balfour's *Cyclopædia*, s.v. " Samadhi."

[2] See *ante*, Vol. I, p. 130, *note* 2.   Dr. W. B. O'Shaughnessy contributed many scientific papers to the *Journal of the Asiatic Society of
Bengal* (volumes viii, ix, x, xii, and xvi).

CHAPTER XVII [1]

Subdivisions of Lands—Want of Gradations of Rank—Taxes.

THE country between Delhi and Meerut is well cultivated and rich in the latent power of its soil; but there is here, as everywhere else in the Upper Provinces, a lamentable want of gradations in society, from the eternal subdivision of property in land, and the want of that concentration of capital in commerce and manufactures which characterizes European—or I may take a wider range, and say Christian societies. [2] Where, as in India, the landlords' share of the annual returns from the soil has been always taken by the government as the most legitimate fund for the payment of its public establishments; and the estates of the farmers, and the holdings of the immediate cultivators of the soil, are liable to be subdivided in equal shares among the sons in every succeeding generation, the land can never aid much in giving to society that, without which no society can possibly be well organized—a gradation of rank. Were the government to alter the system, to give up all the rent of the lands, and thereby convert all the farmers into proprietors of their estates, the case would not be much altered, while the Hindoo and Muhammadan law of inheritance remained the same; for the eternal subdivision would still go on, and reduce all connected with the soil to one common level; and the people would be harassed with a multiplicity of taxes, from which they are now free, that would have to

[1] Chap. XXIV of Vol. II of original edition.
[2] This phrase is meant to include America.

be imposed to supply the place of the rent given up. The agricultural capitalists who derived their incomes from the interest of money advanced to the farmers and cultivators for subsistence and the purchase of stock were commonly men of rank and influence in society ; but they were never a numerous class.[1] The mass of the people in India are really not at present sensible that they pay any taxes at all. The only necessary of life, whose price is at all increased by taxes, is salt, and the consumer is hardly aware of this increase. The natives never eat salted meat ; and though they require a great deal of salt, living, as they do, so much on vegetable food, still they purchase it in such small quantities from day to day as they require it, that they really never think of the tax that may have been paid upon it in its progress.[2]

To understand the nature of taxation in India, an Englishman should suppose that all the non-farming land-holders of his native country had, a century or two ago, consented to resign their property into the hands of their sovereign, for the maintenance of his civil functionaries, army, navy, church, and public creditors, and then suddenly

[1] Money lenders have naturally flourished during the long period of internal peace since the Mutiny. They vary in wealth and position from the humblest " gombeen man " to the millionaire banker. Many of these money lenders are now among the largest owners of land in the country. Under native rule interests in land were generally too precarious to be saleable. The author did not foresee that the growth of private property in land would carry with it the right and desire of one party to sell and of another to buy. and would thus favour the growth of large estates, and, to a considerable extent, counteract the evils of subdivision. Of course, like everything else, the large estates have their evils too. Much nonsense is written about sales of land in India, as well as in Ireland. The two countries have more than the initial letter in common.

[2] Theorists declare that it is right that the tax-payers should know what is taken from them, and that, therefore, direct taxes are best ; but practical men who have to govern ignorant and suspicious races, resentful of direct taxation, know that indirect taxation is, for such people, the best.

disappeared from the community, leaving to till the lands merely the farmers and cultivators ; and that their forty millions of rent were just the sum that the government now required to pay all these four great establishments.[1]

To understand the nature of the public debt of England a man has only to suppose one great national establishment, twice as large as those of the civil functionaries, the army, navy, and the church together, and composed of members with fixed salaries, who purchased their commissions from *the wisdom of our ancestors*, with liberty to sell them to whom they please—who have no duty to perform for the public,[2] and have, like Adam and Eve, the privilege of going to "seek their place of rest" in what part of the world they please—a privilege of which they will, of course, be found more and more anxious to avail themselves, as taxation presses on the one side, and prohibition to the import of the necessaries of life diminishes the means of paying them on the other.

The repeal of the Corn Laws may give a new lift to England ; it may greatly increase the foreign demand for the produce of its manufacturing industry ; it may invite back a large portion of those who now spend their incomes in foreign countries, and prevent from going abroad to reside a vast number who would otherwise go. These laws must soon be repealed, or England must reduce one or other of its great establishments—the national debt, the church, the army, or the navy. The Corn Laws press upon England just in the same manner as the discovery of the passage to India by the Cape of Good Hope pressed upon

[1] This illustration would give a very false idea of modern Indian finance.

[2] They have no duty to perform as creditors ; but as citizens of an enlightened nation they no doubt perform many of them, very important ones. [W. H. S.] The author's whimsical comparison between stock-holders and Adam and Eve, and his notion that the creditors of the nation may be regarded as officials without duties only obscure a very simple matter. The emigration of owners of consols never assumed very alarming dimensions.

Venice and the other states whose welfare depended upon the transit of the produce of India by land. But the navigation of the Cape benefited all other European nations at the same time that it pressed upon these particular states, by giving them all the produce of India at cheaper rates than they would otherwise have got it, and by opening the markets of India to the produce of all other European nations. The Corn Laws benefit only one small section of the people of England, while they weigh, like an incubus, upon the vital energies of all the rest; and at the same time injure all other nations by preventing their getting the produce of manufacturing industry so cheap as they would otherwise get it. They have not, therefore, the merit of benefiting other nations, at the same time that they crush their own.[1]

For some twenty or thirty years of our rule, too many of the collectors of our land revenue in what we call the Western Provinces,[2] sought the "bubble reputation" in an increase of assessment upon the lands of their district every five years when the settlement was renewed. The more the assessment was increased, the greater was the praise bestowed upon the collector by the revenue boards, or the revenue secretary to Government, in the name of the Governor-General of India.[3] These collectors found an easy mode of acquiring this reputation—they left the settlements to their native officers, and shut their ears to all complaints of grievances, till they had reduced all the landholders of their districts to one common level of beggary, without stock, character, or credit; and transferred a great

[1] The Corn Laws were repealed in 1846, and the shilling duty which was then left was abolished in 1869. Considering that the author belonged to an agriculturist family, his clear perception of the evils caused by the Corn Laws is remarkable.

[2] By the "Western Provinces" the author means the North-Western Provinces, and the Delhi Territories, which latter are now under the government of the Panjāb.

[3] At the time referred to, the provincial government had not been constituted.

portion of their estates to the native officers of their own
courts through the medium of the auction sales that took
place for the arrears, or pretended arrears, of revenue.   A
better feeling has for some years past prevailed, and
collectors have sought their reputation in a real knowledge
of their duties, and a real good feeling towards the farmers
and cultivators of their districts.   For this better tone of
feeling the Western Provinces are, I believe, chiefly indebted
to Mr. R. M. Bird, of the Revenue Board, one of the most
able public officers now in India.   A settlement for twenty
years is now in progress that will leave the farmers at least
35 per cent. upon the gross collections from the immediate cultivators of the soil; that is, the amount of the
revenue demandable by government from the estate will be
that less than what the farmer will, and would, under any
circumstances, levy from the cultivators in his detailed
settlement.[1]

[1] Fifty per cent. may be considered as the average rate left to the
lessees or proprietors of estates under this new settlement; and, if they
take on an average one-third of the gross produce, government takes
two-ninths. But we may rate the government share of the produce
actually taken at one-fifth as the maximum, and one-tenth as the
minimum. [W. H. S.]

It is unfortunately true that in the short term settlements made
previous to 1822 many abuses of the kinds referred to in the text
occurred.   The traditions of the people and the old records attest
numerous instances.   The first serious attempt to reform the system of
revenue settlements was made by Regulation VII of 1822, but, owing
to an excessive elaboration of procedure, the attempt produced no
appreciable results.   Regulation IX of 1833 established a workable
system, and provided for the appointment of native Deputy Collectors
with adequate powers.   The settlements of the North-Western
Provinces made under this Regulation were, for the most part, reason-
ably fair, and were generally confirmed for a period of thirty years.
Mr. Robert Mertins Bird, who entered the service in 1805, took a
leading part in this great reform.   When the next settlements were
made, between 1860 and 1880, the share of the profit rental claimed by
the State was reduced from two-thirds to one-half.   Full details will be
found in the editor's *Settlement Officer's Manual for the N. W. P.*
(Allahabad, 1882), or in Mr. Baden Powell's recent big book on *Land
Tenures* (Clarendon Press, Oxford).

The farmer lets all the land of his estate out to cultivators, and takes in money this rate of profit for his expense, trouble, and risk; or he lets out to the cultivators enough to pay the government demand, and tills the rest with his own stock, rent-free. When a division takes place between his sons, they either divide the estate, and become each responsible for his particular share, or they divide the profits, and remain collectively responsible to government for the whole, leaving one member of the family registered as the lessee and responsible head.[1]

In the Ryotwār system of Southern India, government officers, removable at the pleasure of the government collector, are substituted for these farmers, or more properly proprietors, of estates ; and a system more prejudicial to the best interests of society could not well be devised by the ingenuity of man.[2] It has been supposed by some theorists, who are practically unacquainted with agriculture in this or any other country, that all who have any interest in land above the rank of cultivator or ploughman are mere *drones*, or useless consumers of that rent, which, under judicious management, might be added to the revenues of government—that all which they get might, and ought to be, either left with the cultivators or taken by the government. At the head of these is the justly celebrated historian, Mr. Mill. But men who understand the subject practically know that the intermediate agency of a farmer, who has a permanent interest in the estate, or an interest

---

[1] Since 1833 the people whom the author calls "farmers" have gradually become full proprietors, subject to the Government lien on the land and its produce for the land revenue. For many years past the ancient custom of joint ownership and collective responsibility has been losing ground. Partitions are now continually demanded, and every year collective responsibility is become more unpopular and more difficult to enforce.

[2] This judgment, I need hardly say, would not be accepted in Madras or Bombay. The issue raised is too large for discussion in footnotes.

for a long period, is a thousand times better both for the government and the people than that of a government officer of any description, much less that of one removable at the pleasure of the collector. Government can always get more revenue from a village under the management of the farmer; the character of the cultivators and village community generally is much better; the tillage is much better; and the produce, from more careful weeding and attention of all kinds, sells much better in the market. The better character of the cultivators enables them to get the loans they require to purchase stock, and to pay the government demand on more moderate terms from the capitalists, who rely upon the farmer to aid in the recovery of their outlays, without reference to civil courts, which are ruinous media, as well in India as in other places. The farmer or landlord finds in the same manner that he can get much more from lands let out on lease to the cultivators or yeomen, who depend upon their own character, credit, and stock, than he can from similar lands· cultivated with his own stock; and hired labourers can never be got to labour either so long or so well. The labour of the Indian cultivating lessee is always applied in the proper quantity, and at the proper time and place—that of the hired field-labourer hardly ever is. The skilful coachmaker always puts on the precise quantity of iron required to make his coach strong, because he knows where it is required; his coach is, at the same time, as light as it can be with safety. The unskilful workman either puts on too much, and makes·his coach· heavy; or he puts it in the wrong place, and leaves it weak.

If government extends the twenty years' settlement now in progress to fifty years or more, they will confer a great blessing upon the people,[1] and they might, perhaps, do it

---

[1] The advantages of very long terms of settlement are obvious; the disadvantages, though equally real, are less obvious. Fluctuations in prices, and above all, in the price of silver, are among the many conditions which complicate the question. Except the Bengal land-owners,

on the condition that the incumbent consented to allow the lease to descend undivided to his heirs by the laws of primogeniture. To this condition all classes would readily agree, for I have heard Hindoo and Muhammadan landholders all equally lament the evil effects of the laws by which families are so quickly and inevitably broken up ; and say that "it is the duty of government to take advantage of their power as the great proprietor and leaser of all the lands to prevent the evil by declaring leases indivisible. "There would then," they say, "be always one head to assist in maintaining the widows and orphans of deceased members, in educating his brothers and nephews ; and by his influence and respectability procuring employment for them." In such men, with feelings of permanent interest in their estates, and in the stability of the government that secured them possession on such favourable terms, and with the means of educating their children, we should by-and-by find our best support, and society its best element. The law of primogeniture at present prevails only where it is most mischievous under our rule, among the feudal chiefs, whose ancestors rose to distinction, and acquired their possessions by rapine in times of invasion and civil wars. This law among them tends to perpetuate the desire to maintain those military establishments by which the founders of their families arose, in the hope that the times of invasion and civil wars may return, and open for them a similar field for exertion. It fosters a class of powerful men, essentially and irredeemably opposed in feeling, not only to our rule, but to settled government under any rule ; and the sooner the Hindoo law of inheritance is allowed by the paramount power to take its course among these feudal chiefs, the better for society. There is always a strong tendency to it in the desire of the younger brothers to share in the loaves and fishes ; and

everybody now admits that the Permanent Settlement of Bengal a century ago was a grievous mistake. It hangs like a millstone round the neck of the Finance Minister.

this tendency is checked only by the injudicious interposition of our authority.[1]

To give India the advantage of free institutions, or all the blessings of which she is capable under an enlightened paternal government, nothing is more essential than the supersession of this feudal aristocracy by one founded upon other bases, and, above all, upon that of the concentration of capital in commerce and manufactures. Nothing tends so much to prevent the accumulation and concentration of capital over India as this feudal aristocracy which tends everywhere to destroy that feeling of security without which men will nowhere accumulate and concentrate it. They do so, not only by the intrigues and combinations against the paramount power, which keep alive the dread of internal wars and foreign invasion, but by those gangs of robbers and murderers which they foster and locate upon their estates to prey upon the more favoured or better governed territories around them. From those gangs of freebooters who are to be found upon the estate of almost every native chief no accumulation of movable property of any value is ever for a moment considered safe, and those who happen to have any such are always in dread of losing, not only their property, but their lives along with it, for these gangs, secure in the protection of such chief, are reckless in their attack, and kill all who happen to come in their way.[2]

---

[1] These two suggestions of the author that the law of primogeniture should be established to regulate the succession to ordinary estates, and abolished in the case of chieftainships, where it already prevails, are obviously open to much criticism. It seems to be sufficient to say that both recommendations are, for many reasons, altogether impracticable. In passing, I may note that the term " feudal " does not express with any approach to correctness the relation of the Native States to the Government of India.

[2] The evils described in this paragraph, though diminished, have not disappeared. Nevertheless, no one would now seriously propose the deliberate supersession of the existing aristocracy by rich merchants and manufacturers. The proposal is too fanciful for discussion. During the long period of peace merchants and manufacturers have naturally risen to a much more prominent position than they occupied in the author's time.

CHAPTER XVIII[1]

Meerut—Anglo-Indian Society.

MEERUT is a large station for military and civil establishments; it is the residence of a civil commissioner, a judge, a magistrate, a collector of land revenue, and all their assistants and establishments. There are the Major-General commanding the division; the brigadier commanding the station; four troops of horse and a company of foot artillery; one regiment of European cavalry, one of European infantry, one of native cavalry, and three of native infantry.[2] It is justly considered the healthiest station in

[1] Chap. XXV. of Vol. II. of original edition.

[2] In India officers have much better opportunities in time of peace to learn how to handle troops than in England; from having them more concentrated in large stations, with fine open plains to exercise upon. During the whole of the cold season, from the beginning of November to the end of February, the troops are at large stations exercised in brigades, and the artillery, cavalry, and infantry together. [W. H. S.]

In 1875 the garrison consisted of—

Horse artillery	. . . . .	2 batteries
Field ,,	. . . . .	2 ,, and head-quarters
European cavalry	. . . .	1 regiment
,, infantry	. . . .	1 ,,
Native cavalry	. . . . .	1 ,,
,, infantry	. . . .	1 ,,

—(*Gazetteer.*)

The present garrison is about the same strength.

The number of civil officers has been increased by the addition of canal engineers and other departmental officials, unknown in the author's time.

India, for both Europeans and natives,[1] and I visited it in the latter end of the cold, which is the healthiest, season of the year; yet the European ladies were looking as if they had all come out of their graves, and talking of the necessity of going off to the mountains to renovate, as soon as the hot weather should set in. They had literally been fagging themselves to death with gaiety, at this the gayest and most delightful of all Indian stations, during the cold months when they ought to have been laying in a store of strength to carry them through the trying seasons of the hot winds and rains. Up every night and all night at balls and suppers, they could never go out to breathe the fresh air of the morning; and were looking wretchedly ill, while the European soldiers from the barracks seemed as fresh as if they had never left their native land. There is no doubt that sitting up late at night is extremely prejudicial to the health of Europeans in India.[2] I have never seen the European, male or female, that could stand it long, however temperate in habits; and an old friend of mine once told me that if he went to bed a little exhilarated every night at ten o'clock, and took his ride in the morning, he found himself much better than if he sat up till twelve or one o'clock without drinking, and lay abed in the mornings. Almost all the gay pleasures of India are enjoyed at night, and as ladies here, as everywhere else in Christian societies, are the life and soul of all good parties, as of all good novels, they often to oblige others sit up late, much against their own inclinations, and even their judgments, aware as they are that they are gradually sinking under the undue exertions.

When I first came to India there were a few ladies of the old school still much looked up to in Calcutta, and among the rest the grandmother of the Earl of Liverpool, the old Bēgam Johnstone, then between seventy and eighty

---

[1] Not now. The cantonments have suffered severely from typhoid fever for several years past.

[2] Few Anglo-Indians will dispute the truth of this dictum.

years of age.[1] All these old ladies prided themselves upon keeping up old usages. They used to dine in the afternoon at four or five o'clock—take their airing after dinner in their carriages; and from the time they returned till ten at night their houses were lit up in their best style and thrown open for the reception of visitors. All who were on visiting terms came at this time, with any strangers whom they wished to introduce, and enjoyed each other's society; there were music and dancing for the young, and cards for the old, when the party assembled happened to be large enough; and a few who had been previously invited stayed supper. I often visited the old Bēgam Johnstone at this hour, and met at her house the first people in the country, for all people, including the Governor-General himself, delighted to honour this old lady, the widow of a Governor-General of India, and the mother-in-law of a Prime Minister of England.[2] She was at Murshidābād when Sirāj-ud-daula marched from that place at the head of the army that took and plundered Calcutta, and caused so many Europeans to perish in the Black Hole; and she was herself saved from

[1] The late Earl of Liverpool, then Mr. Jenkinson, married this old lady's daughter. He was always very attentive to her, and she used with feelings of great pride and pleasure to display the contents of the boxes of millinery which he used every year to send out to her. [W. H. S.] The author came out to India in 1809. Mr. Charles Jenkinson was created Lord Hawkesbury in 1786, succeeded to the baronetcy in 1789, and was created Earl of Liverpool in 1796. His first wife, who died in 1770, was Amelia, daughter of Mr. William Watts, Governor of Fort William, and of the lady described by the author. Their only son succeeded to the earldom in 1808, and died in 1828. The peerage became extinct on the death of the third earl in 1851. (Burke's *Peerage*.)

[2] Lord Liverpool became Prime Minister in 1812, after the murder of Perceval. If the author is correct in saying that the Bēgam was the widow of a Governor-General, the gentleman must apparently have been Mr. John Macpherson, who acted as Governor-General between the departure of Warren Hastings in 1785, and the arrival of Lord Cornwallis in the following year. Mr. Watts was Governor of Fort William, not Governor-General.

becoming a member of his seraglio, or perishing with the rest, by the circumstance of her being far gone in her pregnancy, which caused her to be made over to a Dutch factory.[1]

She had been a very beautiful woman, and had been several times married ; the pictures of all her husbands being hung round her noble drawing-room in Calcutta, covered during the day with crimson cloth to save them from the dust, and uncovered at night only on particular occasions. One evening Mrs. Crommelin, a friend of mine, pointing to one of them, asked the old lady his name. " Really I cannot at this moment tell you, my dear ; my memory is very bad," (striking her forehead with her right hand, as she leaned with her left arm in Mrs. Crommelin's,) " but I shall recollect in a few minutes." The old lady's last husband was a clergyman, Mr. Johnstone, whom she found too gay, and persuaded to go home upon an annuity of eight hundred a year, which she settled upon him for life. The bulk of her fortune went to Lord Liverpool ; the rest to her grandchildren, the Ricketts, Watts, and others.

Since those days the modes of intercourse in India have much altered. Society at all the stations beyond the three capitals of Calcutta, Madras, and Bombay, is confined almost exclusively to the members of the civil and military services, who seldom remain long at the same station—the military officers hardly ever more than three years, and the civil hardly ever so long. At disagreeable stations the civil servants seldom remain so many months. Every new-comer calls in the forenoon upon all that are at the station when he arrives, and they return his call at the same hour soon after. If he is a married man, the married men upon whom he has called take their wives to call upon his ; and he takes his to return the call of theirs. These calls are all indispensable ; and being made in the forenoon, become

[1] The tragedy of the Black Hole occurred in June, 1756.

very disagreeable in the hot season ; all complain of them, yet no one foregoes his claim upon them ; and till the claim is fulfilled, people will not recognize each other as acquaintances.[1]   Unmarried officers generally dine in the evening, because it is a more convenient hour for the mess ; and married civil functionaries do the same, because it is more convenient for their office work.   If you invite those who dine at that hour to spend the evening with you, you must invite them to dinner, even in the hot weather; and if they invite you, it is to dinner.   This makes intercourse somewhat heavy at all times, but more especially so in the hot season, when a table covered with animal food is sickening to any person without a keen appetite, and stupefying to those who have it.   No one thinks of inviting people to a dinner and ball—it would be vandalism ; and when you invite them, as is always the case, to come after dinner, the ball never begins till late at night, and seldom ends till late in the morning. With all its disadvantages, however, I think dining in the evening much better for those who are in health, than dining in the afternoon, provided people can avoid the intermediate meal of tiffin.   No person in India should eat animal food more than once a day ; and people who dine in the evening generally eat less than they would if they dined in the afternoon.   A light breakfast at nine ; biscuit, or a slice of toast with a glass of water, or soda-water, at two o'clock, and dinner after the evening exercise, is the plan which I should recommend every European to adopt as the most agreeable.[2]   When their digestive powers get out of order, people must do as the doctors tell them.

There is, I believe, no society in which there is more real urbanity of manners than in that of India—a more general disposition on the part of its different members to

---

[1] Of late years the rigour of the custom exacting mid-day calls has been in some places relaxed.

[2] Most people would require some training before they could find this very abstemious regimen "the most agreeable."

sacrifice their own comforts and conveniences to those of others, and to make those around them happy, without letting them see that it costs them an effort to do so.[1] There is assuredly no society where the members are more generally free from those corroding cares and anxieties which "weigh upon the hearts" of men whose incomes are precarious, and position in the world uncertain. They receive their salaries on a certain day every month, whatever may be the state of the seasons or of trade; they pay no taxes; they rise in the several services by rotation;[2] religious feelings and opinions are by common consent left as a question between man and his Maker; no one ever thinks of questioning another about them, nor would he be tolerated if he did so. Most people take it for granted that those which they got from their parents were the right ones; and as such they cherish them. They remember with feelings of filial piety the prayers which they in their infancy offered to their Maker, while kneeling by the side of their mothers; and they continue to offer them up through life, with the same feelings and the same hopes.[3]

Differences of political opinion, which agitate society so much in England and other countries where every man be-

[1] It will, I hope, be admitted that this observation still holds good.

[2] These remarks now (1893) read like bitter satire. Hardly a man or woman of English birth in India is now free from corroding cares and anxieties which weigh heavily upon the heart. The currency has been allowed to depreciate until the services have been mulcted of one-third of their salaries, and many officers are on the verge of insolvency and ruin. This depreciation has gone on for twenty years unchecked, and the Government of India has shown no concern for its servants, until at last a point has been reached at which the strain has become unbearable. The absolute necessity of relief to the servants of Government has been grudgingly admitted, but so far (June, 1893) nothing has been done. The little colony of Ceylon long ago arranged to pay its servants honestly; the great Empire of India is said to be too poor to do the same.

[3] This perfect religious freedom is still generally characteristic of Anglo-Indian society, and is one of its greatest charms; and the charms of the country do not increase.

lieves that his own personal interests must always be more
or less affected by the predominance of one party over
another, are no doubt a source of much interest to people
in India, but they scarcely ever excite any angry passions
among them. The tempests by which the political atmosphere of the world is cleared and purged of all its morbid
influences burst not upon us—we see them at a distance—
we know that they are working for all mankind; and we
feel for those who boldly expose themselves to their "pitiless peltings," as men feel for the sailors whom they suppose
to be exposed on the ocean to the storm, while they listen
to it from their beds or winter firesides.[1] We discuss all
political opinions, and all the great questions which they
affect, with the calmness of philosophers; not without
emotion certainly, but without passion; we have no share
in returning members to parliament—we feel no dread of
those injuries, indignities, and calumnies to which those
who have are too often exposed; and we are free from the
bitterness of feelings which always attend them.[2]

How exalted, how glorious has been the destiny of England, to spread over so vast a portion of the globe her
literature, her language, and her free institutions! How
ought the sense of this high destiny to animate her sons in
their efforts to perfect their institutions which they have
formed by slow degrees from feudal barbarism: to make
them in reality as perfect as they would have them appear
to the world to be in theory, that rising nations may love

---

[1] The author had probably in his mind the famous lines of Lucre-
tius :—

> "Suave, mari magnis turbantibus æquora ventis,
> E terra magnum alterius spectare laborem ;
> Non quia vexare quemquam 'st jucunda voluptas,
> Sed, quibus ipse malis careas, quia cernere suave 'st."

> (Book ii, line 1.)

[2] This delightful philosophic calm is no longer an Anglo-Indian
possession ; and the Indian official can no longer congratulate himself
on his immunity from "injuries, indignities, and calumnies."

and honour the source whence they derive theirs, and continue to look to it for improvement.

We return to the society of our wives and children after the labours of the day are over, with tempers unruffled by collision with political and religious antagonists, by unfavourable changes in the season and the markets, and the other circumstances which affect so much the incomes and prospects of our friends at home. We must look to them for the chief pleasures of our lives, and know that they must look to us for theirs; and if anything has crossed us we try to conceal it from them. There is in India a strong feeling of mutual dependence which prevents little domestic misunderstandings between man and wife from growing into quarrels so often as in other countries, where this is less prevalent. Men have not here their clubs, nor their wives their little coteries to fly to when disposed to make serious matters out of trifles;[1] and both are in consequence much inclined to bear and forbear. There are, of course, on the other hand, evils in India that people have not to contend with at home; but, on the whole, those who are disposed to look on the fair, as well as on the dark side of all around them, can enjoy life in India very much, as long as they and those dear to them are free from physical pain. We everywhere find too many disposed to look upon the dark side of all that is present, and the bright side of all that is distant in time and place—always miserable themselves, be they where they will, and making all around them miserable; this commonly arises from indigestion, and the habit of eating and drinking in a hot, as in a cold, climate; and giving their stomachs too much to do, as if they were the only parts of the human frame whose energies were unrelaxed by the temperature of tropical climates.

There is, however, one great defect in Anglo-Indian

---

[1] There are now clubs everywhere, and coteries are said to be not unknown. Few Anglo-Indians of the present day are able to share the author's cheery optimism.

society ; it is composed too exclusively of the servants of government, civil, military, and ecclesiastic, and wants much of the freshness, variety, and intelligence of cultivated societies otherwise constituted. In societies where capital is concentrated for employment in large agricultural, commercial, and manufacturing establishments, those who possess and employ it form a large portion of the middle and higher classes. They require the application of the higher branches of science to the efficient employment of their capital in almost every purpose to which it can be applied; and they require, at the same time, to show that they are not deficient in that conventional learning of the schools and drawing-rooms to which the circles they live and move in attach importance. In such societies we are, therefore, always coming in contact with men whose scientific knowledge is necessarily very precise, and at the same time very extensive, while their manners and conversation are of the highest polish. There is, perhaps, nothing which strikes a gentleman from India so much on his entering a society differently constituted, as the superior precision of men's information upon scientific subjects ; and more especially upon that of the sciences more immediately applicable to the arts by which the physical enjoyments of men are produced, prepared, and distributed all over the world. Almost all men in India feel that too much of their time before they left England was devoted to the acquisition of the dead languages ; and too little to the study of the elements of science. The time lost can never be regained—at least they think so, which is much the same thing. Had they been well grounded in the elements of physics, physiology, and chemistry before they left their native land, they would have gladly devoted their leisure to the improvement of their knowledge ; but to go back to elements, where elements can be learnt only from books, is, unhappily, what so few can bring themselves to, that no man feels ashamed of acknowledging that he has never studied them at all till he returns to England, or enters a society differently constituted, and finds that he has lost the support of the great majority that always surrounded him in India.[1] It will, perhaps, be said that the members of the official aristocracy of all countries have more or less of the same defects, for certain it is that they everywhere attach paramount or undue importance to the conventional learning of the grammar-school and the drawing-room, and the ignorant and the indolent have everywhere the support of a great majority. Johnson has, however, observed :—

"But the truth is that the knowledge of external nature and the sciences, which that knowledge requires or includes, are not the great or the frequent business of the human mind. Whether we provide for action or conversation, whether we wish to be useful or pleasing, the first requisite is the religious and moral knowledge of right and wrong ; the next is an acquaintance with the history of mankind, and with those examples which may be said to embody truth, and prove by events the reasonableness of opinions.[2] Prudence and justice are virtues and excellencies of all times, and of all places— we are perpetually moralists ; but we are geometricians only by chance. Our intercourse with intellectual nature is necessary ; our speculations upon matter are voluntary and at leisure. Physiological learning is of such rare emergence, that one may know another half his life, without being able to estimate his skill in hydrostatics or astronomy ; but his moral and prudential character

---

[1] In this matter also time has wrought great changes. The scientific branches of the Indian services, the medical, engineering, forestry, geological survey, and others, have greatly developed, and many Indian officials now occupy high places in the world of science.

[2] Compare Bolingbroke's observation, already quoted, that "history is philosophy teaching by example."

immediately appears.   Those authors, therefore, are to be read at schools that supply most axioms of prudence, most principles of moral truth, and most materials for conversation ; and these purposes are best served by poets, orators, and historians." (*Life of Milton.*)

CHAPTER XIX[1]

Pilgrims of India.

THERE is nothing which strikes a European more in travelling over the great roads in India than the vast number of pilgrims of all kinds which he falls in with, particularly between the end of November (*sic*), when all the autumn harvest has been gathered, and the seed of the spring crops has been in the ground. They consist for the most part of persons, male and female, carrying Ganges water from the point at Hardwār, where the sacred stream emerges from the hills, to the different temples in all parts of India, dedicated to the gods Vishnu and Siva. There the water is thrown upon the stones which represent the gods, and when it falls upon these stones it is called "Chandamirt," or holy water, and is frequently collected and reserved to be drunk as a remedy "for a mind diseased."[2]

This water is carried in small bottles, bearing the seals of the presiding priest at the holy place whence it was brought. The bottles are contained in covered baskets, fixed to the ends of a pole, which is carried across the shoulder. The people who carry it are of three kinds—those who carry it for themselves as a votive offering to some shrine; those who are hired for the purpose by others as salaried servants; and, thirdly, those who carry it for sale. In the

---

[1] Chapter XXVI of Vol. II of original edition.

[2] Tavernier notes that Ganges water is often given at weddings, "each guest receiving a cup or two, according to the liberality of the host." "There is sometimes," he says, "2,000 or 3,000 rupees' worth of it consumed at a wedding." (Ball's *Tavernier*, vol. ii, p.p. 231–254.)

interval between the sowing and reaping of the spring crops, that is, between November and March, a very large portion of the Hindoo landholders and cultivators of India devote their leisure to this pious duty. They take their baskets and poles with them from home, or purchase them on the road ; and having poured their libations on the head of the god, and made him acquainted with their wants and wishes, return home. From November to March three-fourths of the number of these people one meets consist of this class. At other seasons more than three-fourths consist of the other two classes—of persons hired for the purpose as servants, and those who carry the water for sale.

One morning the old Jemadār, the marriage of whose mango-grove with the jasmine I have already described,[1] brought his two sons and a nephew to pay their respects to me on their return to Jubbulpore from a pilgrimage to Jagannāth.[2] The sickness of the youngest, a nice boy of about six years of age, had caused this pilgrimage. The eldest son was about twenty years of age, and the nephew about eighteen.

After the usual compliments, I addressed the eldest son : —" And so your brother was really very ill when you set out ? "

" Very ill, sir ; hardly able to stand without assistance."

" What was the matter with him ? "

" It was what we call a drying-up, or withering of the system."

" What were the symptoms ? "

" Dysentery."

" Good ; and what cured him, as he now seems quite well ? "

" Our mother and father vowed five pair of baskets of Ganges water to Gajādhar, an incarnation of the god Siva,

---

[1] *Ante*, Vol. I, Chap. V, p. 39.

[2] Jagannāth (corruptly Juggernaut, &c.), or Puri, on the coast of Orissa, is probably the most venerated shrine in India. The principal deity there worshipped is a form of Vishnu.

at the temple of Baijnāth, and a visit to the temple of Jagannāth."

"And having fulfilled these vows, your brother recovered?"

"He had quite recovered, sir, before we set out on our return from Jagannāth."

"And who carried the baskets?"

"My mother, wife, cousin, myself, and little brother, all carried one pair each."

"This little boy could not surely carry a pair of baskets all the way?"

"No, sir, we had a pair of small baskets made especially for him; and when within about three miles of the temple he got down from his little pony, took up his baskets, and carried them to the god. Up to within three miles of the temple the baskets were carried by a Brahman servant, whom we had taken with us to cook our food. We had with us another Brahman, to whom we had to pay only a trifle, as his principal wages were made up of fees from families in the town of Jubbulpore, who had made similar vows, and gave him so much a bottle for the water he carried in their several names to the god."

"Did you give all your water to the Baijnāth temple, or carry some with you to Jagannāth?"

"No water is ever offered to Jagannāth, sir; he is an incarnation of Vishnu."[1]

"And does Vishnu never drink?"

"He drinks, sir, no doubt; but he gets nothing but offerings of food and money."

"From this to Bindāchal on the Ganges, two hundred and thirty miles; thence to Baijnāth, a hundred and fifty miles; and thence to Jagannāth, some four or five hundred miles more."[2]

[1] Water may not be offered to Jagannāth, but the facts stated in this chapter show that it is offered in other temples of Vishnu.

[2] Bindāchal is in the Mirzāpur district of the North-Western Provinces. Baijnāth is in the Shāhābād district of Bihār.

" And your mother and wife walked all the way with their baskets ? "

" All the way, sir, except when either of them got sick, when she mounted the pony with my little brother till she felt well again."

Here were four members of a respectable family walking a pilgrimage of between twelve and fourteen hundred miles, going and coming, and carrying burthens on their shoulders for the recovery of the poor sick boy; and millions of families are every year doing the same from all parts of India. The change of air, and exercise, cured the boy, and no doubt did them all a great deal of good; but no physician in the world but a religious one, could have persuaded them to undertake such a journey for the same purpose.

The rest of the pilgrims we meet are for the most part of the two monastic orders of Gosāins, or the followers of Siva, and Bairāgīs, or followers of Vishnu, and Muhammadan Fakīrs. A Hindoo of any caste may become a member of these monastic orders. They are all disciples of the high priests of the temples of their respective gods ; and in their name they wander over all India, visiting the celebrated temples which are dedicated to them. A part of the revenues of these temples is devoted to subsisting these disciples as they pass ; and every one of them claims the right of a day's food and lodging, or more, according to the rules of the temple. They make collections along the roads ; and when they return, commonly bring back some surplus as an offering to their apostle, the high priest who has adopted them. Almost every high priest has a good many such disciples, as they are not costly; and from their returning occasionally, and from the disciples of others passing, these high priests learn everything of importance that is going on over India, and are well acquainted with the state of feeling and opinion.

What these disciples get from secular people is given not only from feelings of charity and compassion, but as a religious or propitiatory offering: for they are all considered to be armed by their apostle with a vicarious power of blessing or cursing; and as being in themselves men of God whom it might be dangerous to displease. They never condescend to feign disease or misery in order to excite feelings of compassion, but demand what they want with a bold front, as holy men who have a right to share liberally in the superfluities which God has given to the rest of the Hindoo community. They are in general exceedingly intelligent men of the world, and very communicative. Among them will be found members of all classes of Hindoo society, and of the most wealthy and respectable families.[1] While I had charge of the Narsinghpur district in 1822 a Bairāgī, or follower of Vishnu, came and settled himself down on the border of a village near my residence. His mild and paternal deportment pleased all the little community so much that they carried him every day more food than he required. At last, the proprietor of the village, a very respectable old gentleman, to whom I was much attached, went out with all his family to ask a blessing of the holy man. As they sat down before him, the tears were seen stealing down his cheeks as he looked upon the old man's younger sons and daughters. At last, the old man's wife burst into tears, ran up, and fell upon the holy man's neck, exclaiming, " My lost son, my lost son ! " He was indeed her eldest son. He had disappeared suddenly twelve years before, became a disciple of the high priest of a distant temple, and visited almost every celebrated temple in India, from Kedarnāth in the eternal snows to Sītā Baldī Rāmesar, opposite the island of Ceylon.[2] He

[1] Pandit Saligrām, who was Postmaster-General of the North-Western Provinces some years ago, is said to have become one of these wandering friars.

[2] Seet Buldee Ramesur in original edition. The temple alluded to is that in the small island of Ramisseram at the entrance of Palk's Passage in the Straits of Manaar, which is distinguished by its magnificent colonnade and corridors. The island forms part of the so-called

remained with the family for nearly a year, delighting them and all the country around with his narratives.. At last, he seemed to lose his spirits, his usual rest and appetite ; and one night he again disappeared. He had been absent for some years when I last saw the family, and I know not whether he ever returned.

The real members of these monastic orders are not generally bad men ; but there are a great many men of all kinds who put on their disguises, and under their cloak commit all kinds of atrocities.[1] The security and convenience which the real pilgrims enjoy upon our roads, and the entire freedom from all taxation, both upon these roads, and at the different temples they visit, tend greatly to attach them to our rule, and through that attachment, a tone of good feeling towards it is generally disseminated over all India. They come from the native states, and become acquainted with the superior advantages the people under us enjoy, in the greater security of property, the greater freedom with which it is enjoyed and displayed ; the greater exemption from taxation, and the odious right

Adam's Bridge, by which Ceylon is said to have been connected with the continent of India up to the year A.D. 1480.

[1] The author's other works show that the Thugs often assumed the guise of ascetics, and much of the secret crime of India is known to be committed by men who adopt the garb of holiness. A man disguised as a fakír is often sent on by dacoits (gang-robbers) as a spy and decoy. " Three-fourths of these religious mendicants, whether Hindoos or Muhammadans, rob and steal, and a very great portion of them murder their victims before they rob them ; but they have not any of them as a class been found to follow the trade of murder so exclusively as to be brought properly within the scope of our operations. . . . There is hardly any species of crime that is not throughout India perpetrated by men in the disguise of these religious mendicants ; and almost all such mendicants are really men in disguise ; for Hindoos of any caste can become Bairāgîs and Gosāins ; and Muhammadans of any grade can become Fakírs." (A Report on the System of Megpunnaism, 1839, p. 11.) In the same little work the author advises the compulsory registration of "every disciple belonging to every high priest, whether Hindoo or Muhammadan," and a stringent Vagrant Act.

of search which it involves, the greater facilities for travelling in good roads and bridges ; the greater respectability and integrity of public servants, arising from the greater security in their tenure of office and more adequate rate of avowed salaries ; the entire freedom of the navigation of our great rivers, on which thousands and tens of thousands of laden vessels now pass from one end to the other without any one to question whence they come or whither they go. These are tangible proofs of good government, which all can appreciate ; and as the European gentleman, in his rambles along the great roads, passes the lines of pilgrims with which the roads are crowded during the cold season, he is sure to hear himself hailed with grateful shouts, as one of those who secured for them and the people generally all the blessings they now enjoy.[1]

One day my sporting friend, the Rājā of Maihar, told me that he had been purchasing some water from the Ganges at its source, to wash the image of Vishnu which stood in one of his temples. I asked him whether he ever drank the water after the image had been washed in it. "Yes," said he, "we all occasionally drink the 'chandamirt.'" " And do you in the same manner drink the water in which the god Siva has been washed ?" " Never," said the Rājā. "And why not ?" " Because his wife, Devi, one day in a domestic quarrel cursed him and said, ' The water which falls from thy head shall no man henceforward drink.' From that day," said the Rājā, "no man has ever drunk of the water that washes his image, lest Devi should punish him." " And how is it, then, Rājā Sahib, that mankind continue to drink the water of the Ganges, which is supposed to flow from her husband Siva's top-knot ?" "Because," replied the Rājā, " this sacred river first flows from the right foot of the god Vishnu, and thence passes over the head of Siva. The three gods," continued the Rājā, "govern the world turn and turn about, twenty years

---

[1] This incident still happens occasionally.

at a time. While Vishnu reigns, all goes on well; rain descends in good season, the harvests are abundant, and the cattle thrive. When Brahmā reigns, there is little falling off in these matters; but during the twenty years that Siva reigns, nothing goes on well—we are all at cross purposes, our crops fail, our cattle get the murrain, and mankind suffer from epidemic diseases." The Rājā was a follower of Vishnu, as may be guessed.

CHAPTER XX[1]

The Bēgam Sumroo.

On the 7th of February [1836] I went out to Sardhana and visited the church built and endowed by the late Bēgam Sombre, whose remains are now deposited in it.[2] It was designed by an Italian gentleman, M. Reglioni,[3] and is a fine but not a striking building. I met the bishop, Julius Cæsar, an Italian from Milan, whom I had known a quarter of a century before, a happy and handsome young man—he is still handsome, though old; but very miserable because the Bēgam did not leave him so large a legacy as he expected. In the revenues of her church he had, she thought, quite enough to live upon; and she said that priests without wives or children to care about ought to be satisfied with this; and left him only a few thousand rupees. She made him the medium of conveying a donation to the See of Rome of one hundred and fifty thousand rupees,[4] and thereby procured for him the bishopric of Amartanta in the island of Cyprus; and got her grandson, Dyce Sombre, made a chevalier of the order of Christ, and presented with a splint from the real cross, as a relic.

The Bēgam Sombre was by birth a Saiyadanī, or lineal descendant from Muhammad, the founder of the Musalmān faith; and she was united to Walter Reinhard, when very

[1] Chapter XXVII of Vol. II of original edition.

[2] The reader will observe that the lady's name is spelt Sumroo in the heading and Sombre in the text. The form Samrū, or Shamrū, transliterates the Hindustānī spelling.

[3] Perhaps identical with General Regholini, who was in the Bēgam's service at the time of her death. (*N. W. P. Gazetteer*, vol. iii, p. 295.)

[4] The Bēgam's benefactions are detailed *post*, p.p. 286–288.

young, by all the forms considered necessary by persons of
her persuasion when married to men of another.[1] Reinhard
had been married to another woman of the Musalmān
faith, who still lives at Sardhana,[2] but she had become
insane, and has ever since remained so.   By this first wife
he had a son, who got from the Emperor the title of Zafar
Yāb Khān, at the request of the Bēgam, his step-mother;
but he was a man of weak intellect; and so little thought of
that he was not recognized even as the nominal chief on
the death of his father.

Walter Reinhard was a native of Salzburg.   He enlisted
as a private soldier in the French service, and came to
India, where he entered the service of the East India
Company, and rose to the rank of sergeant.[3]   Reinhard
got the soubriquet of Sombre from his comrades while in
the French service from the sombre cast of his countenance

[1] "This remarkable woman was the daughter, by a concubine, of
Asad Khān, a Musalmān of Arab descent settled in the town of
Kutāna in the Meerut district.   She was born about the year 1753 A.D.
[see *post*, p. 273 note].   On the death of her father, she and her mother
became subject to ill-treatment from her half-brother, the legitimate
heir, and they consequently removed to Delhi about 1760.   There she
entered the service of Sumru, and accompanied him through all his
campaigns.   Sumru, on retiring to Sardhana, found himself relieved of
all the cares and troubles of war, and gave himself entirely up to a life
of ease and pleasure, and so completely fell into the hands of the
Bēgam that she had no difficulty in inducing him to exchange the title
of mistress for that of wife."   (Mr. E. T. Atkinson in *N. W. P.
Gazetteer*, vol. ii, p. 95.   The authorities for the history of Bēgum
Samrū are very conflicting.   Mr. Atkinson has examined them criti-
cally, and his account is, I think, the best in existence.)

[2] This first wife died at Sardhana during the rainy season of 1838.
She must have been above one hundred years of age ; and a good
many of the Europeans that lie buried in the Sardhana cemetery had
lived above a hundred years. [W. H. S.]   She was a concubine,
named Bahā Bēgam. (*Gazetteer*, vol. iii, p. 96.)

[3] His name is spelled Reinhard on his tombstone, as in the text.
It is also spelled Renard.   According to some authorities, his birthplace was Trèves, not Salzburg.   He was a butcher by trade, and
deserted both from the French and the English services.

and temper.[1] An Armenian, by name Gregory, of a Calcutta family, the virtual minister of Kāsim Ali Khān,[2] under the title of Gorgin Khān,[3] took him into his service when the war was about to commence between his master and the English. Kāsim Ali was a native of Kāshmīr, and not naturally a bad man ; but he was goaded to madness by the injuries and insults heaped upon him by the servants of the East India Company, who were not then paid, as at present, in adequate salaries, but in profits upon all kinds of monopolies ; and they would not suffer the recognized sovereign of the country in which they traded to grant to his subjects the same exemption that they claimed for themselves exclusively ; and a war was the consequence.[4]

Mr. Ellis, one of these civil servants and chief of the factory at Patna, whose opinions had more weight with the council in Calcutta than all the wisdom of such men as Vansittart and Warren Hastings, because they happened to be more consonant with the personal interests of the majority, precipitately brought on the war, and assumed the direction of all military operations, of which he knew nothing, and for which he seems to have been totally unfitted by the violence of his temper. All his enterprises

[1] A more probable explanation is that the name is a corruption of an alias, Summers, assumed by the deserter.

[2] Kāsim Ali Khān is generally referred to in the histories under the name of Mīr Kāsim (Meer Cossim). Mīr Jāfir was deposed in 1760, and Mīr Kāsim was placed on the throne of Bengal in his stead by the English. The history of Mīr Kāsim is told in detail by Thornton in his sixth chapter.

[3] This name may be a corruption of " Georgian."

[4] Mill observes upon these transactions :—" The conduct of the Company's servants upon this occasion furnishes one of the most remarkable instances upon record of the power of self-interest to extinguish all sense of justice and even of shame. They had hitherto insisted, contrary to all right and all precedent, that the government of the country should exempt all their goods from duty ; they now insisted that it should impose duties upon all other traders, and accused it as guilty of a breach of the peace towards the English nation, because it proposed to remit them." [W. H. S.]

failed—the city and factory were captured by the enemy, and the European inhabitants taken prisoners. The Nawāb, smarting under the reiterated wrongs he had received, and which he attributed mainly to the counsels of Mr. Ellis, no sooner found the chief within his grasp, than he determined to have him and all who were taken with him, save a Doctor Fullarton, to whom he owed some personal obligations, put to death. His own native officers were shocked at the proposal, and tried to dissuade him from the purpose, but he was resolved, and not finding among them any willing to carry it into execution he applied to Sumroo, who readily undertook and, with some of his myrmidons, performed the horrible duty in 1763.[1] At the suggestion of Gregory and Sombre, Kāsim Ali now attempted to take the small principality of Nepāl, as a kind of basis for his operations against the English. He had four hundred excellent rifles with flint locks and screwed barrels made at Monghyr (Mungīr) on the Ganges, so as to fit into small boxes. These boxes were sent up on the backs of four hundred brave volunteers for this forlorn hope. Gregory had got a passport for the boxes as rare merchandise for the palace of the prince at Kathmandū, in whose presence alone they were to be opened. On reaching the palace at night, these volunteers were to open their boxes, screw up the barrels, destroy all the inmates, and possess themselves of the palace, where it is supposed Kāsim Ali had already secured many friends. Twelve thousand soldiers had advanced to the foot of the hills near Betiya, to support the attack, and the volunteers were in the fort of Makwānpur, the only strong fort between the plain and the capital. They had been treated with great consideration by the garrison, and were to set out at daylight

---

[1] The 3rd of October was the day of slaughter at Patna. The Europeans at other places in Mīr Kāsim's power were also massacred; and the total number slain, men, women, and children, amounted to about two hundred. Sumroo personally butchered about one hundred and fifty at Patna.

the next morning; but one of the attendants, who had been let into the secret, got drunk, and in a quarrel with one of the garrison, told him that he should see in a few days who would be master of that garrison. This led to suspicion ; the boxes were broken open, the arms discovered, and the whole of the party, except three or four, were instantly put to death ; the three or four who escaped gave intelligence to the army at Betiyā, and the whole retreated upon Monghyr. But for this drunken man, Nepāl had perhaps been Kāsim Ali's.[1]

[1] Our troops, under Sir David Ochterlony, took the fort of Makwān-pur in 1815, and might in five days have been before the defenceless capital ; but they were here arrested by the romantic chivalry of the Marquis of Hastings. The country had been virtually conquered ; the prince, by his base treachery towards us and outrages upon others, had justly forfeited his throne ; but the Governor-General, by perhaps a misplaced lenity, left it to him without any other guarantee for his future good behaviour than the recollection that he had been soundly beaten. Unfortunately he left him at the same time a sufficient quantity of fertile land below the hills to maintain the same army with which he had fought us, with better knowledge how to employ them, to keep us out on a future occasion. Between the attempt of Kāsim Ali and our attack upon Nepāl, the Gurkha masters of the country had, by a long series of successful aggressions upon their neighbours, rendered themselves in their own opinion and in that of their neigh-bours the best soldiers of India. They have, of course, a very natural feeling of hatred against our government, which put a stop to the wild career of conquest, and wrested from their grasp all the property and all the pretty women from Kathmandū to Kashmir. To these beauti-ful regions they were what the invading Huns were in former days to Europe, absolute fiends. Had we even exacted a good road into their country with fortifications at the proper places, it might have checked the hopes of one day resuming the career of conquest that now keeps up the army and military spirit, to threaten us with a renewal of war whenever we are embarrassed on the plains. [W. H. S.]

The author's uneasiness concerning the attitude of Nepāl was fully justified. During the Afghan troubles of 1838-1843 the Nepalese Government was in constant communication with the enemies of the Indian Government. The late Maharāja Sir Jang Bahādur obtained power in 1846, and, after his visit to England in 1850, decided to abide by the English alliance. He did valuable service in 1857 and 1858,

Kāsim Alī Khān was beaten in several actions by our gallant little band of troops under their able leader, Colonel Adams; and at last driven to seek shelter with the Nawāb Wazīr of Oudh, into whose service Sumroo afterwards entered. This chief being in his turn beaten, Sumroo went off and entered the service of the celebrated chief of Rohilkhand, Hāfiz Rahmat Khān. This he soon quitted from fear of the English. He raised two battalions in 1772, which he soon afterwards increased to four; and let out always to the highest bidder—first, to the Jāt chiefs of Dīg, then to the chief of Jaipur, then to Najaf Khān, the prime minister, and then to the Marāthās. His battalions were officered by Europeans, but Europeans of respectability were unwilling to take service under a man so precariously situated, however great their necessities; and he was obliged to content himself for the most part with the very dross of society—men who could neither read nor write, nor keep themselves sober. The consequence was that the battalions were often in a state of mutiny, committing every kind of outrage upon the persons of their officers, and at all times in a state of insubordination bordering on mutiny. These battalions seldom obtained their pay till they put their commandant into confinement, and made him dig up his hidden stores, if he had any, or borrow from bankers, if he had none. If the troops felt pressed for time, and their commander was of the necessary character, they put him astride upon a hot gun without his trousers. When our battalion had got its pay out of him in this manner, he was often handed over to another for the same purpose. The poor old Bēgam had been often subjected to the starving stage of this proceeding before she came under our protection; but had never, I believe, been *grilled* upon a gun. It was a rule, it was said, with Sombre, to enter the field of battle at the safest point, form line facing the enemy, fire

and the two governments have ever since maintained an unbroken, though reserved, friendship. The Gūrkha regiments in the English service are recruited in Nepāl.

a few rounds in the direction where they stood, without regard to the distance or effect, form square, and await the course of events. If victory declared for the enemy, he sold his unbroken force to him to great advantage; if for his friends, he assisted them in collecting the plunder, and securing all the advantages of the victory. To this prudent plan of action his corps afterwards steadily adhered; and they never took or lost a gun till they came in contact with our forces at Ajantā and Assaye.[1]

Sombre died at Agra on the 4th of May, 1778, and his remains were at first buried in his garden. They were afterwards removed to the consecrated ground in the Agra churchyard by his widow the Bēgam,[2] who was baptized, at the age of forty,[3] by a Roman Catholic priest, under the name of Joanna,[4] on the 7th of May, 1781.

On the death of her husband she was requested to take command of the force by all the Europeans and natives that composed it, as the only possible mode of keeping them together, since the son was known to be altogether unfit. She consented, and was regularly installed in the

---

[1] Assaye (Assye, Asāi) is in the Nizām's dominions. Here, on the 23rd of September, 1803, Sir Arthur Wellesley, afterwards Duke of Wellington, with about 4,500 men, defeated the Marāthā host of abou. 50,000 men, including more than 10,000 under European leaders. Ajantā, or Ajantā Ghāt, is in the same region.

[2] His tombstone bears a Portuguese inscription:—

"Aqui iazo Walter Reinhard morreo aos 4 de Mayo no anno. de 1778."

(*Gazetteer*, vol. ii, p. 96.)

[3] According to this statement she must have been born in or about 1741, not in 1753 as stated by Mr. Atkinson. If the earlier date is correct, she was ninety-five when she died in 1836. Mr. Higginbotham, referring to Bacon's work, says she died at the age of eighty-nine, which places her birth in 1747. According to Mr. Beale, she was aged eighty-eight lunar years when she died, on the 27th January, 1836, equivalent to about eighty-five solar years. This computation places her birth in 1751 A.D., which may be taken as the correct date.

[4] She added the name Nobilis, when she married Le Vaisseau. (*Gazetteer*, vol. ii, p. 106, note.)

charge by the Emperor Shāh Alam. Her chief officer was a Mr. Paoli, a German, who soon after took an active part in providing the poor imbecile old Emperor with a prime minister, and got himself assassinated on the restoration, a few weeks after, of his rival.[1] The troops continued in the same state of insubordination, and the Bēgam was anxious for an opportunity to show that she was determined to be obeyed.

While she was encamped with the army of the prime minister of the time at Mathurā,[2] news was one day brought to her that two slave girls had set fire to her houses at Agra, in order that they might make off with their paramours, two soldiers of the guard she had left in charge. These houses had thatched roofs, and contained all her valuables, and the widows, wives, and children of her principal officers. The fire had been put out with much difficulty and great loss of property; and the two slave girls were soon after discovered in the bazaar at Agra, and brought out to the Bēgam's camp. She had the affair investigated in the usual summary form; and their guilt being proved to the satisfaction of all present, she had them flogged till they were senseless, and then thrown into a pit dug in front of her tent for the purpose, and buried alive. I had heard the story related in different ways, and I now took pains to ascertain the truth; and this short narrative may, I believe, be relied upon.[3]

---

[1] The author spells the German's name Pauly; I have followed Mr. Atkinson's spelling. The man was assassinated in 1783.

[2] This indication shows that the execution of the slave girls took place in 1782. (See *Gazetteer*, vol. ii, p. 91.)

[3] "The darker side of the Bēgam's character is shown by the story of the slave girl's murder. By some it is said that the girl's crime consisted in her having attracted the favourable notice of one of the Bēgam's husbands. Whatever may have been the offence, her barbarous mistress visited it by causing the girl to be buried alive. The time chosen for the execution was the evening, the place the tent of the Bēgam; who caused her bed to be arranged immediately over the grave, and occupied it until the morning, to prevent any attempt to

An old Persian merchant, called the Agā, still resided at Sardhana, to whom I knew that one of the slave girls belonged. I visited him, and he told me that his father had been on intimate terms with Sombre, and when he died his mother went to live with his widow, the Bēgam—that his slave girl was one of the two—that his mother at first protested against her being taken off to the camp, but became on inquiry satisfied of her guilt—and that the Bēgam's object was to make a strong impression upon the turbulent spirit of her troops by a severe example. " In this object," said the old Agā, " she entirely succeeded ; and for some years after her orders were implicitly obeyed ; had she faltered on that occasion she must have lost the command—she would have lost that respect, without which it would have been impossible for her to retain it a month. I was then a boy ; but I remember well that there were, besides my mother and sisters, many respectable females that would have rather perished in the flames than come out to expose themselves to the crowd that assembled to see the fires ; and had the fires not been put out, a great many lives must have been lost ; besides, there were many old people and young children who could not have escaped." The old Agā was going off to take up his quarters at Delhi

rescue the miserable girl beneath. By acts like this the Bēgam inspired such terror that she was never afterwards troubled with domestic dissensions." (*N. W. P. Gazetteer*, vol. ii, p. 110.) It will be observed that this version mentions only one girl. According to Mr. Higginbotham (*Men whom India has Known*, s.v. " Sumroo ") this execution took place on the evening of the day on which Le Vaisseau perished in 1795. (See *post*.) He adds that " it is said that this act preyed upon her conscience in after life." This account professes to be based on Bacon's *First Impressions and Studies from Nature in Hindustan,* which is said to be " the most reliable, as the author saw the Bēgam, attended and conversed with her at one of her levées, and gained all his information at her Court." But Bacon's account of the Bēgam's history, as quoted by Mr. Higginbotham, is full of gross errors ; and I am of opinion that Sir William Sleeman may be relied on as giving the most accurate obtainable version of the horrid story. He had the best possible opportunities, as well as a desire, to ascertain the truth.

when this conversation took place ; and I am sure that he told me what he thought to be true. This narrative corresponded exactly with that of several other old men from whom I had heard the story. It should be recollected that among natives there is no particular mode of execution prescribed for those who are condemned to · die ; nor, in a camp like this, any court of justice save that of the commander in which they could be tried, and, supposing the guilt to have been established, as it is said to have been to the satisfaction of the Bēgam and the principal officers, who were all Europeans and Christians, perhaps the punishment was not much greater than the crime deserved, and the occasion demanded. But it is possible that the slave girls may not have set fire to the buildings, but merely availed themselves of the occasion of the fire to run off ; indeed, slave girls are under so little restraint in India, that it would be hardly worth while for them to burn down a house to get out. I am satisfied that the Bēgam believed them guilty, and that the punishment, horrible as it was, was merited. It certainly had the desired effect. My object has been to ascertain the truth in this case, and to state it, and not to eulogize or defend the old Bēgam.

After Paoli's death, the command of the troops under the Bēgam devolved successively upon Baours, Evans, Dudrenec, who, after a short time, all gave it up in disgust at the beastly habits of the European subalterns, and the overbearing insolence to which they and the want of regular pay gave rise among the soldiers. At last the command devolved upon Monsieur Le Vaisseau, a French gentleman of birth, education, gentlemanly deportment, and honourable feelings.[1] The battalions had been

[1] Mr. Atkinson (*Gazetteer*, vol. ii, p. 106) uses the spelling Le Vaisseau, which is probably correct, and observes that the name is also written Le Vassont. The author writes Le Vassoult ; and Francklin (*Military Memoirs of Mr. George Thomas*, London ed., p. 55) phonetically spells the name as Levasso. "On every occasion he was the declared and inveterate enemy of. Mr. Thomas."

increased to six, with their due proportion of guns and
cavalry; part resided at Sardhana, her capital, and part at
Delhi, in attendance upon the Emperor. A very extraordinary man entered her service about the same time
with Le Vaisseau, George Thomas, who, from a quarter-
master on board a ship, raised himself to a principality in
Northern India.[1] Thomas on one occasion raised his
mistress in the esteem of the Emperor and the people by
breaking through the old rule of central squares : gallantly
leading on his troops, and rescuing his majesty from a

[1] Thomas was an Irishman, born in the county of Tipperary.
" From the best-information we could procure, it appears that Mr.
George Thomas first came to India in a British ship of war, in 1781-2.
His situation in the fleet was humble, having served as a quarter-
master, or, as is affirmed by some, in the capacity of a common
sailor. . . His first service was among the Polygars to the southward,
where he resided a few years. But at length setting out overland, he
spiritedly traversed the central part of the peninsula, and about the
year 1787 arrived at Delhi. Here he received a commission in the service
of the Begam Sumroo . . . Soon after his arrival at Delhi, the Begam,
with her usual judgment and discrimination of character, advanced
him to a command in her army. From this period his military career
in the north-west of India may be said to have commenced." Owing
to the rivalry of Le Vaisseau, Thomas "quitted the Begam Sumroo,
and about 1792 betook himself to the frontier station of the British
army at the post of Anopshire (Anūpshahr). . . Here he waited several
months. . . In the beginning of the year 1793, Mr. Thomas, being
at Anopshire, received letters from Appakandarow (Apakanda Rāo),
a Mahratta chief, conveying offers of service, and promises of a comfortable provision." (*Francklin*, p. 20.) The author states that
Thomas left the Begam's service in 1793, after her marriage with Le
Vaisseau in that year. Francklin (*see also* p. 55) was clearly under
the impression that the marriage did not take place till after Thomas
had thrown up his command under the Begam. He made peace with
her in 1795. The capital of the principality which he carved out for
himself in 1798 was at Hānsī, 89 miles north-west of Delhi. He was
driven out at the close of 1801, entered British territory in January
1802, and died on the 22nd of August in that year at Barhāmpur,
being about forty-six years of age. A son of his was an officer in the
Begam's service at the time of her death in 1836. A great-grand-
daughter of George Thomas was, in 1867, the wife of a writer on a
humble salary in one of the Government offices at Agra. (*Beale.*)

perilous situation in one of his battles with a rebellious subject, Najaf Kulī Khān, where the Bēgam was present in her palankeen, and reaped all the laurels, being from that day called "the most beloved daughter of the Emperor."[1] As his best chance of securing his ascendency against such a rival, Le Vaisseau proposèd marriage to the Bēgam, and was accepted. She was married to Le Vaisseau by Father Gregoris, a Carmelite monk, in 1793, before Saleur and Bernier, two French officers of great merit. George Thomas left her service, in consequence, in 1793, and set up for himself; and was afterwards crushed by the united armies of the Sikhs and Marāthās, commanded by European officers, after he had been recognized as a general officer by the Governor-General of India. George Thomas had latterly twelve small disciplined battalions officered by Europeans. He had good artillery, cast his own guns, and was the first person that applied iron calibres to brass cannon. He was unquestionably a man of very extraordinary military genius, and his ferocity and recklessness as to the means he used were quite in keeping with the times. His revenues were derived from the Sikh states which he had rendered tributary; and he would probably have been sovereign of them all in the room of Ranjīt Singh, had not the jealousy of Perron and other French officers in the Marāthā army interposed.[2]

[1] This incident happened in 1788. (*See N. W. P. Gazetteer*, vol. ii, p. 99.)

[2] "A more competent estimate may perhaps be formed of his abilities if we reflect on the nature and extent of one of his plans, which he detailed to the compiler of these memoirs during his residence at Benares. When fixed in his residence at Hānsi, he first conceived, and would, if unforeseen and untoward circumstances had not occurred, have executed the bold design of extending his conquests to the mouths of the Indus. This was to have been effected by a fleet of boats, constructed from timber procured in the forests near the city of Firōzpur, on the banks of the Satlaj river, proceeding down that river with his army, and settling the countries he might subdue on his route; a daring enterprise, and conceived in the true spirit of an ancient Roman. On the conclusion of this design it was

The Bēgam tried in vain to persuade her husband to receive all the European officers of the corps at his table as gentlemen, urging that not only their domestic peace, but their safety among such a turbulent set, required that the character of these officers should be raised if possible, and their feelings conciliated. Nothing, he declared, should ever induce him to sit at table with men of such habits; and they at last determined that no man should command them who would not condescend to do so. Their insolence and that of the soldiers generally became at last unbearable, and the Bēgam determined to go off with her husband, and seek an asylum in the Honourable Company's territory with the little property she could command, of one hundred thousand rupees in money, and her jewels, amounting perhaps in value to one hundred thousand more. Le Vaisseau did not understand English; but with the aid of a grammar and a dictionary he was able to communicate her wishes to Colonel McGowan, who commanded at that time (1795) an advanced post of our army at Anūpshahr on the Ganges.[1] He proposed that the Colonel should receive them in his cantonments, and assist them in their journey thence to Farrukhābād, where they wished in future to reside, free from the cares and anxieties of such a charge. The Colonel had some scruples, under the impression that he might be censured for aiding in the flight of a public officer of the Emperor. He now addressed the Governor-General of India, Sir John Shore himself, April 1795, who requested Major

his intention to turn his arms against the Panjāb, which he expected to reduce in a couple of years; and which, considering the wealth he would then have acquired, and the amazing resources he would have possessed, these successes combined would doubtless have contributed to establish his authority on a firm and solid basis." He offered to conquer the Panjāb on behalf of the Government of India, for the welfare of his king and country. (*Francklin*, p.p. 334-336.)

[1] A small town in the Bulandshahr district of the North-Western Provinces, 73 miles south-east of Delhi. Its fort used to be considered strong.

Palmer, our accredited agent with Sindhia, who was then
encamped near Delhi, and holding the seals of prime
minister of the empire, to interpose his good offices in
favour of the Bēgam and her husband. Sindhia demanded
twelve lākhs of rupees as the price of the privilege she
solicited to retire ; and the Bēgam, in her turn, demanded
over and above the privilege of resigning the command into
his hands, the sum of four lākhs of rupees as the price of
the arms and accoutrements which had been provided at
her own cost and that of her late husband. It was at last
settled that she should resign the command, and set out
secretly with her husband ; and that Sindhia should confer
the command of her troops upon one of his own officers,
who would pay the son of Sombre two thousand rupees a
month for life. Le Vaisseau was to be received into our
territories, treated as a prisoner of war upon parole, and
permitted to reside with his wife at the French settlement
of Chandernagore. His last letter to Sir John Shore is
dated the 30th April, 1795. His last letters describing
this final arrangement are addressed to Mr. Even, a French
merchant at Mirzapore, and a Mr. Bernier, both personal
friends of his, and are dated 18th of May, 1795.

The battalions on duty at Delhi got intimation of this
correspondence, made the son of Sombre declare himself
their legitimate chief, and march at their head to seize the
Bēgam and her husband. Le Vaisseau heard of their
approach, and urged the Bēgam to set out with him at
midnight for Anūpshahr, declaring that he would rather
destroy himself than submit to the personal indignities
which he knew would be heaped upon him by the infuriated
ruffians who were coming to seize them. The Bēgam consented, declaring that she would put an end to her life with
her own hand should she be taken. She got into her
palankeen with a dagger in her hand, and as he had seen
her determined resolution and proud spirit before exerted
on many trying occasions, he doubted not that she would
do what she declared she would. He mounted his horse

and rode by the side of her palankeen, with a pair of pistols in his holsters, and a good sword by his side. They had got as far as Kabrī, about three miles from Sardhana,[1] on the road to Meerut, when they found the battalions from Sardhana, who had got intimation of the flight, gaining fast upon the palankeen. Le Vaisseau asked the Bēgam whether she remained firm in her resolve to die rather than submit to the indignities that threatened them. "Yes," replied she, showing him the dagger firmly grasped in her right hand. He drew a pistol from his holster without saying anything, but urged on the bearers. He could have easily galloped off, and saved himself, but he would not quit his wife's side. At last the soldiers came up close behind them. The female attendants of the Bēgam began to scream; and looking in, Le Vaisseau saw the white cloth that covered the Bēgam's breast stained with blood. She had stabbed herself, but the dagger had struck against one of the bones of her chest, and she had not courage to repeat the blow. Her husband put his pistol to his temple and fired. The ball passed through his head, and he fell dead on the ground. One of the soldiers who saw him told me that he sprang at least a foot off the saddle into the air as the shot struck him. His body was treated with every kind of insult by the European officers and their men;[2] and the Bēgam was taken back into Sardhana, kept under a gun for seven days, deprived of all kinds of food, save what she got by stealth from her female servants, and subjected to all manner of insolent language.

At last the officers were advised by George Thomas, who had instigated them to this violence out of pique against the Bēgam for her preference of the Frenchman,[3] to set

---

[1] Francklin says that the troops overtook the fugitives "at the village of Kerwah, in the begum's jaghire, four miles distant from her capital." (P. 58.)

[2] "For three days it lay exposed to the insults of the rabble, and was at length thrown into a ditch." (*Francklin*, p. 60.)

[3] According to George Thomas (whose version of the story is given

aside their puppet and reseat the Bēgam in the command, as the only chance of keeping the territory of Sardhana.[1] "If," said he, "the Bēgam should die under the torture of mind and body to which you are subjecting her, the minister will very soon resume the lands assigned for your payment, and disband a force so disorderly, and so little likely to be of any use to him or the Emperor." A council of war was held—the Bēgam was taken out from under the gun, and reseated on the "masnad." A paper was drawn up by about thirty European officers, of whom only one, Monsieur Saleur, could sign his own name, swearing in the name of God and Jesus Christ,[2] that they would hencefor-

by his biographer), the Bēgam, when the mutiny broke out, was actually preparing to attack Thomas. A German officer, known only as the Liègeois, strenuously dissuaded the Bēgam from the proposed hostilities, and was, in consequence, degraded by Le Vaisseau. The troops then mutinied, and swore allegiance to Zafar Yāb Khān. (*Francklin*, p. 37.)

[1] Thomas says that the overtures came from the Bēgam. "In a manner the most abject and desponding, she addressed Mr. Thomas . . . . implored him to come to her assistance, and, finally, offered to pay any sum of money the Marāthās should require, on condition they would reinstate her in her Jāgīr. On receipt of these letters, Mr. Thomas, by an offer of 120,000 rupees, prevailed on Bāpū Sindhia to make a movement towards Sardhana." After negotiation, Thomas marched to Khātaulī, and "publicly gave out that unless the Bēgam was reinstated in her authority, those who resisted must expect no mercy; and to give additional weight to this declaration, he apprised them that he was acting under the orders of the Marāthā chiefs." After some difficulty, "she was finally reinstated in the full authority of her Jāgīr." This version of the affair, it will be noticed, does not quite agree with that given more briefly by the author.

[2] The paper was written by a Muhammadan, and he would not write Christ *the Son of God*. It is written "In the naiue of God, and his Majesty Christ." The Muhammadans look upon Christ as the greatest of prophets before Muhammad; but the most binding article of their faith is this from the Korān, which they repeat every day :— "I believe in God, who was never begot, nor has ever begotten, nor will ever have an equal,"—alluding to the Christians' belief in the Trinity. [W. H. S.] For Muhammad's opinion of Jesus Christ, see especially chapters iv and v of the Korān.

ward obey her with all their hearts and souls, and recognize no other person whomsoever as commander. They all affixed their seals to this *covenant ;* but some of them, to show their superior learning, put their initials, or what they used as such, for some of these *learned Thebans* knew only two or three letters of the alphabet, which they put down, though they happened not to be their real initials. An officer on the part of Sindhia, who was to have commanded these troops, was present at this reinstallation of the Begam, and glad to take, as a compensation for his disappointment, the sum of one hundred and fifty thousand rupees, which the Begam contrived to borrow for him.

The body of poor Le Vaisseau was brought back to camp, and there lay several days unburied, and exposed to all kinds of indignities. The supposition that this was the result of a plan formed by the Begam to get rid of Le Vaisseau is, I believe, unfounded.[1] The Begam herself gave some colour of truth to the report by retaining the name of her first husband, Sombre, to the last, and never publicly or formally declaring her marriage with Le Vaisseau after his death. The troops in this mutiny pretended nothing more than a desire to vindicate the honour of their old commander Sombre, which had, they said, been compromised by the illicit intercourse between Le Vaisseau and his widow. She had not dared to declare the marriage to them lest they should mutiny on that ground, and deprive her of the command ; and for the same reason she retained the name of Sombre after her restoration, and remained silent on the subject of her second marriage. The marriage was known only to a few European officers, Sir John Shore, Major Palmer, and the other gentlemen with whom Le Vaisseau corresponded. Some grave old native gentlemen who were long in her service have told me that they believed " there really was too much of truth

---

[1] To my mind the circumstances all tend to throw suspicion on the Begam. The author was evidently disposed to form the best possible opinion of her character and acts.

in the story which excited the troops to mutiny on that
occasion—her too great intimacy with the gallant young
Frenchman. God forgive them for saying so of a lady
whose salt they had eaten for so many years." Le Vaisseau
made no mention of the marriage to Colonel McGowan ;
and from the manner in which he mentions it to Sir John
Shore it is clear that he, or she, or both, were anxious to
conceal it from the troops and from Sindhia before their
departure. She stipulated in her will that her heir, Mr.
Dyce, should take the name of Sombre, as if she wished
to have the little episode of her second marriage forgotten.

After the death of Le Vaisseau, the command devolved
on Monsieur Saleur, a Frenchman, the only respectable
officer who signed the covenant ; he had taken no active
part in the mutiny ; on the contrary, he had done all he
could to prevent it ; and he was at last, with George
Thomas, the chief means of bringing his brother officers
back to a sense of their duty. Another battalion was
added to the four in 1797, and another raised in 1798 and
1802 ; five of the six marched under Colonel Saleur to the
Deccan with Sindhia. They were in a state of mutiny the
whole way, and utterly useless as auxiliaries, as Saleur himself declared in many of his letters written in French to
his mistress the Bēgam. At the battle of Assaye, four of
these battalions were left in charge of the Mārāthā camps.
One was present in the action and lost its four guns. Soon
after the return of these battalions, the Bēgam entered into
an alliance with the British government ; the force then
consisted of these six battalions, a party of artillery served
chiefly by Europeans, and two hundred horse. She had a
good arsenal well stored, a foundry for cannon, both within
the walls of a small fortress, built near her dwelling at
Sardhana. The whole cost her about four lākhs of rupees
a year ; her civil establishments eighty thousand, and her
household establishments and expenses about the same ;
total six lākhs of rupees a year. The revenues of Sardhana,
and the other lands assigned at different times for the pay-

ment of the force had been at no time more than sufficient
to cover these expenses ; but under the protection of our
government they improved with the extension of tillage,
and the improvements of the surrounding markets for
produce, and she was enabled to give largely to the support
of charitable institutions, and to provide handsomely for
the support of her family and pensioners after her death."[1]

[1] After the Bēgam's death the revenue settlement of the estate was
made by Mr. Plowden, who writes in his report, as quoted in *N. W. P.
Gazetteer*, vol. iii, p. 432, "The rule seems to have been fully
recognized and acted up to by the Bēgam which declared that, according to Muhammadan law, 'there shall be left for every man who
cultivates his lands as much as he requires for his own support, till the
next crop be reaped, and that of his family, and for seed. This much
shall be left to him ; what remains is land-tax, and shall go to the
public treasury?' For, considering her territory as a private estate and
her subjects as serfs, she appropriated the whole produce of their
labour, with the exception of what sufficed to keep body and soul together. It was by these means . . . . that a factitious state of
prosperity was induced and maintained, which, though it might, and,
I believe, did deceive the Bēgam's neighbours into an impression that
her country was highly prosperous, could not delude the population
into content and happiness. Above the surface and to the eye all was
smiling and prosperous, but within was rottenness and misery. Under
these circumstances the smallness of the above arrear is no proof of
the fairness of the revenue. It rather shows that the collections were
as much as the Bēgam's ingenuity could extract, and this balance
being unrealizable, the demand was, by so much at least, too high."
The statistics alluded to are :—

	Rs.
Average demand of the portions of the Bēgam's Territory in the Meerut district . . .	5.86.650
Average collections	5.67.211
Balances	19.439

"Ruin was impending, when the Bēgam's death in January, 1836,
and the consequent lapse of the estate to the British, induced the
cultivators to return to their homes."

Details of the Bēgam's military forces are given in *Gazetteer*, vol. iii,
p. 295. For the last thirty years of her life the Bēgam had no need for
the large force (3,371 officers and men, with 44 guns) which she
maintained. In her excessive expenditure on a superfluous army, in
her niggardly provision for civil administration, and in her merciless

Sombre's son, Zafaryāb Khān, had a daughter who was married to Colonel Dyce, who had for some time the management of the Bēgam's affairs; but he lost her favour long before her death by his violent temper and overbearing manners, and was obliged to resign the management to his son, who, on the Bēgam's death, came in for the bulk of her fortune, or about sixty lākhs of rupees. He has two sisters who were brought up by the Bēgam, one married to Captain Troup, an Englishman, and the other to Mr. Salaroli, an Italian, both very worthy men. Their wives have been handsomely provided for by the Bēgam, and by their brother, who trebled the fortunes left to them by the Bēgam.[1] She built an excellent church at Sardhana, and assigned the sum of 100,000 rupees as a fund to provide for its service and repairs; 50,000 rupees as another [fund] for the poor of the place; and 100,000 as a third, for a college in which Roman Catholic priests might be educated for the benefit of India generally. She sent to Rome 150,000 rupees to be employed as a charity fund at the discretion of the Pope; and to the Archbishop of Canterbury she sent 50,000 for the same purpose. She gave to the Bishop of Calcutta 100,000 rupees to

rack-renting, she followed the evil example of the ordinary native prince, and was superior only in the unusual ability with which she worked an unsound and oppressive system.

[1] Zafaryāb Khān died in 1802. His son-in-law, Colonel Dyce, was employed in the Bēgam's service. "The issue of this marriage was: (1) David Ochterlony Dyce Sombre, who married Mary Anne, daughter of Viscount St. Vincent, by whom he had no issue. He died in Paris in July 1851. In August 1867 his body was conveyed to Sardhana and buried in the cathedral. (2) A daughter, who married Captain Rose Troup. (3) A daughter, who married Paul Salaroli, now Marquis of Briona. The present owner of Sardhana is the Honourable Mary Anne Forester, the widow of David Ochterlony Dyce Sombre, and the successful claimant in the suit against Government which has recently been decided in her favour." (*Gazetteer*, vol. iii (1875), p. 296.) This lady in 1862 married George Cecil-Weld, third Baron Forester, who died without issue in 1886. (Burke's *Peerage*.) Lady Forester died recently.

provide teachers for the poor of the Protestant church in Calcutta. She sent to Calcutta for distribution to the poor, and for the liberation of deserving debtors, 50,000. To the Catholic missions at Calcutta, Bombay, and Madras she gave 100,000 ; and to that of Agra 30,000. She built a handsome chapel for the Roman Catholics at Meerut ; and presented the fund for its support, with a donation of 12,000 ; and she built a chapel for the Church Missionary at Meerut, the Reverend Mr. Richards, at a cost of 10,000, to meet the wants of the native Protestants.[1]

Among all who had opportunities of knowing her she

[1] In the original edition these statistics are given in words. Figures have been used in this edition as being more readily grasped. The amounts stated by the author are approximate round sums. More accurate details are given in *Gazetteer*, vol. iii, p. 295. The Bēgam also subscribed liberally to Hindoo and Muhammadan institutions. Her contemporary, Colonel Skinner, was equally impartial, and is said to have built a mosque and a temple, as well as the church at Delhi.

The Cathedral at Sardhana was built in 1822. St. John's College is intended to train natives as priests. There are about 250 native Christians at Sardhana, partly the descendants of the converts who followed their mistress in change of faith. "The Roman Catholic priests work hard for their little colony, and are greatly revered and respected. At St. John's College some of the boys are instructed for the priesthood, and others taught to read and write the Nāgarī and Urdū characters. The instruction for the priesthood is peculiar. There are some twelve little native boys who can quote whole chapters of the Latin Bible, and nearly all the prayers of the Missal. Those who cannot sympathize with the system must admire the patience and devotion of the Italian priests who have put themselves to the trouble of imparting such instruction. The majority of the Christian population here are cultivators and weavers, while many are the pensioned descendants of the European servants of Bēgam Sumru, and still bear the appellation of Sāhib and Mem Sāhib." (*Gazetteer*, vol. iii, p.p. 273, 430.)

The Bēgam's palace, built in 1834, is chiefly remarkable for a collection of about twenty-five portraits of considerable interest. They comprise likenesses of Sir David Ochterlony, Dyce Sombre, Lord Combermere, and other notable personages. (*Calcutta Review*, vol. lxx, p. 460 ; quoted in *North Indian N. & Q.*, vol. ii, p. 179.)

bore the character of a kind-hearted, benevolent, and good woman ; and I have conversed with men capable of judging, who had known her for more than fifty years. She had uncommon sagacity and a masculine resolution ; and the Europeans and natives who were most intimate with her have told me that though a woman and of small stature, her " ru'b " (dignity, or power of commanding personal respect) was greater than that of almost any person they had ever seen.[1] From the time she put herself under the protection of the British government in 1803, she by degrees adopted the European modes of social intercourse, appearing in public on an elephant, in a carriage, and occasionally on horseback with her hat and veil, and dining at table with gentlemen. She often entertained Governors-General and Commanders-in-Chief, with all their retinues, and sat with them and their staff at table, and for some years past kept an open house for the society of Meerut ; but in no situation did she lose sight of her dignity. She retained to the last the grateful affections of the thousands who were supported by her bounty, while she never ceased to inspire the most profound respect in the minds of those who every day approached her, and were on the most unreserved terms of intimacy.[2]

[1] A miniature portrait of the Bēgam is given on the frontispiece to volume ii of the original edition. Francklin, describing the events of 1796, in his memoirs of George Thomas, first published in 1803, describes her personal appearance as follows :—" Begum Sumroo is about forty-five years of age, small in stature, but inclined to be plump. Her complexion is very fair, her eyes black, large and animated ; her dress perfectly Hindustany, and of the most costly materials. She speaks the Persian and Hindustany languages with fluency, and in her conversation is engaging, sensible and spirited." (London ed., p. 92, note.) The liberal benefactions of her later years have secured her ecclesiastical approval, and I should not be surprised to hear of her beatification or canonization. Her earlier life was certainly not that of a saint.

[2] In her earlier days she strictly maintained native etiquette. " It has been the constant and invariable usage of this lady to exact from her subjects and servants the most rigid attention to the customs of

Lord William Bentinck was an excellent judge of character ; and the following letter will show how deeply his visit to that part of the country had impressed him with a sense of her extensive usefulness :—

" To Her Highness the Begum Sumroo.

" My esteemed Friend,—I cannot leave India without expressing the sincere esteem I entertain for your highness's character. The benevolence of disposition and extensive charity which have endeared you to thousands, have excited in my mind sentiments of the warmest admiration ; and I trust that you may yet be preserved for many years, the solace of the orphan and widow, and the sure resource of your numerous dependants. To-morrow morning I embark for England ; and my prayers and best wishes attend you, and all others who, like you, exert themselves for the benefit of the people of India.

" I remain,

" With much consideration,

" Your sincere friend,

(Signed) " M. W. BENTINCK.[1]

" Calcutta, March 17th, 1835."

Hindoostan. She is never seen out of doors or in her public durbar unveiled.

" Her officers and others, who have business with her, present themselves opposite the place where she sits. The front of her apartment is furnished with *chicques* or Indian screens, these being let down from the roof. In this manner she gives audience, and transacts business of all kinds. She frequently admits to her table the higher ranks of her European officers, but never admits the natives to come within the enclosure." (*Francklin*, p. 92.)

[1] The Governor-General's name was William Henry Cavendish Bentinck. I do not understand the signature M. W. Bentinck, which may be a misprint. The eulogium seems odd to a reader who remembers that the recipient had been for fifteen years the mistress and wife of the Butcher of Patna. But when it was written, the memory of the massacre had been dimmed by the lapse of seventy-two years.

CHAPTER XXI[1]

ON THE SPIRIT OF MILITARY DISCIPLINE IN THE NATIVE ARMY OF INDIA.

Abolition of Corporal Punishment—Increase of Pay with Length of Service—Promotion by Seniority.

THE following observations on a very important and interesting subject were not intended to form a portion of the present work.[2] They serve to illustrate, however, many passages in the foregoing chapters touching the character of the natives of India ; and the Afghan war having occurred since they were written, I cannot deny myself the gratification of presenting them to the public, since the courage and fidelity, which it was my object to show the British government had a right to expect from its native troops and might always rely upon in the hour of need, have been so nobly displayed.

I had one morning (November 14th, 1838) a visit from the senior native officer of my regiment, Shaikh Mahūb Ali, a very fine old gentleman, who had recently attained the rank of " Sardār Bahādur," and been invested with the new

___

[1]. Chapter XXVIII of Vol. II. of original edition.

[2] This chapter and the following one were printed as a separate tract at Calcutta in 1841 (*see* Bibliography). That small volume included an Introduction and two statistical tables which the author did not reprint. He has utilized extracts from the Introduction in various parts of the *Rambles and Recollections*. I am not sure that the tract was ever published, though it was printed ; for the author says in his Introduction,—"They (*scil.* these two essays) may never be published ; but I cannot deny myself the gratification of printing them."

Order of British India.[1] He entered the service at the age of fifteen, and had served fifty-three years with great credit to himself, and fought in many an honourable field. He had come over to Jubbulpore as president of a native general court-martial, and paid me several visits in company with another old officer of my regiment who was a member of the same court. The following is one of the many conversations I had with him, taken down as soon as he left me.

"What do you think, Sardār Bahādur, of the order prohibiting corporal punishment in the army; has it had a bad or a good effect?"

"It has had a very good effect."

"What good has it produced?"

"It has reduced the number of courts-martial to one quarter of what they were before, and thereby lightened the duties of the officers; it has made the good men more careful, and the bad men more orderly than they used to be."

"How has it produced this effect?"

"A bad man formerly went on recklessly from small offences to great ones in the hope of impunity; he knew that no regimental, cantonment, or brigade court-martial could sentence him to be dismissed the service; and that they would not sentence him to be flogged, except for great crimes, because it involved at the same time dismissal from the service. If they sentenced him to be flogged, he still hoped that the punishment would be remitted. The general or officer confirming the sentence was generally unwilling to order it to be carried into effect, because the man must, after being flogged, be turned out of the service, and the marks of the lash upon his back would prevent his getting service anywhere else. Now he knows that these courts can sentence him to be dismissed from the service—that he is liable to lose his bread for ordinary transgressions,

---

[1] This order is confined to the native army.

and be sentenced to work on the roads for graver ones.[1]
He is in consequence much more under restraint than he
used to be."

"And how has it tended to make the well-disposed more
careful ? "

"They were formerly liable to be led into errors by the
example of the bad men, under the same hope of impunity ;
but they are now more on their guard. They have all
relations among the native officers, who are continually
impressing upon them the necessity of being on their guard,
lest they be sent back upon their families—their mothers
and fathers, wives and children, as beggars. To be dismissed from a service like that of the Company is a very
great punishment ; it subjects a man to the odium and
indignation of all his family. When in the Company's
service, his friends know that a soldier gets his pay regularly,
and can afford to send home a very large portion of it.
They expect that he will do so ; he feels that they will
listen to no excuse, and he contracts habits of sobriety and
prudence. If a man gets into the service of a native chief,
his friends know that his pay is precarious, and they continue to maintain his family for many years without receiving a remittance from him, in the hope that his circumstances may one day improve. He contracts bad habits,
and is not ashamed to make his appearance among them,
knowing that his excuses will be received as valid. If one
of the Company's sepoys[2] were not to send home remittances for six months, some members of the family would
be sent to know the reason why. If he could not explain,
they would appeal to the native officers of the regiment,
who would expostulate with him ; and, if all failed, his
wife and children would be turned out of his father's house,
unless they knew that he was gone to the wars ; and he
would be ashamed ever to show his face among them again."

[1] The punishment of working on the roads is long obsolete.
[2] The author spells this word " sipahee." I have thought it better to
use throughout the now familiar corruption.

" And the gradual increase of pay with length of service has tended to increase the value of the service, has it not ? "

" It has very much ; there are in our regiment, out of eight hundred men, more than one hundred and fifty sepoys, who get the increase of two rupees a month, and the same number that get the increase of one. This they feel as an immense addition to the former seven rupees a month. A prudent sepoy lives upon two, or at the utmost three, rupees a month in seasons of moderate plenty, and sends all the rest to his family. A great number of the sepoys of our regiment live upon the increase of two rupees, and send all their former seven to their families. The dismissal of a man from such a service as this distresses, not only him, but all his relations in the higher grades, who know how much of the comfort and happiness of his family depend upon his remaining and advancing in it ; and they all try to make their young friends behave as they ought to do."

" Do you think that a great portion of the native officers of the army have the same feelings and opinions on the subject as you have ? "

" They have all the same ; there is not, I believe, one in a hundred that does not think as I do upon the subject. Flogging was an odious thing. A man was disgraced, not only before his regiment, but before the crowd that assembled to witness the punishment. Had he been suffered to remain in the regiment he could never have hoped to rise after having been flogged, or sentenced to be flogged ; his hopes were all destroyed, and his spirit broken, and the order directing him to be dismissed was good ; but, as I have said, he lost all hope of getting into any other service, and dared not show his face among his family at home."

" You know who ordered the abolition of flogging ? "

" Lord Bentinck."[1]

[1] General Orders by the Commander-in-Chief of the 5th of January, 1797, declare that no sepoy or trooper of our native army shall be dis-

"And you know that it was at his recommendation the Honourable Company gave the increase of pay with, length of service?"

"We have heard so; and we feel towards him as we

missed from the service by the sentence of any but a general court-martial. General Orders by the Commander-in-Chief, Lord Combermere, of the 19th of March, 1827, declare that his Excellency is of opinion that the quiet and orderly habits of the native soldiers are such that it can very seldom be necessary to have recourse to the punishment of flogging, which might be almost entirely abolished with great advantage to their character and feelings; and directs that no native soldier shall in future be sentenced to corporal punishment unless for the crime of *stealing, marauding, or gross insubordination*, where the individuals are deemed unworthy to continue in the ranks of the army. No such sentence by a regimental, detachment, or brigade court-martial was to be carried into effect till confirmed by the general officer commanding the division. When flogged the soldier was invariably to be discharged from the service.

A circular letter from the Commander-in-Chief, Lord Combermere, on the 16th of June, 1827, directs that sentence to corporal punishment is not to be restricted to the three crimes of *theft, marauding, and gross insubordination;* but that it is not to be awarded except for very serious offences against discipline, or actions of a disgraceful or infamous nature, which show those who committed them to be unfit for the service; that the officer who assembles the court may remit the sentence of corporal punishment, and the dismissal involved in it; but cannot carry it into effect till confirmed by the officer commanding the division, except when an immediate example is indispensably necessary, as in the case of plundering and violence on the part of soldiers in the line of march. In all cases the soldier who has been flogged must be dismissed.

A circular letter by the Commander-in-Chief, Sir E. Barnes, 2nd of November, 1832, dispenses with the duty of submitting the sentence of regimental, detachment and brigade courts-martial for confirmation to the general officer commanding the division; and authorizes the officer who assembles the court to carry the sentence into effect without reference to higher authority; and to mitigate the punishment awarded, or remit it altogether; and to order the dismissal of the soldier who has been sentenced to corporal punishment, though he should remit the flogging, "for it may happen that a soldier may be found guilty of an offence which renders it improper that he should remain any longer in the service, although the general conduct of the man has been such that an example is unnecessary; or he may have

felt towards Lord Wellesley, Lord Hastings, and Lord Lake."

"Do you think the army would serve again now with the same spirit as they served under Lord Lake?"

"The army would go to any part of the world to serve

relations in the regiment of excellent character, upon whom some part of the disgrace would fall if he were flogged." Still no court-martial but a general one could sentence a soldier to be simply dismissed. To secure his dismissal, they must first sentence him to be flogged.

On the 24th of February, 1835, the Governor-General of India in Council, Lord William Bentinck, directed that the practice of punishing soldiers of the native army by the cat-o'-nine-tails, or rattan, be discontinued at all the presidencies; and that henceforth it shall be competent to any regimental, detachment, or brigade court-martial to sentence a soldier of the native army to dismissal from the service for any offence for which such soldier might now be punished by flogging, provided such sentence of dismissal shall not be carried into effect unless confirmed by the general or other officer commanding the division."

For crimes involving higher penalties, soldiers were, as heretofore, committed for trial before general courts-martial.

By Act 23 of 1839, passed by the Legislative Council of India on the 23rd of September, it is made competent for courts-martial to sentence soldiers of the native army in the service of the East India Company to the punishment of dismissal, and to be imprisoned, with or without hard labour, for any period not exceeding two years, if the sentence be pronounced by a general court-martial; and not exceeding one year, if by a garrison or line court-martial; and not exceeding six months, if by a regimental or district court-martial. Imprisonment for any period with hard labour, or for a term exceeding six months without hard labour, to involve dismissal. Act 2 of 1840 provides for such sentences of imprisonment being carried into execution by magistrates or other officers in charge of the gaols. [W. H. S.]

This last paragraph has been brought up from the end of the volume where it is printed in the original edition.

The army has been completely reorganized since the author's time, and the regulations have been much modified.

In October, 1833, Lord William Bentinck had assumed the command of the army, on the retirement of Sir Edward Barnes, and thus combined the offices of Governor-General and Commander-in-Chief, as the Marquis Cornwallis and the Marquis of Hastings had done before him.

such masters—no army had ever masters that cared for
them like ours. We never asked to have flogging abolished; nor did we ever ask to have an increase of pay
with length of service; and yet both have been done for us
by the Company Bahādur."

The old Sardār Bahādur came again to visit me on the
1st of December, with all the native officers. who had
come over from Sāgar to attend the court, seven in number.
There were three very smart, sensible men among them;
one of whom had been a volunteer at the capture of Java,[1]
and the other at that of the Isle of France.[2] They all
told me that they considered the abolition of corporal
punishment a great blessing to the native army. "Some
bad men who had already lost their character, and consequently all hope of promotion, might be in less dread than
before; but they were very few, and their regiments would
soon get rid of them under the new law that gave the power
of dismissal to regimental courts-martial."

"But I find the European officers are almost all of
opinion that the abolition of flogging has been, or will be,
attended with bad consequences."

"They, sir, apprehend that there will not be sufficient
restraint upon the loose characters of the regiment; but
now that the sepoys have got an increase of pay in proportion to length of service there will be no danger of that.
Where can they ever hope to get such another service if
they forfeit that of the Company? If the dread of losing
such a service is not sufficient to keep the bad in order,
that of being put to work upon the roads in irons will.

[1] Batavia was occupied by Sir Samuel Auchmuty in August, and the
whole island was taken possession of in September, 1811. But at the
general peace which followed the great war the island of Java, with its
dependencies, was restored to the Dutch.

[2] The Isle of France, otherwise called the Mauritius, which is still
British territory, was gallantly taken at the end of November, 1810,
by Commodore Rowley and Major-General Abercrombie. Full
details of the Java and Mauritius expeditions are given in Thornton's
twenty-second chapter.

The good can always be kept in order by lighter punishments, when they have so much a stake as the loss of such a service by frequent offences. Some gentlemen think that a soldier does not feel disgraced by being flogged, unless the offence for which he has been flogged is in itself disgraceful. There is no soldier, sir, that does not feel disgraced by being tied up to the halberts and flogged in the face of all his comrades and the crowd that may choose to come and look at him ; the sepoys are all of the same respectable families as ourselves, and they all enter the service in the hope of rising in time to the same stations as ourselves, if they conduct themselves well ; their families look forward with the same hope. A man who has been tied up and flogged knows the disgrace that it will bring upon his family, and will sometimes rather die than return to it ; indeed, as head of a family he could not be received at home.[1] But men do not feel disgraced in being flogged with a rattan at drill. While at the drill they consider themselves, and are considered by us all, as in the relation of scholars to their schoolmasters. Doing away with the rattan at drill had a very bad effect. Young men were formerly, with the judicious use of the rattan, made fit to join the regiment at furthest in six months ; but since the abolition of the rattan it takes twelve months to make them fit to be seen in the ranks. There was much

---

[1] The funeral obsequies which are everywhere offered up to the manes of parents by the surviving head of the family during the last fifteen days of the month Kuār (September) were never considered as acceptable from the hands of a soldier in our service who had been tied up and flogged, whatever might have been the nature of the offence for which he was punished ; any head of a family so flogged lost by that punishment the most important of his civil rights—that, indeed, upon which all others hinged, for it is by presiding at the funeral ceremonies that the head of the family secures and maintains his recognition. [W. H. S.] I have invariably found that natives of position, who happen to be interested in an offender, care nothing for the disgraceful nature of the offender's crime, while they dread the disgrace of the punishment, however just it may be.

virtue in the rattan, and it should never have been given up. We have all been flogged with the rattan at the drill, and never felt ourselves disgraced by it—we were *shāgirds* (scholars), and the drill-sergeant, who had the rattan, was our *ustād* (schoolmaster); but when we left the drill, and took our station in the ranks as sepoys, the case was altered, and we should have felt disgraced by a flogging, whatever might have been the nature of the offence we committed. The drill will never get on so well as it used to do, unless the rattan be called into use again; but we apprehend no evil from the abolition of corporal punishment afterwards. People are apt to attribute to this abolition offences that have nothing to do with it; and for which ample punishments are still provided. If a man fires at his officer, people are apt to say it is because flogging has been done away with; but a man who deliberately fires at his officer is prepared to undergo worse punishment than flogging."[1]

"Do you not think that the increase of pay with length of service to the sepoys will have a good effect in tending to give to regiments more active and intelligent native officers? Old sepoys who are not so will now have less cause to complain if passed over, will they not?"

[1] The worst feature of this abolition measure is unquestionably the odious distinction which it leaves in the punishments to which our European and our native soldiers are liable, since the British legislature does not consider that it can be safely abolished in the British army. This odious distinction might be easily removed by an enactment declaring that European soldiers in India should be liable to corporal punishment for only two offences; first, mutiny, or gross insubordination; second, plunder or violence while the regiment or force to which the prisoner belongs is in the field, or marching. The same enactment might declare the soldiers of our native army liable to the same punishments for the same offences. Such an enactment would excite no discontent among our native soldiery; on the contrary, it would be applauded as just and proper. [W. H. S.]

Flogging in the British army in time of peace was abolished in April, 1868, by an amendment to the Mutiny Bill, and was completely abolished by the Army Discipline Act of 1881.

"If the sepoys thought that the increase of pay was given with this view, they would rather not have it at all. To pass over men merely because they happen to have grown old, we consider very cruel and unjust. They all enter the service young, and go on doing their duty till they become old, in the hope that they shall get promotion when it comes to their turn. If they are disappointed, and young men, or greater favourites with their European officers, are put over their heads, they become heart-broken. We all feel for them, and are always sorry to see an old soldier passed over, unless he has been guilty of any manifest crime, or neglect of duty. He has always some relations among the native officers who know his family, for we all try to get our relations into the same regiment with ourselves, when they are eligible. They know what that family will suffer when they learn that he has no longer any hopes of rising in the service, and has become miserable. Supersessions create distress and bad feelings throughout a regiment, even when the best men are promoted, which cannot always be the case; for the greatest favourites are not always the best men. Many of our old European officers, like yourself, are absent on staff or civil employments; and the command of companies often devolves upon very young subalterns, who know little or nothing of the character of their men. They recommend those whom they have found most active and intelligent, and believe to be the best; but their opportunities of learning the characters of the men have been few. They have seen and observed the young, active, and forward; but they often know nothing of the steady, unobtrusive old soldier, who has done his duty ably in all situations, without placing himself prominently forward in any. The commanding officers seldom remain long with the same regiment, and, consequently, seldom know enough of the men to be able to judge of the justice of the selections for promotion. Where a man has been guilty of a crime, or neglected his duty, we feel no sympathy for him; and are not ashamed to tell him so, and put him down[1] when he complains."

Here the old Sūbadār, who had been at the taking of the Isle of France, mentioned that when he was senior Jemadār of his regiment, and a vacancy had occurred to bring him in as Sūbadār, he was sent for by his commanding officer, and told that, by orders from headquarters, he was to be passed over, on account of his advanced age, and supposed infirmity. " I felt," said the old man, "as if I had been struck by lightning, and *fell down dead*. The colonel was a good man, and had seen much service. He had me taken into the open air ; and when I recovered, he told me that he would write to the Commander-in-Chief, and represent my case. He did so, and I was promoted ; and I have since done my duty as Sūbadār for ten years."[2]

The Sardār Bahādur told me that only two men in our regiment had been that year superseded, one for insolence, and the other for neglect of duty ; and that officers and sepoys were all happy in consequence—the young, because they felt more secure of being promoted if they did their duty ; and the old, because they felt an interest in their young relations. "In those regiments," said he, "where supersessions have been more numerous, old and young are dispirited and unhappy. They all feel that the *good old rule of right* (*hakk*), as long as a man does his duty well, can no longer be relied upon."

When two companies of my regiment passed through Jubbulpore a few days after this conversation on their way from Sāgar to Seonī, I rode out a mile or two to meet

---

[1] The author also gives the Hindustānī word as "kaelkur-hin." I am not sure what he means by this.

[2] No wonder that the native army, pampered in this sentimental fashion, gradually became more and more inefficient, till it needed the fires of the mutiny to purge away its humours. No army could be efficient when its subordinate officers on the active list were men of sixty or seventy years of age.

them. They had not seen me for sixteen years, but almost all the native commissioned and non-commissioned officers were personally known to me. They were all very glad to see me, and I rode along with them to their place of encampment, where I had ready a feast of sweetmeats. They liked me as a young man, and are, I believe, proud of me as an old one. Old and young spoke with evident delight of the rigid adherence on the part of the present commanding officer, Colonel Presgrave, to the good old rule of "hakk" (right) in the recent promotions to the vacancies occasioned by the annual transfer to the invalid establishment. We might, no doubt, have in every regiment a few smarter native officers by disregarding this rule than by adhering to it; but we should, in the diminution of the good feeling towards the European officers and the Government, lose a thousand times more than we gained. They now go on from youth to old age, from the drill to the retired pension, happy and satisfied that there is no service on earth so good for them.[1] With admirable *moral*, but little or no *literary* education, the native officers of our regiments never dream of aspiring to anything more than is now held out to them, and the mass of the soldiers are inspired with devotion to the service, and every feeling with which we could wish to have them inspired, by the hope of becoming officers in time, if they discharge their duties faithfully and zealously. Deprive the mass of this hope, give the commissions to an *exclusive class* of natives, or to a favoured few, chosen often, if not commonly, without reference to the feelings or qualifications we most want in our native officers, and our native army will soon cease to have the same feelings of devotion towards the Govern-

[1] The sepoys were quite right; no other service in the world was managed on such principles. The illusion of the old Company's officers about the gratitude and affection of the men generally was rudely dispelled nineteen years after the conversations recorded in the text. But, even in 1857, a noble minority remained faithful, and did devoted service.

ment, and of attachment and respect towards their
European officers that they now have. The young,
ambitious, and aspiring native officers will soon try to
teach the great mass that their interest and that of
the European officers and European Government are by
no means one and the same, as they have been hitherto
led to suppose; and it is upon the good feeling of
this great mass that we have to depend for support.
To secure this good feeling, we can well afford to sacrifice a little efficiency at the drill. It was unwise in
one of our commanders-in-chief to direct that no soldier
in our Bengal native regiments should be promoted unless
he could read and write—it was to prohibit the promotion of the best, and direct the promotion of the worst,
soldiers in the ranks. In India a military officer is
rated as a gentleman by his birth, that is *caste*, and by
his deportment in all his relations of life, not by his
knowledge of books.

The Rājpūt, the Brahman, and the proud Pathān who
attains a commission, and deports himself like an officer,
never thinks himself, or is thought by others, deficient in
anything that constitutes the gentleman, because he happens
not to be at the same time a clerk. He has from his
childhood been taught to consider the quill and the sword
as two distinct professions, both useful and honourable
when honourably pursued; and having chosen the sword,
he thinks he does quite enough in learning how to use and
support it through all grades, and ought not to be expected
to encroach on the profession of the penman. This is a
tone of feeling which it is clearly the interest of government
rather to foster than discourage, and the order which
militated so much against it has happily been either
rescinded or disregarded.

Three-fourths of the recruits of our Bengal native
infantry are drawn from the Rājpūt peasantry of the
kingdom of Oudh, on the left bank of the Ganges, where
their affections have been linked to the soil for a long series

of generations.[1] The good feelings of the families from which they are drawn continue through the whole period of their service to exercise a salutary influence over their conduct as men and as soldiers. Though they never take their families with them, they visit them on furlough every two or three years, and always return to them when the surgeon considers a change of air necessary to their recovery from sickness. Their family circles are always present to their imaginations; and the recollections of their last visit, the hopes of the next, and the assurance that their conduct as men and as soldiers in the interval will be reported to those circles by their many comrades, who are annually returning on furlough to the same parts of the country, tend to produce a general and uniform propriety of conduct, that is hardly to be found among the soldiers of any other army in the world, and which seems incomprehensible to those unacquainted with its source—veneration for parents cherished through life, and a never impaired love of home, and of all the dear objects by which it is constituted.

Our Indian native army is perhaps the only *entirely* voluntary standing army that has been ever known, and it is, to all intents and purposes, *entirely* voluntary, and as such must be treated.[2] We can have no other native army in India, and without such an army we could not maintain our dominion a day. Our best officers have always understood this quite well; and they have never tried to flog and

[1] The best troops now are the Sikhs, Gūrkhās, and frontier Muhammadans. Oudh men still enlist in large numbers, but do not enjoy their old prestige. The army known to the author comprised no Sikhs, Gūrkhās, or frontier Muhammadans. The recruitment of Gūrkhās only began in 1838, and the other two classes of troops were obtained by the annexation of the Panjāb.

[2] I do not understand the qualifying clause "to all intents and purposes." Enlistment in the native army is absolutely voluntary, and does not even require to be stimulated by a bounty. A subsequent passage shows that the author refuses to describe the British army as an "entirely voluntary" one, because a soldier when once enlisted is bound to serve for a definite term; whereas the sepoy could resign when he chose.

harass men out of all that we find good in them for our
purposes. Any regiment in our service might lay down
their arms and disperse to-morrow, without our having a
chance of apprehending one deserter among them all.[1]

When Frederick the Great of Prussia reviewed his army
of sixty thousand men in Pomerania, previous to his invasion
of Silesia, he asked the Prince d'Anhalt, who accompanied
him, what he most admired in the scene before him.

"Sire," replied the prince, "I admire at once the fine
appearance of the men, and the regularity and perfection of
their movements and evolutions."

"For my part," said Frederick, "this is not what excites
my astonishment, since with the advantage of money, time,
and care, these are easily attained. It is that you and I,
my dear cousin, should be in the midst of such an army as
this in perfect safety. Here are sixty thousand men who
are all *irreconcilable enemies to both you and myself;* not one
among them that is not a man of more strength and better
armed than either, yet they all tremble at our presence,
while it would be folly on our part to tremble at theirs—
such is the wonderful effect of order, vigilance, and subordination."

But a reasonable man might ask, what were the circumstances which enabled Frederick to keep in a state of order
and subordination an army composed of soldiers who were
"irreconcilable enemies" of their Prince and of their
officers? He could have told the Prince d'Anhalt, had he
chose to do so; for Frederick was a man who thought
deeply. The chief circumstance favourable to his ambition
was the imbecility of the old French government, then in
its dotage, and unable to see that an army of involuntary
soldiers was no longer compatible with the state of the
nation. This government had reduced its soldiers to a
condition worse than that of the common labourers upon
the roads, while it deprived them of all hope of rising, and

---

[1] Desertions are frequent among the regiments recruited on the
Afghan frontier. These regiments did not exist in the author's day.

all feeling of pride in the profession.[1] Desertion became easy from the extension of the French dominion and from the circumstance of so many belligerent powers around requiring good soldiers ; and no odium attended desertion, where everything was done to degrade, and nothing to exalt the soldier in his own esteem and that of society.

Instead of following the course of events and rendering the condition of the soldier less odious by increasing his pay and hope of promotion, and diminishing the labour and disgrace to which he was liable, and thereby filling her regiments with voluntary soldiers when involuntary ones could no longer be obtained, the government of France reduced the soldier's pay to one-half the rate of wages which a common labourer got on the roads, and put them under restraints and restrictions that made them feel every day, and every hour, that they were slaves. To prevent desertions by severe examples under this high pressure system, they had recourse first to slitting the noses and cutting off the ears of deserters, and, lastly, to shooting them as fast as they could catch them.[2] But all was in vain ; and Frederick of Prussia alone got fifty thousand of the finest soldiers in the world from the French regiments, who composed one-third of his army, and enabled him to keep all the rest in that state of discipline that improved so much its efficiency, in the same manner as the deserters from the Roman

---

[1] An ordinance issued in France so late as 1778 required that a man should produce proof of four quarterings of nobility before he could get a commission in the army. [W. H. S.]

[2] "*Est et alia causa, cur attenuatæ sint legiones*," says Vegetius. "*Magnus in illis labor est militandi, graviora arma, sera munera, severior disciplina. Quod vitantes plerique, in auxiliis festinant militiæ sacramenta percipere, ubi et minor sudor, et maturiora sunt premia.*" *Lib.* II. *cap.* 3. [W. H. S.] Vegetius, according to Gibbon and his most recent editor (*recensuit Carolus Lang. Editio altera. Lipsiæ. Teubner,* 1885), flourished during the reign of Valentinian III. (A.D. 425–455). His "Soldier's Pocket-book" is entitled "Flavi Vegeti Renati, Epitoma Rei Militaris."

legions, which took place under similar circumstances, became the flower of the army of Mithridates.[1]

Frederick was in position and disposition a despot. His territories were small, while his ambition was boundless. He was unable to pay a large army the rate of wages necessary to secure the services of voluntary soldiers ; and he availed himself of the happy imbecility of the French government to form an army of involuntary ones. He got French soldiers at a cheap rate, because they dared not return to their native country, whence they were hunted down and shot like dogs, and these soldiers enabled him to retain his own subjects in his ranks upon the same terms. Had the French government retraced its steps, improved the condition of its soldiers, and mitigated the punishment for desertion during the long war, Frederick's army would have fallen to pieces "like the baseless fabric of a vision."

"*Parmi nous,*" says Montesquieu, "*les désertions sont fréquentes parceque les soldats sont la plus vile partie de chaque nation, et qu'il n'y en a aucun qui aie, ou qui croie avoir un certain avantage sur les autres. Chez les Romains elles étaient plus rares—des soldats tirés du sein d'un peuple si fier, si orgueilleux, si sûr de commander aux autres, ne pouvaient guère penser à s'aviler jusqu' à cesser*

---

[1] Montesquieu thought that "the government had better have stuck to the old practice of slitting noses and cutting off ears, since the French soldiers, like the Roman dandies under Pompey, must necessarily have a greater dread of a disfigured face than of death." It did not occur to him that France could retain her soldiers by other and better motives. See *Spirit of Laws*, book vi. chap. 12. See *Necker on the Finances*, vol. ii. c. 5 ; vol. iii. c. 34. A day-labourer on the roads got fifteen sous a day ; and a French soldier only six, at the very time that the mortality of an army of forty thousand men sent to the colonies was annually thirteen thousand three hundred and thirty-three, or about one in three. In our native army the sepoy gets about double the wages of an ordinary day-labourer ; and his duties, when well done, involve just enough of exercise to keep him in health. The casualties are perhaps about one in a hundred. [W. H. S.]

d'être Romains."[1] But was it the poor soldiers who were to blame if they were "vile," and had "no advantage over others," or the government that took them from the vilest classes, or made their condition when they got them worse than that of the lowest class in society? The Romans deserted under the same circumstances, and, as I have stated, formed the *élite* of the army of Mithridates and the other enemies of Rome; but they respected their military oath of allegiance long after perjury among senators had ceased to excite any odium, since as a fashionable or political vice it had become common.

Did not our day of retribution come, though in a milder shape, to teach us a great political and moral lesson, when so many of our brave sailors deserted our ships for those of America, in which they fought against us?[2] They deserted from our ships of war because they were there treated like dogs, or from our merchant ships because they were every hour liable to be seized like felons and put on

---

[1] Just precisely what the French soldiers were after the revolution had purged France of all "the perilous stuff that weighed upon the heart" of its people. Gibbon, in considering the chance of the civilized nations of Europe ever being again overrun by the barbarians from the North, as in the time of the Romans, says:—"If a savage conqueror should issue from the deserts of Tartary, he must repeatedly vanquish the robust peasantry of Russia, the numerous armies of Germany, the gallant nobles of France, and the intrepid free men of Britain." Never was a more just, yet more unintended satire upon the state of a country. Russia was to depend upon her "robust peasantry"; Germany upon her "numerous armies"; England upon her "intrepid free men"; and poor France upon her "gallant nobles" alone; because, unhappily, no other part of her vast population was then ever thought of. When the hour of trial came, those pampered nobles who had no feeling in common with the people were shaken off "like dew-drops from the lion's mane"; and the hitherto spurned peasantry of France, under the guidance and auspices of men who understood and appreciated them, astonished the world with their powers. [W. H. S.]

[2] The allusion is to the now half-forgotten war with the United States in the years 1812–1814, during the course of which the English captured the city of Washington, and the Americans gained some unexpected naval victories.

board the former. When " England expected every man to
do his duty " at Trafalgar, had England done its duty to
every man who was that day to fight for her ? Is not the
intellectual stock which the sailor acquires in scenes of
peril "upon the high and giddy mast" as much his property as that which others acquire in scenes of peace at
schools and colleges ? And have not our senators, morally
and religiously, as much right to authorize their sovereign
to seize clergymen, lawyers, and professors, for employment
in his service, upon the wages of ordinary uninstructed
labour, as they have to authorize him to seize able sailors
to be so employed in her navy ? A feeling more base
than that which authorized the able seaman to be
hunted down upon such conditions, torn from his
wife and children, and put like Uriah in front of those
battles upon which our welfare and honour depended,
never disgraced any civilized nation with whose history
we are acquainted.[1]

Sir Matthew Decker, in a passage quoted by Mr.
McCulloch, says, "The custom of impressment puts a
freeborn British sailor on the same footing as a Turkish
slave. The Grand Seignior cannot do a more absolute act
than to order a man to be dragged away from his family,
and against his will run his head against the mouth of a
cannon ; and if such acts should be frequent in Turkey
upon any one set of useful men, would it not drive them
away to other countries, and thin their numbers yearly ?
And would not the remaining few double or triple their
wages, which is the case with our sailors in time of war, to
the great detriment of our commerce ? " The Americans
wisely relinquished the barbarous and unwise practice of
their parent land, and, as McCulloch observes, "While the
wages of all labourers and artisans are uniformly higher in
the United States than in England, those of sailors are
generally lower," as the natural consequence of manning

[1] The author has already denounced the practice of impressment,
ante, Vol. I, p.p. 223, 224.

their navy by means of voluntary enlistment alone.   At the
close of the last war, sixteen thousand British sailors were
serving on board of American ships ; and the wages of our
seamen rose from forty or[1] fifty to a hundred or one hundred and twenty shillings a month, as the natural consequence of our continuing to resort to impressment after the
Americans had given it up.[2]

Frederick's army consisted of about one hundred and
fifty thousand men.   Fifty thousand of these were French
deserters, and a considerable portion of the remaining
hundred thousand were deserters from the Austrian army,
in which desertion was punished in the same manner with
death.   The dread of this punishment if they quitted his
ranks, enabled him to keep up that state of discipline that
improved so much the efficacy of his regiments, at the
same time that it made every individual soldier his "irreconcileable enemy."   Not relying entirely upon this dread
on the part of deserters to quit his ranks under his high
pressure system of discipline, and afraid that the soldiers of
his own soil might make off in spite of all their vigilance,
he kept his regiments in garrison towns till called on actual
service ; and that they might not desert on their way from
one garrison to another during relief, he never had them
relieved at all.   A trooper was flogged for falling from his
horse, though he had broken a limb in his fall ; it was
difficult, he said, to distinguish an involuntary fault from
one that originated in negligence, and to prevent a man
hoping that his negligence would be forgiven, all blunders
were punished, from whatever cause arising.   No soldier
was suffered to quit his garrison till led out to fight ; and
when a desertion took place, cannons were fired to announce
it to the surrounding country.   Great rewards were given
for apprehending, and severe punishments inflicted for har-
bouring, the criminal ; and he was soon hunted down, and

---

[1] "To" in original edition.
[2] *See* McCulloch, *Pol. Econ.*, page 235, first edition, Edinburgh,
1825. [W. H. S.]

brought back. A soldier was, therefore, always a prisoner and a slave.

Still, all this rigour of Prussian discipline, like that of our navy, was insufficient to extinguish that ambition which is inherent in our nature to obtain the esteem and applause of the circle in which we move ; and the soldier discharged his duty in the hour of danger, in the hope of rendering his life more happy in the esteem of his officers and comrades. " Every tolerably good soldier feels," says Adam Smith, " that he would become the scorn of his companions if he should be supposed capable of shrinking from danger, or of hesitating either to expose or to throw away his life, when the good of the service required it." So thought the philosopher, King of Prussia, when he let his regiments out of garrison to go and face the enemy. The officers were always treated with as much lenity in the Prussian as any other service, because the king knew that the hope of promotion would always be sufficient to bind them to their duties ; but the poor soldiers had no hope of this kind to animate them in their toils and their dangers.

We took our system of drill from Frederick of Prussia ; and there is still many a martinet who would carry his high pressure system of discipline into every other service over which he had any control, unable to appreciate the difference of circumstances under which they may happen to be raised and maintained.[1]

---

[1] Many German princes adopted the discipline of Frederick in their little petty states, without exactly knowing why or wherefore. The Prince of Darmstadt conceived a great passion for the military art ; and when the weather would not permit him to worry his little army of five thousand men in the open air, he had them worried for his amusement under sheds. But he was soon obliged to build a wall round the town in which he drilled his soldiers for the sole purpose of preventing their running away—round this wall he had a regular chain of sentries to fire at the deserters. Mr. Moore thought that the discontent in this little band was greater than in the Prussian army, inasmuch as the soldiers saw no object but the prince's amusement. A fight, or the prospect of a fight, would have been a feast to them. [W. H. S.]

The sepoys of the Bengal army, the only part of our native army with which I am much acquainted, are educated as soldiers from their infancy—they are brought up in that feeling of entire deference for constituted authority which we require in soldiers, and which they never lose through life. They are taken from the agricultural classes of Indian society—almost all the sons of yeomen—cultivating proprietors of the soil, whose families have increased beyond their means of subsistence. One son is sent one after another to seek service in our regiments as necessity presses at home, from whatever cause—the increase of taxation, or the too great increase of numbers in families.[1] No men can have a higher sense of the duty they owe to the state that employs them, or whose " salt they eat " ; nor can any men set less value on life when the service of that state requires that it shall be risked or sacrificed. No persons are brought up with more deference for parents. In no family from which we drew our recruits is a son through infancy, boyhood, or youth, heard to utter a disrespectful word to his parents—such a word from a son to his parents would shock the feelings of the whole community in which the family resides, and the offending member would be visited with their highest indignation. When the father dies the eldest son takes his place, and receives the same marks of respect, the same entire confidence and deference as the father. If he be a soldier in a distant land, and can afford to do so, he resigns the service, and returns home to take his post as the head of the family. If he cannot afford to resign, if the family still

---

[1] Speaking of the question whether recruits drawn from the country or the towns are best, Vegetius says :—" *De quâ parte numquam credo potuisse dubitari, aptiorem armis rusticam plebem, quae sub divo et in labore nutritur ; solis patiens ; umbrae negligens ; balnearum nescia ; deliciarum ignara ; simplicis animi ; parvo contenta ; duratis ad omnem laborem membris ; cui gestare ferrum, fossam ducere, onus ferre, consuetudo de rure est.*" (*De Re Militari*, Lib. i, cap. 3.) [W. H. S.] The passage quoted is disfigured by many misprints in the original edition.

want the aid of his regular monthly pay, he remains with his regiment, and denies himself many of the personal comforts he has hitherto enjoyed, that he may increase his contribution to the general stock.

The wives and children of his brothers, who are absent on service, are confided to his care with the same confidence as to that of the father.   It is a rule to which I have through life found but few exceptions that those who are most disposed to resist constituted authority are those most disposed to abuse such authority when they get it.   The members of these families, disposed, as they always are, to pay deference to such authority, are scarcely ever found to abuse it when it devolves upon them ; and the elder son, when he succeeds to the place of his father, loses none of the affectionate attachment of his younger brothers.

They never take their wives or children with them to their regiments, or to the places where their regiments are stationed.[1]   They leave them with their fathers or elder brothers, and enjoy their society only when they return on furlough.   Three-fourths of their incomes are sent home to provide for their comfort and subsistence, and to embellish that home in which they hope to spend the winter of their days.   The knowledge that any neglect of the duty they owe their distant families will be immediately visited by the odium of their native officers and brother soldiers, and ultimately communicated to the heads of their families, acts as a salutary check on their conduct ; and I believe that there is hardly a native regiment in the Bengal army in which the twenty drummers who are Christians, and have their families with the regiment, do not cause more trouble to the officers than the whole eight hundred sepoys.

To secure the fidelity of such men all that is necessary is to make them feel secure of three things—their regular pay, at the handsome rate at which it has now been fixed ; their retiring pensions upon the scale hitherto enjoyed ; and

---

[1] As the Madras sepoys do.

promotion by seniority, like their European officers, unless
they shall forfeit all claims to it by misconduct or neglect
of duty.[1] People talk about a *demoralized* army, and *dis-
contented* army ! No army in the world was certainly ever
more moral or more contented than our native army; or
more satisfied that their masters merit all their devotion
and attachment; and I believe none was ever more
devoted or attached to them.[2] I do not speak of the

[1] The writing of the bulk of this work was completed in 1839.
These concluding supplementary chapters on the Bengal army seem to
have been written a little later, perhaps in 1841, the year in which they
were first printed. The publication of the complete work took place
in 1844. The mutiny broke out in 1857, and proved that the fidelity
of the sepoys could not be so easily assured as the author supposed.

[2] I believe the native army to be better now than it ever was—better
in its disposition and in its organization. The men have now a better
feeling of assurance than they formerly had that all their rights will be
secured to them by their European officers; that all those officers are
men of honour, though they have not all of them the same fellow-feeling that their officers had with them in former days. This is because
they have not the same opportunity of seeing their courage and fidelity
tried in the same scenes of common danger. Go to Afghānistan and
China, and you will find the feeling between officers and men as fine
as ever it was in days of yore, whatever it may be at our large and gay
stations, where they see so little of each other. [W. H. S.]

The author's reputation for sagacity and discernment could not be
made to rest upon the above remarks. His judgment was led astray
by his lifelong association with and affection for the native troops.
Lord William Bentinck took a far juster view of the situation, and
understood far better the real nature of the ties which bind the native
army to its masters. His admirable minute dated 13th March, 1835,
has been published for the first time in Mr. D. Boulger's well-written
little book, and is still well worthy of study. As a corrective to the
author's too effusive sentiment some brief passages from the Governor-
General's minute may be quoted. "In considering the question of
internal danger," he observes, "those officers most conversant with
Indian affairs who were examined before the Parliamentary Committee
apprehend no danger to our dominion as long as we are assured of the
fidelity of our native troops. To this opinion I entirely subscribe.
But others again view in the native army itself the source of our
greatest peril. In all ages the military body has been often the prime
cause, but generally the instrument, of all revolutions; and proverbial

European officers of the native army. They very generally believe that they have had just cause of complaint, and sufficient care has not always been taken to remove that impression. In all the junior grades the Honourable Company's officers have advantages over the Queen's in India. In the higher grades the Queen's officers have advantages over those of the Honourable Company. The reasons it does not behove me here to consider.

In all armies composed of involuntary soldiers, that is, of soldiers who are anxious to quit the ranks and return to peaceful occupations, but cannot do so, much of the drill to which they are subjected is adopted merely with a view to keep them from pondering too much upon the miseries of their present condition, and from indulging in those licentious habits to which a strong sense of these miseries, and the recollection of the enjoyments of peaceful life which they have sacrificed, are too apt to drive them. No

almost as is the fidelity of the native soldier to the chief whom he serves, more especially when he is justly and kindly treated, still we cannot be blind to the fact that many of those ties which bind other armies to their allegiance are totally wanting in this. Here is no patriotism, no community of feeling as to religion or birthplace, no influencing attachment from high considerations, or great honours and rewards. Our native army also is extremely ignorant, capable of the strongest religious excitement, and very sensitive to disrespect to their persons or infringement of their customs. . . . . In the native army alone rests our internal danger, and this danger may involve our complete subversion. . . .

" All these facts and opinions seem to me to establish incontrovertibly that a large proportion of European troops is necessary for our security under all circumstances of peace and war. . . .

" I believe the sepoys have never been so good as they were in the earliest part of our career ; none superior to those under De Boigne. . . . I fearlessly pronounce the Indian army to be the least efficient and most expensive in the world."

The events of 1857–1859 proved the truth of Lord William Bentinck's wise words. The native army is no longer inefficient as a whole, though large sections of it still are so, but the less that is said about the supposed affection of mercenary troops for a foreign government, the better.

portion of this is necessary for the soldiers of our native army, who have no miseries to ponder over, or superior enjoyments in peaceful life to look back upon ; and a very small quantity of drill is sufficient to make a regiment go through its evolutions well, because they have all a pride and pleasure in their duties, as long as they have a commanding officer who understands them.   Clarke, in his *Travels*, speaking of the three thousand native infantry from India whom he saw paraded in Egypt under their gallant leader, Sir David Baird, says, " Troops in such a state of military perfection, or better suited for active service, were never seen—not even on the famous parade of the chosen ten thousand belonging to Bonaparte's legions, which he was so vain of displaying before the present war in the front of the Tuileries at Paris.   Not an unhealthy soldier was to be seen.   The English, inured to the climate of India, considered that of Egypt as temperate in its effects, and the sipāhees seemed as fond of the Nile as the Ganges."[1]

It would be much better to devise more innocent amusements to lighten the miseries of European soldiers in India than to be worrying them every hour, night and day, with duties which are in themselves considered to be of no importance whatever, and imposed merely with a view to prevent their having time to ponder on these miseries.[2]

[1] " General Baird had started from Bombay in the end of December 1800, but only arrived at Kossir, on the coast of Upper Egypt, on the 8th of June.   In nine days, with a force of 6,400 British and native troops, he traversed 140 miles of desert to the Nile, and reached Cairo on 10th August with hardly any loss.   The united force then marched down on Alexandria, and on 31st August Menou capitulated, and the whole French army evacuated Egypt." (Balfour's *Cyclopædia, s.v.* " Egypt.")   The Indian native army again did brilliant service in the Egyptian campaign of 1882.

[2] Great progress has been made in the task of lightening the miseries of European soldiers in India by the provision of innocent amusements.   Lord Roberts during his long tenure of the office of Commander-in-Chief pre-eminently showed himself to be the soldier' friend.

But all extra and useless duties to a soldier become odious, because they are always associated in his mind with the ideas of the odious and degrading punishment inflicted for the neglect of them.   It is lamentable to think how much of misery is often wantonly inflicted upon the brave soldiers of our European regiments of India on the pretence of a desire to preserve order and discipline."[1]

Sportsmen know that if they train their horses beyond a certain point they " train off ; " that is, they lose the spirit and with it the condition they require to support them in their hour of trial.   It is the same with soldiers ; if drilled beyond a certain point, they "drill off," and lose the spirit which they require to sustain them in active service, and before the enemy.   An over-drilled regiment will seldom go through its evolutions well, even in ordinary review before its own general.   If it has all the mechanism, it wants all the real spirit of military discipline—it becomes dogged, and is, in fact, a body without a soul.   The martinet, who is seldom a man of much intellect, is satisfied as long as the bodies of his men are drilled to his liking ; his narrow mind comprehends only one of the principles which influence mankind—fear ; and upon this he acts with all the pertinacity of a slave-driver.   If he does not disgrace himself when he comes before the enemy, as he commonly does, by his own incapacity, his men will perhaps try to disgrace him, even at the sacrifice of what they hold dearer than their lives—their reputation.   The real soldier, who is generally a man of more intellect, cares more about the feelings than the bodies of his men ; he wants to command their affections as well as their limbs,

---

[1] Their commanding officers say, as Pharaoh said to the Israelites, "Let there be more work laid upon them, that they may labour therein, and not enter into vain discourses."   Life to such men becomes intolerable ; and they either destroy themselves, or commit murder, that they may be taken to a distant court for trial.   [W. H. S.] The quotation is from Exodus v. 9.   The authorized version is, " Let there be more work laid upon the men, that they may labour therein ; and let them not regard vain words."

and he inspires them with a feeling of enthusiasm that renders them insensible to all danger—such men were Lord Lake, and Generals Ochterlony, Malcolm, and Adams, and such are many others well known in India.

Under the martinet the soldiers will never do more than what a due regard for their own reputation demands from them before the enemy, and will sometimes do less. Under the real soldier, they will always do more than this ; his reputation is dearer to them even than their own, and they will do more to sustain it. The army of the consul, Appius Claudius, exposed themselves to almost inevitable destruction before the enemy to disgrace him in the eyes of his country, and the few survivors were decimated on their return ; he cared nothing for the spirit of his men. The army of his colleague, Quintius, on the contrary, though from the same people, and levied and led out at the same time, covered him with glory because they loved him.[1] We had an instance of this in the war with Nepāl in 1815, in which a king's regiment played the part of the army of Appius.[2] There were other martinets, king's and company's, commanding divisions in that war, and they all

---

[1] See Livy, lib. ii, cap. 59. The infantry under Fabius had refused to conquer, that their general, whom they hated, might not triumph ; but the whole army under Claudius, whom they had more cause to detest, not only refused to conquer, but determined to be conquered, that he might be involved in their disgrace. All the abilities of Lucullus, one of the ablest generals Rome ever had, were rendered almost useless by his disregard to the feelings of his soldiers. He could not perceive that the civil wars under Marius and Sylla had rendered a different treatment of Roman soldiers necessary to success in war. Pompey, his successor, a man of inferior military genius, succeeded much better because he had the sagacity to see that he now required not only the confidence but the affections of his soldiers. Cæsar to abilities even greater than those of Lucullus united the conciliatory spirit of Pompey. [W. H. S.]

[2] This curious incident is not mentioned by Thornton in the detailed account of the Nepalese war given in his twenty-fourth chapter. The war was notable for the number of blunders and failures which marked its course.

signally failed; not, however, except in the above one
instance, from backwardness on the part of their
troops, but from utter incapacity when the hour of
trial came.   Those who succeeded were men always noted
for caring something more about the hearts than the
whiskers and. buttons of their men. · That the officer who
delights in harassing his regiment in times of peace will
fail with it in times of war and scenes of peril seems to me
to be a rule almost as well established as that he, who in
the junior ranks of the army delights most to kick against
authority, is always found the most disposed to abuse it
when he gets to the higher.   In long intervals of peace,
the only prominent military characters are commonly such
martinets ; and hence the failures so generally experienced
in the beginning of a war after such an interval. White-
locks are chosen for command, till Wolfes and Wellingtons
find Chathams and Wellesleys to climb up by.

To govern those whose mental and physical energies we
require for our subsistence and support by the lash alone is
so easy, so simple a mode of bending them to our will, and
making them act strictly and instantly in conformity to it,
that it is not at all surprising to find so many of those who
have been accustomed to it, and are not themselves liable
to have the lash inflicted upon them, advocating its free use.
In China the Emperor has his generals flogged, and finds
the lash so efficacious in bending them to his will that
nothing would persuade him that it could ever be safely
dispensed with.   In some parts of Germany they had the
officers flogged, and princes and generals found this so very
efficacious in making those act in conformity to their will
that they found it difficult to believe that any army could
be well managed without it.   In other Christian armies the
officers are exempted from the lash, but they use it freely
upon all under them ; and it would be exceedingly difficult
to convince the greater part of these officers that the free
use of the lash is not indispensably necessary, nay, that
the men do not themselves like to be flogged, as eels like

to be skinned, when they once get used to it. Ask the slave-holders of the southern states of America whether any society can be well constituted unless the greater part of those upon the sweat of whose brow the community depends for their subsistence are made by law liable to be bought, sold, and driven to their daily labour with the lash; they will one and all say No; and yet there are doubtless many very excellent and amiable persons among these slave-holders. If our army, as at present constituted, cannot do without the free use of the lash, let its constitution be altered; for no nation with free institutions should suffer its soldiers to be flogged. "*Laudabiliores tamen duces sunt, quorum exercitum ad modestiam labor et usus instituit, quam illi, quorum milites, ad obedientiam suppliciorum formido compellit.*"[1]

Though I reprobate that wanton severity of discipline in which the substance is sacrificed to the form, in which unavoidable and trivial offences are punished as deliberate and serious crimes, and the spirit of the soldier is entirely disregarded, while the motion of his limbs, cut of his whiskers, and the buttons of his coat are scanned with microscopic eye, I must not be thought to advocate idleness. If we find the sepoys of a native regiment, as we sometimes do at a healthy and cheap station, become a little unruly like schoolboys, and ask an old native officer the reason, he will probably answer others as he has me by another question,—"*Ghorā ārā kyūn? Pānī sarā kyūn?*" "Why does the horse become vicious? Why does the water become putrid?"—For want of exercise. Without proper attention to this exercise no regiment is ever kept in order; nor has any commanding officer ever the respect or the affection of his men unless they see that he understands well all the duties which his government intrusts to him, and is resolved to have them performed in all situa-

[1] Vegetius, *De Re Militari*, Lib. iii, cap. 4. If corporal punishment be retained at all, it should be limited to the two offences I have already mentioned; [W. H. S.] namely, (1) mutiny or gross insubordination, (2) plunder or violence in the field or on the march. (*Ante*, p. 298 *note*.)

tions and under all circumstances.   There are always some
bad characters in a regiment, to take advantage of any
laxity of discipline, and lead astray the younger soldiers,
whose spirits have been rendered exuberant by good health
and good feeding ; and there is hardly any crime to which
they will not try to excite these young men, under an officer
careless about the discipline of his regiment, or disinclined,
from a mistaken *esprit de corps*, or any other cause, to have
those crimes traced home to them and punished.[1]

[1] Polybius says that "as the human body is apt to get out of order
under good feeding and little exercise, so are states and armies."   (B.
11, chap. 6.)—Wherever food is cheap, and the air good, native regiments should be well exercised without being worried.

I must here take the liberty to give an extract from a letter from one
of the best and most estimable officers now in the Bengal army :—
" As connected with the discipline of the native army, I may here
remark that I have for some years past observed on the part of many
otherwise excellent commanding officers a great want of attention to
the instruction of the young European officers on first joining their
regiments.   I have had ample opportunities of seeing the great value
of a regular course of instruction drill for at least six months.   When
I joined my first regiment, which was about forty years ago, I had the
good fortune to be under a commandant and adjutant who, happily for
me and many others, attached great importance to this very necessary
course of instruction.   I then acquired a thorough knowledge of my
duties, which led to my being appointed an adjutant very early in life.
When I attained the rank of lieutenant-colonel I had, however,
opportunities of observing how very much this essential duty had been
neglected in certain regiments, and made it a rule in all that I commanded to keep all young officers on first joining at the instruction
drill till thoroughly grounded in their duties.   Since I ceased to command a regiment, I have taken advantage of every opportunity to
express to those commanding officers with whom I have been in
correspondence my conviction of the great advantages of this system
to the rising generation.   In going from one regiment to another I
found many curious instances of ignorance on the part of young officers
who had been many years with their corps.   It was by no means an
easy task to convince them that they really knew nothing, or at least
had a great deal to learn ; but when they were made sensible of it,
they many of them turned out excellent officers, and now, I believe,
bless the day they were first put under me."

The advantages of the system here mentioned cannot be questioned ;

There can be no question that a good tone of feeling between the European officers and their men is essential to the well-being of our native army ; and I think I have found this tone somewhat impaired whenever our native regiments are concentrated at large stations. In such places the European society is commonly large and gay ; and the officers of our native regiments become too much occupied in its pleasures and ceremonies to attend to their native officers or sepoys. In Europe there are separate classes of people who subsist by catering for the amusements of the higher classes of society, in theatres, operas, concerts, balls, &c., &c. ; but in India this duty devolves entirely upon the young civil and military officers of the government, and at large stations it really is a very laborious one, which often takes up the whole of a young man's time. The ladies must have amusement ; and the officers must find it for them, because there are no other persons to undertake the arduous duty. The consequence is that they often become entirely alienated from their men, and betray signs of the greatest impatience while they listen to the necessary reports of their native officers, as they come on or go off duty.[1]

It is different when regiments are concentrated for active service. Nothing tends so much to improve the tone of feeling between the European officers and their men, and between European soldiers and sepoys, as the concentration

and it is much to be regretted that it is not strictly enforced in every regiment in the service. Young officers may find it irksome at first ; but they soon become sensible of the advantages, and learn to applaud the commandant who has had the firmness to consult their permanent interests more than their present inclinations. [W. H. S.]

[1] Among the many changes produced in India by the development of the railway system and by other causes one of the most striking is the abolition of small military stations. Almost all these have disappeared, and the troops are now massed in large cantonments, where they can be handled much more effectively than in out-stations. The discipline of small detached bodies of troops is generally liable to deterioration.

of forces on actual service, where the same hopes animate, and the same dangers unite them in common bonds of sympathy and confidence. "*Utrique alteris freti, finitimos armis aut metu sub imperium cogere, nomen gloriamque sibi addidere.*" After the campaigns under Lord Lake, a native regiment passing Dinapore, where the gallant King's 76th, with whom they had fought side by side, was cantoned, invited the soldiers to a grand entertainment provided for them by the sepoys. They consented to go on one condition—that the sepoys should see them all back safe before morning. Confiding in their sable friends, they all got gloriously drunk, but found themselves lying every man upon his proper cot in his own barracks in the morning. The sepoys had carried them all home upon their shoulders. Another native regiment, passing within a few miles of a hill on which they had buried one of their European officers after that war, solicited permission to go and make their "salām" to the tomb, and all went who were off duty.[1]

The system which now keeps the greater part of our native infantry at small stations of single regiments in times of peace tends to preserve this good tone of feeling between officers and men, at the same time that it promotes the general welfare of the country by giving confidence everywhere to the peaceful and industrious classes.

I will not close this chapter without mentioning one thing which I have no doubt every Company's officer in India will concur with me in thinking desirable to improve the good feeling of the native soldiery—that is, an increase in the pay of the Jemadārs. They are commissioned officers, and seldom attain the rank in less than from twenty-five to thirty years;[2] and they have to provide them-

---

[1] Many instances of semi-religious honour paid by natives to the tombs of Europeans have been noticed.

[2] There are, I believe, many Jemadārs who still wear medals on their breasts for their service in the taking of Java and the Isle of France more than thirty years ago. Indeed I suspect that some will

selves with clothes of the same costly description as those
of the Sūbadār ; to be as well mounted, and in all respects
to keep the same respectability of appearance, while their
pay is only twenty-four rupees and a half a month ; that is,
ten rupees a month only more than they had been receiving
in the grade of Hāvildārs, which is not sufficient to meet
the additional expenses to which they become liable as commissioned officers. Their means of remittance to their
families are rather diminished than increased by promotion,
and but few of them can hope ever to reach the next grade
of Sūbadār. Our government, which has of late been so
liberal to its native civil officers, will, I hope, soon take
into consideration the claims of this class, who are
universally admitted to be the worst paid class of native
public officers in India. Ten rupees a month addition to
their pay would be of great importance ; it would enable
them to impart some of the advantages of promotion to
their families, and improve the good feeling of the circles
around them towards the government they serve.[1]

be found who accompanied Sir David Baird to Egypt. [W. H. S.]
Such old men must have been perfectly useless as officers. Sir David
Baird's operations took place in 1801.

[1] The rate of pay of Jemadārs in the Bengal Native Infantry now is
either forty or fifty rupees monthly. Half of the officers of this rank
in each regiment receive the higher rate. The grievance complained
of by the author has, therefore, been remedied. The pay of a
Havīldār is still fourteen rupees a month.

CHAPTER XXII[1]

Invalid Establishment.

I HAVE said nothing in the foregoing chapter of the invalid establishment, which is probably the greatest of all bonds between the government and its native army, and consequently the greatest element in the "spirit of discipline." Bonaparte, who was, perhaps, with all his faults, "the greatest man that ever floated on the tide of time," said at Elba, "There is not even a village that has not brought forth a general, a colonel, a captain, or a prefect, who has raised himself by his especial merit, and illustrated at once his family and his country." Now we know that the families and the village communities in which our invalid pensioners reside never read newspapers,[2] and feel but little interest in the victories in which these pensioners may have shared. They feel that they have no share in the *éclat* or glory which attend them ; but they everywhere admire and respect the government which cherishes its faithful old servants, and enables them to spend the " winter of their days " in the bosoms of their families ; and they spurn the man who has failed in his duty towards that government in the hour of need.

No sepoy taken from the Rājpūt communities of Oudh or any other part of the country can hope to conceal from his family circle or village community any act of cowardice, or anything else, which is considered disgraceful to a soldier,

---

[1] Chapter XXIX of Volume II of original edition.
[2] This can no longer be safely assumed as true.

or to escape the odium which it merits in that circle and community.

In the year 1819 I was encamped near a village in marching through Oudh, when the landlord, a very cheerful old man, came up to me with his youngest son, a lad of eighteen years of age, and requested me to allow him (the son) to show me the best shooting grounds in the neighbourhood. I took my " Joe Manton " and went out. The youth showed me some very good ground, and I found him an agreeable companion, and an excellent shot with his matchlock. On our return we found the old man waiting for us. He told me that he had four sons, all by God's blessing tall enough for the Company's service, in which one had attained the rank of " havīldār " (sergeant), and two were still sepoys. Their wives and children lived with him ; and they sent home every month two-thirds of their pay, which enabled him to pay all the rent of the estate, and appropriate the whole of the annual returns to the subsistence and comfort of the numerous family. He was, he said, now growing old, and wished his eldest son, the sergeant, to resign the service and come home to take upon him the management of the estate ; that as soon as he could be prevailed upon to do so, his old wife would permit my sporting companion, her youngest son, to enlist, but not before.

I was on my way to visit Fyzabad, the old metropolis of Oudh,[1] and on returning a month afterwards in the latter end of January, I found that the wheat, which was all then in ear, had been destroyed by a severe frost. The old man wept bitterly, and he and his old wife yielded to the wishes of their youngest son to accompany me and enlist in my regiment, which was then stationed at Partābgarh.

We set out, but were overtaken at the third stage by the poor old man, who told me that his wife had not eaten or

----

[1] Fyzābād (Faizābād) was the capital for a short time of the Nawāb Wazīrs of Oudh. In 1775 Asaf-ud-daula moved his court to Lucknow. The city of Ajodhya adjoining Fyzabad is of immense antiquity.

slept since the boy left her, and that he must go back and
wait for the return of his eldest brother, or she certainly
would not live. The lad obeyed the call of his parents,
and I never saw or heard of the family again.

There is hardly a village in the kingdom of Oudh without families like this depending upon the good conduct
and liberal pay of sepoys in our infantry regiments, and
revering the name of the government they serve, or have
served. Similar villages are to be found scattered over the
provinces of Bihār and Benares, the districts between the
Ganges and Jumna, and other parts where Rājpūts and the
other classes from which we draw our recruits have been
long established as proprietors and cultivators of the soil.

These are the feelings on which the spirit of discipline
in our native army chiefly depends, and which we shall, I
hope, continue to cultivate, as we have always hitherto
done, with care ; and a commander must take a great deal
of pains to make his men miserable, before he can render
them, like the soldiers of Frederick, " the irreconcileable
enemies of their officers and their government."

In the year 1817 I was encamped in a grove on the
right bank of the Ganges below Monghyr,[1] when the
Marquis of Hastings was proceeding up the river in his
fleet, to put himself at the head of the grand division of
the army then about to take the field against the Pindhārīs
and their patrons, the Marāthā chiefs. Here I found an
old native pensioner, above a hundred years of age. He
had fought under Lord Clive at the battle of Plassey, A.D.
1757, and was still a very cheerful, talkative old gentleman,
though he had long lost the use of his eyes. One of his
sons, a grey-headed old man, and a Sūbadār (captain) in a
regiment of native infantry, had been at the taking of Java,
and was now come home on leave to visit his father.
Other sons had risen to the rank of commissioned officers,
and their families formed the aristocracy of the neighbour-

[1] Monghyr (Mungīr) is the chief town of the district of the same
name, which lies to the east of Patna.

hood. In the evening, as the fleet approached, the old gentleman, dressed in his full uniform of former days as a commissioned officer, had himself taken out close to the bank of the river, that he might be once more during his life within sight of a British Commander-in-Chief, though he could no longer see one. There the old patriarch sat listening with intense delight to the remarks of the host of his descendants around him, as the Governor-General's magnificent fleet passed along,[1] every one fancying that he had caught a glimpse of the great man, and trying to describe him to the old gentleman, who in return told them (no doubt for the thousandth time) what sort of a person the great Lord Clive was. His son, the old Sūbadār, now and then, with modest deference, venturing to imagine a resemblance between one or the other, and his *beau idéal* of a great man, Lord Lake. Few things in India have interested me more than scenes like these.

I have no means of ascertaining the number of military pensioners in England or in any other European nation, and cannot, therefore, state the proportion which they bear to the actual number of forces kept up. The military pensioners in our Bengal establishment on the 1st of May, 1841, were 22,381; and the family pensioners, or heirs of soldiers killed in action, 1,730; total 24,111, out of an army of 82,027 men. I question whether the number of retired soldiers maintained at the expense of government bears so large a proportion to the number actually serving in any other nation on earth.[2] Not one of the twenty-four thousand has been brought on, or retained upon, the list from political interest or court favour; every one receives his pension for long and faithful services, after he has been pronounced by a board of European surgeons as no longer fit for the active duties of his profession; or gets it

[1] Such a spectacle is no longer to be seen in India. Four or five inconspicuous railway carriages now take the place of the "magnificent fleet."

[2] The percentage is 29½.

for the death of a father, husband, or son, who has been killed in the service of government.

All are allowed to live with their families, and European officers are stationed at central points in the different parts of the country, where they are most numerous to pay them their stipends every six months. These officers are at— 1st, Barrackpore; 2nd, Dinapore; 3rd, Allahabad; 4th, Lucknow; 5th, Meerut. From these central points they move twice a year to the several other points within their respective circles of payment where the pensioners can most conveniently attend to receive their money on certain days, so that none of them have to go far, or to employ any expensive means to get it—it is, in fact, brought home as near as possible to their doors by a considerate and liberal government.[1]

Every soldier is entitled to a pension when pronounced by a board of surgeons as no longer fit for the active duties of his profession, after fifteen years' active service; but to be entitled to the pension of his rank in the army, he must have served in such rank for three years. Till he has done so he is entitled only to the pension of that immediately below it. A sepoy gets four rupees a month, that is, about one-fourth more than the ordinary wages of common uninstructed labour throughout the country.[2] But it will be better to give the rate of pay of the native officers and men of our native infantry, and that of their retired pensions in one table.

[1] These arrangements have all been changed. Military pensioners are now paid through the civil authorities of each district.
[2] Wages are now generally higher.

TABLE OF THE RATE OF PAY AND RETIRED PENSIONS OF THE NATIVE OFFICERS AND SOLDIERS OF OUR NATIVE INFANTRY.

RANK.	Rate of Pay per Mensem.	Rate of Pension per Mensem.
	RUPEES.	RUPEES.
A Sepoy, or private soldier. (NOTE.— After sixteen years' service eight rupees a month, after twenty years he gets nine rupees a month) . .	7.0	4.0
A Nāik, or corporal . . .	12.0	7.0
A Havīldār, or sergeant . . .	14.0	7.0
A Jemadār, subaltern commissioned officer	24.8	13.0
Sūbadār, or captain . . .	67.0	25.0
Sūbadār Major	92.0	0.0[1]
A Sūbadār, after forty years' service	0.0	50.0
A Sardār Bahādur of the Order of British India, First Class, two rupees a day extra ; Second Class, one rupee a day extra. This extra allowance they enjoy after they retire from the service during life.[2]		

[1] I presume this means that no special rate of pension was fixed for the rank of Sūbadār Major.

[2] The monthly rates of pay and pension now in force for native officers and men of the Bengal army are as follows :—

RANK.	Pay.		Pension.	
	Ordinary.	Superior.	Ordinary.	Superior.
	Rs.	Rs.	Rs.	Rs.
Sūbadār	80	100*	30	50
Jemadār.	40	50*	15	25
Havīldār	14	—	7	12
Naick (nāik)	12	—	7	12
Drummer or Bugler . .	7	—		
Sepoy	7	—	4	7

* Half of this rank in each regiment receive the higher rate of pay.

The circumstances which, in the estimation of the people, distinguish the British from all other rulers in India, and make it grow more and more upon their affections, are these :—The security which public servants enjoy in the tenure of their office; the prospect they have of advancement by the gradation of rank ; the regularity and liberal scale of their pay ; and the provision for old age, when they have discharged the duties entrusted to them ably and faithfully.[1] In a native state almost every public officer knows that he has no chance of retaining his office beyond the reign of the present minister or favourite ; and that no present minister or favourite can calculate upon retaining his ascendency over the mind of his chief for more than a few months or years. Under us they see secretaries to government, members of council, and Governors-General themselves going out and coming into office without causing any change in the position of their subordinates, or even the apprehension of any change, as long as they discharge their duties ably and faithfully.

In a native state the new minister or favourite brings with him a whole host of expectants who must be provided for as soon as he takes the helm ; and if all the favourites of his predecessor do not voluntarily vacate their offices for them, he either turns them out without ceremony, or his favourites very soon concoct charges against them, which causes them to be turned out in due form, and perhaps put into jail till they have "paid the uttermost farthing." Under us the Governors-General, members of council, the secretaries of state, the members of the

[1] This sentence might mislead readers unacquainted with the details of Indian administration. Every official who satisfies the formal rules of the Accounts department gets his pension, as a matter of course, in accordance with those rules, whether his service has been able and faithful or not. The pension ist is often the last refuge of incompetent and dishonest officials, to which they are gladly consigned by code-bound superiors, who cannot otherwise get rid of them. Nor am I certain that British rule " grows more and more upon the affections " of those subject to it.

judicial and revenue boards, all come into office and take
their seats unattended by a single expectant. No native
officer of the revenue or judicial department, who is
conscious of having done his duty ably and honestly, feels
the slightest uneasiness at the change. The consequence
is a degree of integrity in public officers never before known
in India, and rarely to be found in any other country. In
the province where I now write,[1] which consists of six
districts, there are twenty-two native judicial officers,
Munsifs, Sadr Amins, and Principal Sadr Amins ;[2] and in
the whole province. I have never heard a suspicion
breathed against one of them ; nor do I believe that
the integrity of one of them is at this time suspected.
The only one suspected within the two and a half years that I
have been in the province was, I grieve to say, a Christian ;
and he has been removed from office, to the great satisfaction of the people, and is never to be employed again.[3]

The only department in which our native public servants
do not enjoy the same advantages of security in the tenure
of their office, prospect of rise in the gradation of rank,
liberal scale of pay, and provision for old age, is the
police ; and it is admitted on all hands that there they are
everywhere exceedingly corrupt. Not one of them, indeed,
ever thinks it possible that he can be supposed honest ;
and those who really are so are looked upon as a kind of
martyrs or penitents, who are determined by long suffering
to atone for past crimes ; and who, if they could not get

---

[1] The Sāgar and Nerbudda (Narbadā) Territories, now included in
the Central Provinces.

[2] The designations Sadr Amin and Principal Sadr Amin have been
superseded by the title of Subordinate Judge. The officers referred
to have only civil jurisdiction, which does not include revenue and
rent causes.

[3] Most experienced officers will, I think, agree with me that the
author was exceptionally fortunate in his experience. So far as I can
make out, the standard of integrity among the higher native officials
has risen considerably during the last sixty years, but it is still a long
way from the perfection indicated by the author's remarks.

into the police, would probably go long pilgrimages on all fours, or with unboiled peas in their shoes.[1]

He who can suppose that men so inadequately paid, who have no promotion to look forward to, and feel no security in their tenure of office, and consequently no hope of a provision for old age, will be zealous and honest in the discharge of their duties, must be very imperfectly acquainted with human nature—with the motives by which men are influenced all over the world. Indeed, no man does in reality suppose so ; on the contrary, every man knows that the same motives actuate public servants in India as elsewhere. We have acted successfully upon this knowledge in all other branches of the public service, and shall, I trust, at no distant period act upon the same in that of the police ; and then, and not till then, can it prove to the people what we must all wish it to be, a blessing.

The European magistrate of a district has, perhaps, a million of people to look after.[2] The native officers next under him are the Thānadārs of the different subdivisions of the district, containing each many towns and villages, with a population of perhaps one hundred thousand people. These officers have no grade to look forward to, and get a salary of *twenty-five rupees a month each.*

They cannot possibly do their duties unless they keep each a couple of horses or ponies, with servants to attend to them ; indeed, they are told so by every magistrate who cares about the peace of his district. The people, seeing how much we expect from the Thānadār, and how little we give him, submit to his demands for contribution without a

---

[1] These observations on the police are merely a repetition of the remarks in chapter XIV of this volume, which have been discussed in the notes to that chapter.

[2] The districts in the North-Western Provinces and Oudh are much smaller than those in Bengal or Madras, but even in Northern India a district with only a million of inhabitants is considered to be rather a small one. Some districts have a population of more than three millions each.

murmur, and consider almost any demand venial from a man so employed and paid. They are confounded at our inconsistency, and say, where they dare to speak their minds, "We see you giving high salaries and high prospects of advancement to men who have nothing on earth to do but to collect your revenues and to decide our disputes about pounds, shillings, and pence, which we used to decide much better among ourselves when we had no other court but that of our elders to appeal to ; while those who are to protect life and property, to keep peace over the land, and enable the industrious to work in security, maintain their families and pay the government revenue, are left without any prospect of rising, and almost without any pay at all." ·

There is really nothing in our rule in India which strikes the people so much as this glaring inconsistency, the evil effects of which are so great and so manifest. The only way to remedy the evil is to give the police what the other branches of the public service already enjoy—a feeling of security in the tenure of office, a higher rate of salary, and, above all, a gradation of rank which shall afford a prospect of rising to those who discharge their duties ably and honestly. For this purpose all that is required is the interposition of an officer between the Thānadār and the magistrate, in the same way as the Sadr Amin is now interposed between the Munsif and the Judge.[1] On an

---

[1] The author's note to this passage repeats the quotation from Hobbes's *Leviathan*, Part ii, sec. 30, which has been already cited in the text, page 214 of this volume, and need not be repeated here. The note continues :—"Almost every Thānadār in our dominions is a little Tarquin in his way, exciting the indignation of the people against his master. When we give him the proper incentives to good, we shall be able with better conscience to punish him severely for bad conduct. The interposition of the officers I propose between him and the magistrate will give him the required incentive to good conduct, at the same time that it will deprive him of all hope of concealing his 'evil ways,' should he continue in them." [W. H. S.] He still manages to continue in his evil ways, and generally to conceal them.

average there are, perhaps, twelve Thānas, or police sub-
divisions in each district, and one such officer to every four
Thānas would be sufficient for all purposes. The Governor-
General who shall confer this boon on the people of India
will assuredly be hailed as one of their greatest benefactors.[1] I should, I believe, speak within bounds when I say
that the Thānadārs throughout the country give at present
more than all the money which they receive in avowed
salaries from government as a share of indirect perquisites
to the native officers of the magistrate's court, who have to
send their reports to them, and communicate their orders,
and prepare the cases of the prisoners they may send in
for commitment to the Sessions courts.[2] The intermediate
officers here proposed would obviate all this; they
would be to the magistrate at once the *tapis* of Prince
Husain, and the telescope of Prince Ali—media that
would enable them to be everywhere, and see everything.

I may here seem to be "travelling beyond the record,"
but it is not so. In treating on the spirit of military discipline in our native army I advocate, as much as in me lies,
the great general principle upon which rests, I think, not
only our *power* in India, but what is more, the *justification
of that power*. It is our wish, as it is our interest, to give
to the Hindoos and Muhammadans a liberal share in all
the duties of administration, in all offices, civil and military,

---

[1] This statement seems almost like sarcasm to a reader who knows
what manner of men well-paid Inspectors of Police commonly are, and
how they are regarded by the non-official population. They are not
usually reverenced as "protectors of the poor."

[2] The reader who is not practically acquainted with the work of
administration in India will probably think that the magistrate who
allows such intrigues to go on must be very careless and inefficient.
But that thought, though very natural, would be unjust. The author
was one of the best possible district magistrates, and yet was unable
to suppress the evils which he describes, nor have the remedies which
he advocated, and which have been adopted, proved effectual. The
Thānadār now has generally to pay the Inspector and the people in the
District Superintendent's office, in addition to "the native officers of
the magistrate's court."

and to show the people in general the incalculable advantages of a strong and settled government, which can secure life, property, and character, and the free enjoyment of all their blessings throughout the land ; and give to those who perform duties as public servants ably and honestly a sure prospect of rising by gradation, a feeling of security in their tenure of office, a liberal salary while they serve, and a respectable provision for old age.

It is by a steady adherence to these principles that the Indian Civil Service has been raised to its present high character for integrity and ability ; and the native army made what it really is, faithful and devoted to its rulers, and ready to serve them in any quarter of the world. I deprecate any innovation upon these principles in the branches of the public service to which they have already been applied with such eminent success ; and I advocate their extension to all other branches as the surest means of making them what they ought, and what we must all most fervently wish them to be.

The native officers of our judicial and revenue establishments, or of our native army, are everywhere a bond of union between the governing and the governed.[1] Discharging everywhere honestly and ably their duties to their employers, they tend everywhere to secure to them the respect and affection of the people. His Highness Muhammad S'aīd Khān, the reigning Nawāb of Rāmpur, still talks with pride of the days when he was one of our Deputy Collectors in the adjoining district of Badāon, and of the useful knowledge he acquired in that office. He has still one brother a Sadr Amīn in the district of Mainpurī, and another a Deputy Collector in the Hamīrpur district ; and neither would resign his situation under the Honourable Company to take office in Rāmpur at three

---

[1] This statement requires to be guarded by many qualifications. The author's following remarks only illustrate the well-known fact that in India official rank is ardently desired by the classes eligible for it, and carries with it great social advantages.

times the rate of salary, when invited to do so on the accession of the eldest brother to the "masnad." What they now enjoy they owe to their own industry and integrity ; and they are proud to serve a government which supplies them with so many motives for honest exertion, and leaves them nothing to fear, as long as they exert themselves honestly. To be in a situation which it is generally understood that none but honest and able men can fill[1] is of itself a source of pride, and the sons of native princes and men of rank, both Hindoo and Muhammadan, everywhere prefer taking office in our judicial and revenue establishments to serving under native rulers, where everything depends entirely upon the favour or frown of men in power, and ability, industry, and integrity can secure nothing.[2]

[1] This description of the class of officials alluded to is somewhat idealized, though it applies to a considerable proportion of the class.

[2] These propositions were, doubtless, literally correct in the author's time, but they are not fully applicable to the existing state of affairs.

THE END.

INDEX

INDEX

A A

Muhammad, journey to heaven of, II, 202, 203

Muhammad, prince, son of Aurangzēb, II, 177

Muhammad Shāh, reign and tomb of, II, 168

Muhammadābād, fort, II, 140

Muhammadan toleration, I, 406*n*.

—— law of succession, I, 220, 290, 335

—— feeling towards Government, II, 122

—— notions about resurrection, II, 181

—— tombs, II, 131, 181

—— education, II, 132, 183

—— processions, II, 133

—— lunar year, II, 134

—— prayers, II, 142*n*.

—— doctrine of predestination, II, 197-200

—— doctrine concerning the devil, II, 199

—— notions of astronomy, II, 202

—— opinion of Jesus Christ, II, 204

—— attitude towards science, I, 45*n*. ; II, 205

—— military government, I, 340, 343

—— land revenue law, II, 285*n*.

Muhammadanism, numerous converts to, II, 64

Muhammadans and modern science, I, 45*n*.

—— sects of, I, 59*n*.

Muharram celebration, II, 134

Muīn-ud-dīn Chishtī, saint, I, 423 ; II, 165*n*.

Mumtāz-i-Mahall, empress, names of, I, 393*n*.

—— pedigree of, I, 397*n*.

Municipal institutions, II, 47

Munro, Sir Thomas, on Indian civilization, I, 4

Murād Baksh, son of Aurangzēb, I, 330, 332, 374*n*. ; II, 171*n*.

Murādābād for some time headquarters of author, I, xviii

Murder of Mr. William Fraser at Delhi, II, 59, 106-125, 160

—— of Mr. Cherry at Benares, II, 123

—— by Thugs (see "Thugs"), I, 110*n*.

—— see "Poisoners" and "Robbers"

Musēl, a kind of grass, I, 151

Mutiny at Barrackpore in 1824, I, 2

Mutiny of 1857, dispelled illusions, II, 300*n*., 301*n*., 314*n*.

—— at Gwālior, I, 329*n*.

—— at Jhānsī, I, 267*n*.

Muzaffarnagar, criminal tribes of, I, 284

Myths, formation of, I, 157*n*.

Nādir Shāh, chronology of, I, 349*n*.

—— sack of Delhi by, II, 176, 177*n*.

Nāgaudh (Nagode), also called Uchahara, I, 40*n*.

Nāgpur State, annexation of, I, 346*n*.

—— Bhonslā Rājās of, I, 126*n*., 346 ; II, 13*n*.

Nahavend, battle of, I, 167*n*.

Nālkī, a state litter, I, 165

Names, Hindoo customs concerning, I, 93

Nānak Shāh, founder of Sikh religion, II, 127*n*.

Nandi, the bull ridden by Siva, I, 67*n*.

Narbadā (Narmadā), see "Nerbudda"

Narhar Sā, last Gond Rājā of Garhā Mandlā, I, 69